Enjoy Cooking
THE COSTCO WAY™

Spinach Salad with Fennel, Oranges,
Grapes and Kiwi recipe on page 64.

Enjoy Cooking
THE COSTCO WAY™

Mealtime magic using Costco products

Stephanie E. Ponder
Editorial Director

With a foreword by
Dennis Knapp and Jeff Lyons

Issaquah, Washington

*Senior Vice President
E-commerce and Publishing:* Ginnie Roeglin

Publisher: David W. Fuller

Editorial Director: Stephanie E. Ponder

Art Director: Doris Winters

Associate Editorial Director: Tim Talevich

Associate Art Director: Lory Williams

Associate Editor: Judy Gouldthorpe

Senior Designer: Brenda Shecter

Photographers: Darren Emmens
Ryan Castoldi
Devin Seferos

Food Stylists: Amy Muzyka-McGuire
Christine W. Jackson

Kitchen Manager: Linda Carey

Studio Assistant: Alicia Deal

Business Manager: Jane Klein-Shucklin

Advertising Manager: Melanie Woods

Assistant Advertising Manager: Kathi Tipper

Advertising Assistant: Jordan Maughan

Production Manager: Pam Sather

Prepress Supervisor/Color Specialist: MaryAnne Robbers

Assistant Production Manager: Antolin Matsuda

Online Editor: David Wight

Print Management: James Letzel and
Patricia Cartmell, GSSI

Distribution: Rossie Cruz

Photography by Iridio Photography, Seattle, Washington.

Contents

50

67

96

158

232

To Our Valued Members

We are delighted to offer you a gift—the 12th annual book in *The Costco Way* cookbook series—in time for the holidays to thank you for your business and your loyal membership. This book has been made possible through the support of Costco's many food suppliers.

As in past years, we've asked our suppliers to develop recipes that showcase products of theirs that we sell at Costco. Their response has resulted in our biggest cookbook yet, at 250 pages.

Returning in this edition is our special "Chef's Choice" section in the middle of the book, with 22 chefs, compared with last year's 15. It features recipes from many of our favorite celebrity chefs, including Ree Drummond, Ina Garten, Carla Hall and Ethan Stowell. These top chefs have worked their magic to develop recipes using their favorite ingredients from Costco to create everything from appetizers and snacks to entrées and desserts.

I'd like to take a moment to note the title: *Enjoy Cooking The Costco Way*. These days cooking can seem like just another to-do item that gets lumped in with work, picking up the kids and other daily tasks. My hope is that this collection of recipes will help you not only prepare delicious meals, but also rediscover the magic that happens when quality ingredients are combined in just the right way.

If a quick snack or meal is occasionally the key to enjoying time in the kitchen, look for the "Quick and Easy" logo to find fast and delicious recipes that require minimal effort when your schedule is a little tight.

The secret of all the great dishes, old and new, featured in this book is top-quality ingredients. When you purchase your ingredients from Costco, you know you are getting the best—and at a great price.

We hope you like *Enjoy Cooking The Costco Way* and that you try out our recipes with your family and friends. You can also find our past years' cookbooks online at Costco.com. Just type "Costco cookbooks" in the search window on our home page.

Bon appétit from all of us at Costco.

Ginnie Roeglin
Senior Vice President,
E-commerce and Publishing

Foreword

In this, the 12th installment of *The Costco Way* series, you will find both new and traditional recipes that help showcase the wonderful variety of foods sold in Costco warehouses. One of our strengths as a company can be seen in the many top-quality vendors that help us deliver great products to you, our members, every day.

The title of this year's cookbook is pretty straightforward: *Enjoy Cooking The Costco Way*. Whether your enjoyment comes from the process of making a culinary masterpiece or rave reviews from family and friends, we believe time spent cooking should be rewarding.

With that in mind, we are positive you will find a wide array of delicious recipes to pick from this holiday season and for years to come. Whether you are looking for an entrée or a unique side dish for that special meal, you can be sure Costco will stay true to form and deliver excellent quality at remarkable value.

While none of us here have our own cooking show, we do have some insight into how to have more fun in the kitchen. First, start with quality ingredients. Fresh meat, fruit, vegetables, seasonings and more are key to making dishes that will have people asking for seconds, or even thirds. Second, rest assured that our buyers work hard to make sure the items you buy are of consistent quality so that your dishes are perfect every time. Third, use these recipes as a starting point and make them your own by experimenting with seasonings and alternate ingredients.

Please take a few moments to review the ideas, creativity and mouthwatering recipes in this year's cookbook. Innovative dishes made with fresh, high-quality products at a great value: We can't think of a better way to enjoy cooking. Inspiration is just the turn of a page away.

Dennis Knapp
Senior Vice President,
Foods and Sundries

Jeff Lyons
Senior Vice President,
Fresh Foods

About This Book

Welcome to the 12th annual cookbook in *The Costco Way* series. As with our earlier books, *Enjoy Cooking The Costco Way* will be handed out to members on a first-come, first-served basis the weekend after Thanksgiving as a token of our appreciation for their membership.

Like Costco itself, the format of the book is simple and direct. The book is arranged with sections for breakfasts, appetizers and beverages, salads and soups, side dishes, entrées and desserts.

The index at the back of the book contains listings by recipe and key ingredients. The "Supplier Listing" section provides contact information for all of the participating food suppliers.

Every recipe has been identified with the supplier's name and logo. We want to thank each of these suppliers for their support of this book. (Please note that some branded products may not be sold in your part of the country. In such cases, you should substitute a similar product.)

Again this year, some of the recipes list nutritional information. This is helpful for anybody watching calories and following a controlled, healthful diet.

Our popular "Chef's Choice" chapter offers 57 pages of recipes developed by some of the country's most accomplished chefs. All of these chefs have achieved national or international renown with their own cookbooks, television shows and/or exceptional restaurants. Thanks to all of them for helping to make this another exciting addition to *The Costco Way* cookbook series.

Please have fun with this year's recipes, aimed as always at helping you enjoy cooking.

David W. Fuller
Publisher

Enjoy Cooking
THE COSTCO WAY™

Breakfasts

Pear Pancakes
Columbia Marketing International

¾ cup milk

2 tablespoons apple cider vinegar

1 cup unbleached all-purpose flour

1 teaspoon baking powder

½ teaspoon baking soda

⅓ cup granulated sugar, divided

¼ teaspoon ground cinnamon

½ teaspoon salt

1 large egg, lightly beaten

2 tablespoons butter, melted

2 CMI D'Anjou, Bartlett or Bosc pears

Cooking spray

Syrup, confectioners' sugar or pear preserves, for serving

In a small bowl, mix milk and vinegar together. Set aside.

In a large bowl, combine flour, baking powder, baking soda, 2 tablespoons sugar, cinnamon and salt. Mix with a fork to evenly blend.

Whisk egg and melted butter into the milk mixture. Pour over the flour mixture a little at a time, stirring to remove any lumps.

Cut pears in half lengthwise and scoop out seeds with a spoon. Slice the pears ¼ inch thick vertically, creating pear-shaped slices. Dip both sides of each slice into the remaining sugar.

Spray a griddle or skillet with cooking spray and set over medium-low heat. Place a pear slice on the griddle. Cook for 1 minute, and then flip. Cook another minute, and then spoon about 3 tablespoons of batter over and around the pear.

Cook for 2 minutes, until small bubbles start to appear all over the surface of the batter. Then carefully flip and cook another 2 minutes. Move to a plate, respray the pan, and continue with the remaining pear slices and batter.

Serve with syrup, confectioners' sugar or pear preserves. Makes 8-10 pancakes.

Recipe courtesy of Lara Ferroni, food writer and epicurean from the Pacific Northwest.

Cara Cara Orange Syrup
SunWest Fruit Company

Juice of 3 SunWest Cara Cara navel oranges (about 1 cup)

1 tablespoon butter

1½ cups granulated sugar

½ teaspoon Kirkland Signature pure vanilla extract

¼ teaspoon Kirkland Signature cinnamon or pumpkin pie spice

In a small saucepan, combine orange juice and butter. Bring to a boil.

Add sugar and cook over medium heat until completely dissolved, stirring frequently, about 1-2 minutes.

Stir in vanilla and cinnamon until well blended.

Remove from the heat and let cool. The syrup will thicken as it cools.

This is especially good on Belgian waffles. Makes 8-10 servings.

Tip: For a thicker syrup, use more sugar; for thinner, use less.

Berrylicious Breakfast Crêpes
Sun Belle

12 ounces Sun Belle blackberries
½ cup sugar, divided
½ teaspoon vanilla extract, divided
12 ounces Sun Belle raspberries
1 cup Sun Belle blueberries

CRÊPES

6 tablespoons unsalted butter
3 cups milk
6 large eggs
½ teaspoon salt
2 tablespoons sugar
2 cups unbleached flour

In a blender, puree blackberries, ¼ cup sugar, ¼ teaspoon vanilla and ¼ cup water. Strain out the seeds. In a saucepan, combine raspberries, ¼ cup sugar and ¼ teaspoon vanilla. Cook over medium heat, stirring constantly, until the berries break down, about 10 minutes.

Prepare the crêpes: Microwave butter in a heatproof glass bowl until melted. Add milk; microwave for 2 minutes. Whisk in eggs, salt, sugar and then flour until smooth.

Heat a 10-inch greased nonstick skillet on medium-high. For each crêpe pour ¼ cup batter into the pan, swirling to spread evenly. Cook for 45 seconds; flip and cook for 45 seconds. Stack the crêpes on a warm plate. Spread blackberry sauce on each crêpe; fold in half twice to make a triangle. Overlap 2 crêpes on each plate. Add raspberry sauce and blueberries. Makes 12 servings.

Nutella Breakfast Granola Parfaits

Nutella

1 cup low-fat granola

½ cup Nutella hazelnut spread

1¼ cup plain or vanilla Greek-style, nonfat yogurt

1 cup diced mixed fresh fruit (pineapple, strawberries, cantaloupe, honeydew melon, etc.) or berries

4 mint sprigs, for garnish (optional)

For each serving, in a tall 10- to 12-ounce sundae/parfait glass or a to-go plastic glass, dollop with layers as follows:

2 tablespoons granola

1 tablespoon Nutella

2 tablespoons yogurt

¼ cup diced fresh fruit

2 tablespoons yogurt

2 tablespoons granola

1 tablespoon Nutella

Top with a spoonful of yogurt and a mint sprig. Makes 4 servings.

Asparagus Frittata
Altar Produce

6 large eggs

2 tablespoons whipping cream

½ teaspoon salt, plus a pinch

¼ teaspoon freshly ground black pepper

1 tablespoon olive oil

1 tablespoon butter

12 ounces asparagus, trimmed, cut into ¾-inch pieces

1 tomato, seeded and diced

3 ounces Fontina cheese, diced

Preheat the broiler.

In a medium bowl, whisk eggs, cream, ½ teaspoon salt and pepper. Set aside.

Heat olive oil and butter in a 9½-inch nonstick ovenproof skillet over medium heat. Add asparagus and sauté until crisp and tender, about 2 minutes.

Raise the heat to high. Add tomato and a pinch of salt; sauté for 2 minutes.

Pour the egg mixture over the asparagus mixture and cook for a couple of minutes, until the eggs start to set. Sprinkle with cheese.

Reduce the heat to medium-low and cook until the frittata is almost set but the top is still runny, about 2 minutes.

Place the skillet under the broiler. Broil until the top is set and golden brown, about 5 minutes. Remove from the oven and let stand for 2 minutes. Makes 4 servings.

ALTAR
PRODUCE LLC

Sausage, Apple and Gouda Breakfast Pizzas
Jimmy Dean

4 6-inch pita bread rounds

1 tablespoon butter

1 small onion, thinly sliced

1 large apple, cored and cut into thin slices (about 2 cups)

1 tablespoon brown sugar

½ teaspoon ground cinnamon

6 Jimmy Dean Fully Cooked Turkey Sausage Links, cut into ¼-inch pieces

1 cup baby spinach leaves

1 cup (4 ounces) shredded Gouda cheese

Preheat oven to 375°F. Place pita bread rounds on a baking sheet.

Melt butter in a medium skillet over medium heat. Add onion and cook, stirring, for 4-6 minutes, or until lightly browned and softened. Add apple, brown sugar and cinnamon; cook and stir for 2 minutes, or until a light glaze forms. Stir in sausage and heat through.

Place about 4-5 spinach leaves (about ¼ cup) on top of each pita. Divide the apple-sausage mixture among the pizzas. Sprinkle each with ¼ cup cheese.

Bake for 8-10 minutes, or until the cheese is melted and the crust is lightly browned. Makes 4 servings.

Ham and Swiss Baked Omelet

Kirkland Signature/Carando

1½ cups diced Kirkland Signature/
  Carando hickory-smoked ham

3 tablespoons sliced green onions

1 cup (4 ounces) shredded Swiss cheese

9 eggs

½ cup milk

½ cup sour cream

¼ teaspoon ground pepper

Preheat oven to 325°F. Layer ham, green onions and cheese in a greased 9-inch square baking dish. In a bowl, beat together eggs, milk, sour cream and pepper.

Pour over the ham and cheese. Bake for 50-55 minutes, or until the eggs are set and a knife inserted in the center comes out clean. Let stand for 10 minutes before slicing. Makes 6-8 servings.

French Onion Brunch Strata

Plats du Chef

2 pucks Plats du Chef French Onion Soup, thawed

4 large eggs, beaten

⅓ cup half-and-half

7 cups cubed baguette or other crusty bread

1 cup chopped fresh spinach

½ cup chopped roasted red peppers, dried with paper towel

¼ cup chopped prosciutto or ham

2 tablespoons butter, melted

Fresh oregano, for garnish (optional)

Strain thawed soups, reserving cheese and croutons separately. Whisk the broth with eggs and half-and-half.

In a large bowl, toss bread cubes with spinach, peppers, prosciutto, the broth mixture and half the reserved cheese and croutons until evenly combined. Soak for 20 minutes. Arrange in a greased 9-inch deep-dish pie plate.

Scatter remaining cheese and croutons over the top. (Strata can be refrigerated, covered, overnight.)

Preheat oven to 350°F. Drizzle strata evenly with butter. Tent with foil; bake for 45 minutes. Uncover and bake for 20 minutes longer, or until golden and set.

Cool for 10 minutes; slice into wedges. Garnish with fresh oregano, if desired. Makes 8 servings.

Tip: Thaw soup in the refrigerator overnight. Or to quick-thaw, place unwrapped pucks in a microwave-safe bowl and microwave on medium for 8 minutes, stopping occasionally to scoop off topping as it thaws to prevent the cheese from melting.

Black Forest Ham Green Chile Breakfast Pie

Cargill Meat Solutions

1 prepared single 9-inch pie crust

3 large eggs

1 cup shredded Pepper Jack cheese

½ cup milk

½ cup heavy cream

1 cup chopped Kirkland Signature Black Forest ham

½ cup chopped canned green chiles

¼ cup thinly sliced green onions

Bake pie crust according to package directions until golden brown.

Turn the oven to 325°F.

Whisk remaining ingredients in a bowl. Pour the mixture into the precooked crust. Bake until just set, about 20 minutes. Makes 6-8 servings.

Tips: Serve with hash browns. To serve for lunch, add a simple salad.

Hearty Huevos Skillet
ConAgra Foods

PAM Original No-Stick Cooking Spray

1 16-ounce can Rosarita No Fat Traditional Refried Beans

¾ cup Egg Beaters Original

1 10-ounce can Ro*Tel Original Diced Tomatoes & Green Chilies, drained

8 6-inch yellow corn tortillas

¼ cup shredded sharp Cheddar cheese

2 tablespoons sliced green onions

Spray a large (11- to 12-inch) nonstick skillet with cooking spray. Spread beans in the bottom of the skillet. Make 4 deep depressions (about 3½ inches across) in the beans, pushing the beans to the center and sides of the skillet. Fill the depressions with Egg Beaters. Cover the skillet. Cook over medium heat for 7-10 minutes, or until the Egg Beaters are set. Meanwhile, place drained tomatoes in a medium microwave-safe bowl. Microwave on high for 1-1½ minutes, or until hot. Wrap tortillas in paper towels. Microwave on high for 45-60 seconds, or until warm. Sprinkle cheese and onions over the beans and Egg Beaters. Overlap 2 tortillas on each serving plate. Top with beans and Egg Beaters. Serve with tomatoes. Makes 4 servings.

ConAgra Foods
Food you love

California Avocado Toast Three Ways

California Avocado Commission/Calavo Growers/Del Rey Avocado/Eco Farms/Giumarra Escondido/
Index Fresh/McDaniel Fruit Co./Mission Produce/West Pak Avocado, Inc.

1 slice bread (try thick, crusty artisan
   bread – sourdough, rye, wheat,
   multigrain or whatever you prefer)

½ large ripe fresh California Avocado,
   washed, peeled, seeded and
   mashed or sliced

1 egg (optional)

2 slices heirloom or beefsteak
   tomato (optional)

2 slices cooked bacon – try maple,
   peppercorn, turkey or veggie
   bacon for variety (optional)

Sea salt (optional)

Fresh cracked pepper (optional)

CALIFORNIA AVOCADO TOAST WITH FRIED EGG
Toast bread and spread with avocado (mashed or sliced). Spray a small nonstick
skillet with cooking spray and fry the egg. Place cooked egg on the avocado toast.
Season to taste with salt and pepper.

CALIFORNIA AVOCADO TOAST WITH HEIRLOOM TOMATO
Toast bread and spread with avocado (mashed or sliced). Top with tomato
slices. Season to taste with salt and pepper.

CALIFORNIA AVOCADO TOAST WITH BACON
Toast bread and spread with avocado (mashed or sliced). Top with bacon.
Makes 1 serving.

Tip: For additional options, try making a sandwich with any combination
of fried egg, tomato and bacon—or all three.

©2013 California Avocado Commission

Pistachio Maple Energy Butter on Grilled Cinnamon Sugar Toast

Kirkland Signature/Setton Pistachio/Setton Farms

1-2 teaspoons neutral-tasting oil

4 slices whole-grain bread

2 teaspoons natural cane sugar

¼ teaspoon ground cinnamon

Dash of sea salt

Fresh berries, for topping (strawberries or blueberries preferred)

PISTACHIO MAPLE ENERGY BUTTER

1 cup Kirkland Signature roasted, salted California pistachio nuts, shelled

3 tablespoons Grade B maple syrup

¼ teaspoon sea salt

¼ teaspoon ground cinnamon

2 tablespoons water, plus 1 tablespoon more if needed

Heat oil in a sauté pan over medium heat. Add bread and grill on each side about 2 minutes, or until golden.

In a small bowl, combine sugar, cinnamon and salt. Slice the grilled toast pieces in half diagonally and sprinkle with cinnamon sugar.

Using a spoon, apply a generous amount of pistachio butter to each piece of toast. Top with berries. Makes 4 servings.

Recipe courtesy of Jenny Engel and Heather Goldberg—sisters, authors, co-owners of Spork Foods, www.sporkfoods.com.

Prepare the pistachio butter: In a high-powered blender or food processor, combine pistachios, maple syrup, salt, cinnamon and water. Blend until smooth, about 1-2 minutes in a high-powered blender or 3-4 minutes in a food processor. Set aside.

Breakfast Cuties Times Two: Scones and Marmalade
Sun Pacific

MARMALADE

2 pounds Cuties clementines

2½ cups sugar

3 tablespoons lemon juice

2 star anise (optional)

SCONES

2 Cuties clementines

6 tablespoons cold butter, cut in pieces

2 cups flour

⅓ cup sugar

1 tablespoon baking powder

½ teaspoon salt

½ cup heavy cream

1 large egg

Pistachios, for topping

Prepare the marmalade: Peel the zest from 2-3 Cuties with a vegetable peeler. Cut into fine slivers to make 2 tablespoons.

Peel the Cuties with a sharp knife, removing the white pith. Roughly chop the Cuties with a knife or food processor. Place in a saucepan with sugar, zest slivers, lemon juice and star anise. Simmer for 45 minutes, or until reduced to 2½-2¾ cups. The marmalade will thicken as it cools. Keep refrigerated.

Prepare the scones: In a food processor, whirl unpeeled Cuties and butter until nearly smooth. Transfer to a bowl and refrigerate for 30-60 minutes, or until firm.

Preheat oven to 350°F. In a large bowl, combine flour, sugar, baking powder and salt. Cut in the Cuties/butter blend with a pastry blender or 2 knives. In another bowl, whisk cream and egg. Stir into the flour mixture. Line a baking sheet with parchment paper. Add the dough, and lightly knead. Pat the dough into an 8-by-6-inch rectangle. Cut into 16 triangles and place 1 inch apart on the baking sheet. Press pistachios on top. Bake for 15-18 minutes, or until golden brown. Serve with marmalade. Makes 16 servings.

Recipe adapted from Rangel Catering, Bakersfield, California.

Apple Sour Cream Coffee Cake
Yakima Fresh

½ cup butter, softened
1 cup granulated sugar
2 large eggs
2 cups sifted all-purpose flour
1 teaspoon baking soda
1 teaspoon baking powder
½ teaspoon salt
1½ cups sour cream

1 teaspoon vanilla extract
4 large Yakima Fresh Gala apples,
　peeled, cored and sliced

TOPPING
⅓ cup packed light brown sugar
¼ cup granulated sugar
1 teaspoon ground cinnamon
1 cup chopped pecans

Preheat oven to 325°F. Spray a 9-by-9-inch baking pan.

Prepare the topping: Combine all ingredients and mix well. Set aside.

In a bowl, cream together butter, sugar and eggs. Add flour, baking soda, baking powder, salt, sour cream and vanilla; mix well.

Pour half of the batter into the pan. Layer with half of the apple slices, then half of the topping. Pour in the remaining batter, layer with the remaining apples (keep 3 slices for decoration), then add the rest of the topping. Arrange the 3 remaining apple slices in a pinwheel on top.

Bake for 1 hour, or until a toothpick inserted in the center comes out clean. Let cool and then refrigerate for at least 1 hour before serving. Makes 8-10 servings.

Banana Mini-Chip Muffins
Splenda

Nonstick cooking spray
2 cups all-purpose flour
2 teaspoons baking powder
½ teaspoon salt
¾ cup light butter, softened
⅓ cup Splenda Sugar Blend
⅓ cup packed Splenda Brown Sugar Blend
1 teaspoon vanilla extract
3 medium ripe bananas, mashed
1 large egg
1 12-ounce package semi-sweet chocolate mini morsels

Preheat oven to 350°F. Spray 48 mini muffin cups with cooking spray or line with paper cups.

In a medium bowl, combine flour, baking powder and salt. Set aside.

In a large bowl, combine butter, Splenda Sugar Blend, Splenda Brown Sugar Blend and vanilla; beat at medium speed with a mixer until creamy. Beat in bananas and egg. Gradually mix in the flour mixture. Stir in chocolate morsels.

Spoon the batter evenly into the prepared pan, filling the cups ⅔ full.

Bake for 15-20 minutes, or until a wooden pick inserted in the center comes out clean. Cool for 10 minutes in the pans on a wire rack. Remove the muffins from the pans to the rack to cool completely. Makes 48 mini muffins.

California Walnut-Banana Bread
Kirkland Signature

2 cups all-purpose flour
⅔ cup sugar
2¼ teaspoons baking powder
¾ teaspoon salt
1 large egg
¾ cup milk
⅓ cup canola or vegetable oil
1 teaspoon vanilla extract
1 cup mashed ripe banana
1⅓ cups chopped Kirkland Signature walnuts, divided

Preheat oven to 350°F. Generously grease a 9-by-5-inch loaf pan.

In a bowl, combine flour, sugar, baking powder and salt; mix well.

In another bowl, combine egg, milk, oil and vanilla; blend well. Add to the flour mixture, stirring just until the dry ingredients are moistened.

Fold in mashed banana and 1 cup walnuts. Spoon into the greased pan. Sprinkle with the remaining ⅓ cup walnuts.

Bake for 45 minutes-1 hour, or until a toothpick inserted in the center comes out clean. Let cool in the pan for 10 minutes. Then remove from the pan and cool on a wire rack. Makes 8 servings.

KIRKLAND *Signature*

Lemon Glazed Almond Poppy Seed Wedges
Dawn Food Products

1 Kirkland Signature almond poppy seed muffin
1½ cups confectioners' sugar
3-4 tablespoons water
2 teaspoons lemon zest

Preheat oven to 350°F. Using a serrated knife, slice muffin into 6 equal wedges. Place the wedges, cut side up, on a cookie-cooling rack and warm in the oven for 8 minutes.

In a small bowl, combine sugar and water, whisking until smooth. Pour into a squeeze bottle. Set aside.

Remove the muffin wedges from the oven and immediately set the rack on a cookie tray. Squeeze the sugar glaze over the hot wedges. Top with lemon zest. Let stand for 15 minutes to let the glaze set. Makes 2 servings.

Appetizers & Beverages

Brie with Lemon Roasted Cashews and Blueberry Sauce

Kirkland Signature/Meduri Farms/Harvest Manor Farms

4½ lemons, divided

1⅓ cups Kirkland Signature whole fancy cashews

¾ cup water

¼ cup sugar

½ cup Kirkland Signature dried blueberries

1 13.4-ounce Kirkland Signature Brie cheese wheel

Lemon wedges and herb sprigs, for garnish

Crackers or rustic bread, for serving

Squeeze the juice from 3½ lemons. Soak cashews in the lemon juice for 30 minutes.

Grate the zest from the remaining lemon and set aside.

Squeeze the juice from the zested lemon into a saucepan and add water. Bring to a boil, then add sugar and stir until dissolved. Add blueberries and return to a boil, then lower the heat and simmer until the sauce thickens, 10-15 minutes. Remove from the heat and let cool.

Preheat oven to 325°F.

Strain the cashews from the lemon juice, and spread them onto a cookie sheet. Bake for 15-20 minutes, stirring occasionally, so they brown evenly. When the nuts are browned, remove them from the oven and spread onto a paper towel to cool. Once the cashews have cooled, chop coarsely.

To serve, remove the rind from the top of the Brie wheel. Press the chopped cashews into the top of the Brie to cover. Spoon the blueberry sauce over the cashews. Garnish with lemon zest, lemon wedges and herb sprigs. Serve with crackers or rustic bread. Makes 20 servings.

Cranberry and Cheddar Pita Bites

Cabot Creamery Cooperative

2 8-inch pita breads, whole wheat or white

½ cup whole-berry cranberry sauce or chutney

5 ounces Cabot 3 Year Cheddar or Cabot Vintage White Extra Sharp Cheddar, grated (about 1¼ cups)

Place one oven rack in the upper position and one in the center. Preheat oven to 375°F. Line a baking sheet with foil.

Cut each pita bread into eight 2-inch rounds with a biscuit or cookie cutter. Split each round in two. Arrange on the baking sheet and bake on the center rack for 6-8 minutes, or until crisp and toasted.

Adjust the heat to broil. Top each toasted pita round with ½ teaspoon cranberry sauce and top with cheese, dividing it evenly among them.

Broil, carefully monitoring and rotating as necessary, for 30 seconds to 3 minutes, or until the cheese is evenly melted. Cool slightly before serving. Makes 32 bites.

Nutritional information: Each 4-bite serving has 147 calories, 5.5 g protein, 18 g carbohydrates, 6 g fat (3 g saturated), 19 mg cholesterol, 1.5 g fiber, 279 mg sodium, 128 mg calcium.

Fuji Apple and Goat Cheese Phyllo Packets
Domex Superfresh Growers

8 ounces fresh goat cheese, crumbled

1 tablespoon minced fresh chives

2 Fuji apples, cored, seeded and cut into ½-inch-thick slices

24 sheets phyllo dough, thawed if frozen (about 9 by 14 inches)

½ cup butter, melted

Preheat oven to 375°F. Set 2 oven racks at the centermost positions. In a small bowl, combine goat cheese and chives; stir to evenly blend. Cut apple slices crosswise into pieces 1-1½ inches wide. Lay 1 sheet of phyllo dough on the work surface with the shorter end facing you (cover the remaining dough with a kitchen towel). Lightly but evenly brush the dough with melted butter. Spoon 1 slightly heaping teaspoon of the goat cheese onto the dough, centered about 3 inches up from the bottom, and top the cheese with a piece of apple.

Fold the bottom edge of the phyllo upward to cover the apple, then fold in both sides evenly toward the center. Lightly brush the exposed strip of phyllo with butter. Fold the packet upward to fully enclose the filling. Set the packet, apple-side upward, on a baking sheet. Repeat with the remaining phyllo dough, cheese and apples, using 2 baking sheets.

Lightly brush the tops with melted butter. Bake until browned and crisp, about 12 minutes, switching the pans halfway through. Set aside to cool for a few minutes, then transfer the packets to a platter for serving. Makes 24 packets.

Cherries and Goat Cheese in Phyllo

Morada Produce

1 pound Morada Produce fresh cherries,
  pitted and chopped

4 large basil leaves, chopped

½ teaspoon almond extract

¼ cup plus 3 tablespoons sugar, divided

8 ounces goat cheese

8 ounces cream cheese

2 tablespoons amaretto

24 sheets phyllo dough,
  thawed if frozen

½ cup butter, melted

Sliced almonds, for garnish
  (optional)

Preheat oven to 350°F for phyllo cups or 375°F for purses.

In a bowl, combine cherries, basil, almond extract and ¼ cup sugar. Mix and let stand for 30 minutes. In a separate bowl, combine goat cheese, cream cheese, amaretto and 3 tablespoons sugar. Beat with an electric mixer until well blended. Place a phyllo sheet on a work surface and brush with melted butter. Layer with 3 more phyllo sheets, brushing each with butter. Cut into 6 rectangles. Make 5 more stacks, for a total of 36 rectangles.

For cups, press each rectangle into the cup of a small muffin pan. Bake for 4-5 minutes, or until golden brown. When cool, fill each cup with 1-2 teaspoons *each* of the cherry and cheese mixtures Garnish with almonds.

For purses, place 1-2 teaspoons of *each* mixture in the center of each rectangle. Pinch the edges together at the top, with the edges fanned out. Place on a baking sheet and bake for 8 minutes, or until golden brown. Remove from the baking sheet and set on a wire rack to cool. Garnish with sliced almonds. Makes 36 servings.

Notes: Ready-made phyllo cups can be used. These toppings can also be served on bruschetta.

MORADA
Produce Company

Stuffed Mini Pointed Peppers with Quinoa and Parsley

Mucci Farms

1 cup quinoa, rinsed well
½ teaspoon salt
2 bunches flat-leaf parsley
8 Mucci Farms Sapori cocktail tomatoes
3 Mucci Farms mini cucumbers, diced
6 green onions, sliced
Juice of 1 lemon
2 tablespoons chopped mint
1 teaspoon ground cumin
½ teaspoon garlic powder
¼ teaspoon black pepper
¼ cup olive oil
½ cup crumbled feta cheese
1.5-pound bag Mucci Farms Sweet to the Point mini pointed peppers

In a medium saucepan, bring quinoa, salt and 1¼ cups water to a boil. Reduce the heat to medium-low, cover, and simmer until the quinoa is tender, about 10 minutes. Remove from the heat and let cool.

Chop parsley leaves, discarding the stems. Dice tomatoes, discarding the seeds and juice.

In a large bowl, combine quinoa, parsley, tomatoes, cucumbers, green onions, lemon juice, mint, cumin, garlic powder, pepper and olive oil. Stir to blend. Sprinkle with feta and toss. Refrigerate the mixture, covered, for a day to let the flavors blend before stuffing.

Cut mini peppers in half and remove seeds, leaving the stems on. Stuff with the quinoa mixture. Makes 10-12 servings.

Tomato Chicken Salad Stackers

Chairmans Foods

4 leaves Bibb lettuce
8 slices red tomato
2 cups Comfort Cuisine Cape Cod Chicken Salad
4 slices yellow tomato
½ cup pecans
Fresh parsley, for garnish

On each lettuce leaf, place 1 red tomato slice.

Using a small dry measuring cup, place ¼ cup chicken salad on the tomato slice; smooth the top and sides with a spoon. Top with 1 yellow tomato slice. Add another ¼ cup chicken salad, smoothing the top and sides. Top with another red tomato slice.

Sprinkle with pecans and garnish with parsley. Makes 4 servings.

Tip: To serve as an entrée, use beefsteak tomatoes and double the amount of chicken salad.

Tomatoes with Mozzarella

NatureSweet

NatureSweet SunBursts tomatoes
Fresh basil leaves
Toothpicks

Fresh buffalo mozzarella balls
Olive oil and vinegar
Salt and pepper

Wash tomatoes and pat dry. Spear 1 basil leaf with a toothpick. Follow with 1 tomato. Add a second basil leaf, and finish with a ball of mozzarella.

Drizzle with olive oil and vinegar. Repeat to make as many individual spears as desired. Sprinkle with salt and pepper to taste.

Flaky Smoked Roasted Salmon Puffs

Marine Harvest

1 16- or 18-ounce package Royal Fjord smoked roasted salmon

½ cup wasabi mayonnaise

½ cup raspberry honey mustard dip

2 12-ounce packages crescent roll dough (8 rolls each)

1 6.5-ounce package Alouette spreadable herb cheese (or any other brand)

Preheat oven to 350°F.

Remove the skin and brown meat from smoked salmon. Cut the salmon into small pieces. Place an equal amount of salmon in 2 bowls.

Add wasabi mayonnaise to one of the bowls and mix gently. Add raspberry honey mustard dip to the second bowl and mix.

Separate the crescent roll dough into triangles. Place 1 tablespoon of the wasabi-salmon mixture on half of the triangles. Repeat with raspberry-salmon mixture on remaining triangles. Top each with 1 teaspoon of herb cheese. Fold the dough over the filling and crimp the edges together to create a pocket.

Place the pastries on an ungreased cookie sheet. Bake until golden brown, about 10-15 minutes. Makes 16 servings.

Shrimp Salad Wraps

Ventura Foods

4 Flatout Traditional Flatbreads

2 cups thinly shredded romaine lettuce

¾ cup diced fresh tomatoes

1 20.5-ounce Kirkland Signature Shrimp Salad

12 slices smoked bacon, cooked

AVOCADO SPREAD

2-4 tablespoons chopped canned chipotle pepper in adobo sauce (see note)

3 ripe avocados, pitted, smashed

4 ounces cream cheese, softened

1 tablespoon chopped fresh cilantro

Prepare the avocado spread: Using an electric mixer, combine all ingredients and beat on high until the mixture is light and fluffy. If this is not being used right away, it can be refrigerated, covered, for 2-3 days.

Lay out flatbreads on a clean cutting board. Spread with equal amounts of the avocado spread.

On one end of the flatbreads, layer the lettuce, tomatoes, shrimp salad and bacon. Roll the flatbread over the mixture, making a tube/sandwich wrap.

Slice the wraps into small pinwheels for a party platter or just in half to make a wonderful sandwich. Makes 8-12 appetizer servings.

Note: Don't use too much of the adobo sauce, as it will make the spread too runny.

◤Ventura Foods™

Salmon Mousse-Stuffed Cucumber with Cranberry-Jalapeño Reduction

Copper River Seafoods

2 English cucumbers
5 cups cranberry juice, divided
½ tablespoon salt
1 pound fresh cranberries
½ cup granulated sugar
1 jalapeño, stemmed, seeded and
   cut in small dice

1 pound smoked Alaska salmon,
   skin removed
2 pounds cream cheese, softened,
   then whipped
1 cup sour cream
1 tablespoon chopped fresh dill
1 teaspoon Worcestershire sauce
½ teaspoon ground white pepper

Cut cucumbers horizontally into 1½-inch sections, and scoop out the seeds. In a bowl, combine cucumbers, 4 cups cranberry juice and salt. Set aside. In a small saucepan, combine cranberries, 1 cup cranberry juice, sugar and jalapeño. Simmer for 5-10 minutes, until thickened. Transfer to a shallow pan and let cool.

Put salmon in a food processor and pulse until the texture is consistently fine. Transfer to a bowl and fold in cream cheese, sour cream, dill, Worcestershire and white pepper. Remove cucumbers from juice and pat dry. Place the salmon mixture in a pastry bag and pipe into the cucumbers. Top with the cranberry reduction and dill sprigs, if desired, and serve. Makes 5-6 servings.

Recipe courtesy of Shane Pennington, executive chef, Norton Sound Seafood House.

Tuna Avocado Spring Rolls with Peanut Dipping Sauce
Kirkland Signature

1 7-ounce can Kirkland Signature solid white albacore tuna, drained

2 teaspoons toasted sesame oil

¼ cup chopped green onion

8 8-inch round rice paper wrappers

1 avocado, cut into 16 even slices

1 cup grated carrot

¼ cup coarsely chopped fresh cilantro

2 tablespoons fresh mint leaves

4 butter or Bibb lettuce leaves, cut in half

PEANUT DIPPING SAUCE

¼ cup natural crunchy peanut butter

3 tablespoons hot water

2 tablespoons rice vinegar

1 tablespoon low-sodium soy sauce

1 tablespoon minced fresh ginger

2 teaspoons brown sugar

1 teaspoon chopped garlic

¼ teaspoon red pepper flakes

In a bowl, combine tuna, sesame oil and green onion. Set aside.

Fill a shallow bowl with cool water. Submerge 1 wrapper in the water until soft, then place on a cutting board. In the center of the wrapper, arrange 2 avocado slices, carrot, cilantro, mint and tuna. Top with a lettuce leaf. Fold one side of the wrapper over the ingredients, roll, and tuck in sides. Repeat with the remaining wrappers.

Prepare the sauce: Combine all ingredients and whisk until smooth. Serve with the spring rolls. Makes 4 servings.

Grilled Littleneck Clams
North Coast Seafoods

½ cup unsalted butter

¼ cup dry white wine

Juice of 1 lemon

2 teaspoons minced garlic

½ teaspoon crushed red pepper flakes

1 tablespoon chopped fresh parsley

2 pounds cleaned littleneck clams

Grilled garlic bread, for serving

Preheat the grill.

In a saucepan, combine butter, wine, lemon juice, garlic, red pepper flakes and parsley. Warm over low heat until the butter is melted. Keep warm.

Place clams on the hot grill and cover until the clams have opened and are cooked through, about 5 minutes.

Carefully remove the clams from the grill—try not to spill the juice—and place on a platter. Spoon butter sauce over each clam. Serve with grilled garlic bread. Makes 4 servings.

Tip: Adding soaked wood chips to the grill gives the clams a delicious smoky flavor.

Grilled Lemon Planks with Salmon and Green Tea/Jasmine Tea Oils

Sunkist Growers

24 uncooked salmon slices, ¼ ounce each, about 1 by ½ inch and ¼ inch thick

Kosher salt

¼ cup Greek-style plain yogurt

1 tablespoon fried shallots

1 tablespoon Korean red pepper threads or crushed red pepper

LEMON PLANKS

2 Sunkist lemons

2 teaspoons extra-virgin olive oil

1 pinch ground black pepper

GREEN TEA OIL

¼ cup olive oil

¼ teaspoon green tea powder

JASMINE TEA OIL

¼ cup virgin olive oil

½ teaspoon jasmine tea powder

Prepare the Lemon Planks: Wash lemons and slice each into 6 lengthwise sections. Toss lemons with olive oil and pepper. Preheat the grill on highest heat. Grill lemons on one side, creating dark-brown grill markings. Remove and place in a single layer on a baking sheet to cool.

Prepare the Green Tea Oil: Whisk all ingredients together. If there are lumps, strain.

Prepare the Jasmine Tea Oil: Whisk all ingredients together.

Preheat the oven broiler on the highest setting for at least 10 minutes. Season salmon with salt to taste. Arrange 2 salmon slices on top of each lemon plank and drizzle with green tea oil. Broil until the salmon is cooked through, about 2 minutes.

Transfer to a plate and garnish each with a small dollop of yogurt, fried shallots and red pepper. Drizzle the plate with both tea oils. Makes 12 servings.

Sunkist

Ceviche-Inspired Wild Alaska Salmon
Copper River Seafoods

1 tablespoon chopped garlic

1 pound skinless Alaska salmon, cut into ½-inch cubes

1 cup diced fresh tomato

1 cup peeled, seeded and diced cucumber

¼ cup finely diced jalapeño, or to taste

¼ cup finely diced red onion

¼ cup chopped fresh cilantro

½ cup lime juice

½ cup lemon juice

1 tablespoon ketchup

Taro chips or tortilla chips, for serving

In a large bowl, combine tomato, cucumber, jalapeño, red onion, cilantro, lime juice, lemon juice and ketchup. Gently fold together. Fold in the salmon, being careful not to break up the pieces. Chill in the refrigerator for 1 hour. Serve with your favorite dippers, such as taro chips or tortilla chips. Makes 4-6 servings.

Recipe courtesy of Shane Pennington, executive chef, Norton Sound Seafood House.

Heat a sauté pan over very low heat. Add garlic and salmon, and cook just until the salmon has no translucence. Spread the salmon on a sheet pan and cool in the refrigerator.

Shrimp Cocktail with Hummus

Sabra Dipping Company

2-4 tablespoons horseradish, to taste
Cheesecloth (see note)
1 cup Sabra Roasted Pine Nut Hummus
½ teaspoon Old Bay seasoning
1 cup chopped romaine lettuce
⅓ cup Bloody Mary mix

16 shrimp, cooked, peeled and chilled
4 thin lemon slices
2 tablespoons chopped green onion
¼ cup diced tomato

Special equipment: 4 martini glasses

Place horseradish in a piece of cheesecloth and squeeze to drain off excess liquid. Stir the hummus garnish thoroughly into the hummus. In a small bowl, combine the hummus, drained horseradish and Old Bay seasoning, stirring to blend.

Place some chopped romaine in each martini glass. Top with the hummus mixture. Drizzle with Bloody Mary mix. Place 4 shrimp and a lemon slice on the rim of each glass. Garnish with green onion and diced tomato. Makes 4 servings.

Note: If cheesecloth is not available, press horseradish against the side of the measuring cup with a fork and tilt to drain off excess liquid.

Raspberry and Brie Crostini
Dole Berry Company

½ cup seedless
 raspberry preserves

2 tablespoons
 Dijon-style mustard

18 slices (½ inch thick)
 baguette, lightly toasted

8 ounces Brie cheese,
 rind intact, cut into
 18 slices or pieces

1 6-ounce container
 Dole raspberries, rinsed
 and drained

Chopped fresh
 (or flat-leaf) parsley

Sea salt (optional)

In a small bowl, combine raspberry preserves and mustard.

Spread toasted bread with the preserve mixture. Top each with a slice of cheese and 2 raspberries.

Garnish with parsley and sprinkle with sea salt, if desired. Makes 9 servings.

Minted Grape Crostini
with Goat Cheese
Fowler Packing

1 cup balsamic vinegar

1 shallot, minced
 and sautéed

1½ cups red seedless
 grapes, quartered

3 tablespoons minced
 green onion

1½ teaspoons chopped
 fresh mint

1 baguette

2 tablespoons olive oil

2 teaspoons minced garlic

Salt and pepper

4 ounces goat cheese

Pour vinegar into a small saucepan and bring to a boil over medium-high heat. Reduce the heat to medium-low and simmer until the vinegar has reduced to about ¼ cup. Let cool.

Combine shallot, grapes, green onion and mint; stir to blend.

Preheat oven to 350°F.

Cut baguette on an angle into ½-inch-thick slices. Brush with oil, garlic, and salt and pepper to taste. Place on a baking sheet and bake for 10 minutes, or until lightly golden brown.

Spread goat cheese over the bread and cook under the broiler for 2 minutes, or until the cheese is slightly melted and lightly browned. Remove from the oven and let cool for 5 minutes.

To serve, top the crostini with the grape mixture and drizzle with ½ teaspoon of the balsamic reduction. Makes about 20 servings. (Serving size varies, based on the size of the baguette.)

Tip: Store leftover balsamic reduction, covered, in the fridge.

Crostini with Prosciutto di Parma, Parmigiano-Reggiano and Figs

Arthur Schuman/Citterio USA

2 cups fresh figs, stemmed, quartered and halved again

¾ cup tawny port (optional)

1 French baguette

3 tablespoons extra-virgin olive oil, divided

1 teaspoon grated orange zest

1 teaspoon grated lemon zest

½ cup ricotta cheese

6-8 ounces Kirkland Signature Parmigiano-Reggiano cheese, divided

Cracked black pepper

1 12-ounce package Citterio Prosciutto di Parma

Combine figs and port; let marinate for 1 hour. Preheat oven to 325°F. Cut twelve ¼- to ½-inch-thick slices from the baguette. Brush the slices with olive oil. Place on an ungreased baking sheet. Bake until crisp and lightly browned, about 3-4 minutes. (Or use a panini press.) Remove from the heat and let cool.

In a bowl, mix orange zest, lemon zest, ricotta and ¼ cup grated Parmigiano-Reggiano. Add pepper to taste. Spread the ricotta mixture on the crostini. Fold 1 slice of prosciutto over the cheese mixture on each slice. Top with a spoonful of figs and a few shavings of Parmigiano-Reggiano. Arrange the crostini on a plate. Garnish the plate with nuggets of Parmigiano-Reggiano and drizzle the entire plate with olive oil and port. Makes 8-10 servings.

Pomegranate Relish
POM Wonderful

3 tablespoons finely diced shallots

1 teaspoon lemon juice

¼ teaspoon kosher salt, plus more to taste

¼ cup extra-virgin olive oil

½ cup arils from POM Wonderful pomegranates, or ½ cup POM POMS fresh arils

1 tablespoon sliced flat-leaf parsley

Freshly ground black pepper

Toasted crostini and Brie cheese, for serving

POM MOLASSES

3 cups juice from POM Wonderful pomegranates, or 3 cups POM Wonderful 100% pomegranate juice

¼ cup sugar

Juice of 1 lemon

Prepare the molasses: In a saucepan, combine pomegranate juice, sugar and lemon juice. Bring to a simmer and cook until a very thick syrup forms that coats the back of a spoon. Remove from the heat and let cool to room temperature.

In a small bowl, combine shallots, lemon juice and salt; let sit for 5 minutes. Whisk in 1 tablespoon POM molasses and then olive oil. Stir in arils, parsley and pepper to taste. Taste for balance and seasoning.

Serve on crostini with Brie. Makes 2-4 servings.

Tip: The remaining molasses can be stored, covered, in the refrigerator.

Pesto Potato "Crostini"
Alsum Farms & Produce, Inc./RPE

Cooking spray

1½ pounds Wisconsin russet potatoes, peeled and cut into ½-inch-thick slices

½ teaspoon seasoned salt, divided

¾ cup cream cheese, softened

¼ cup prepared pesto

¼-½ teaspoon hot pepper sauce (optional)

¼ cup finely chopped prepared roasted red peppers

Small basil leaves, for garnish (optional)

Preheat oven to 400°F. Spray a baking sheet with cooking spray.

On the baking sheet, arrange sliced raw potatoes in a single layer. Spray lightly with cooking spray to coat the tops of the potatoes. Sprinkle evenly with ¼ teaspoon seasoned salt.

Roast the potatoes for 20-25 minutes, or until tender and browned, turning the potatoes over once and sprinkling with the remaining seasoned salt.

While the potatoes are cooking, mix together cream cheese, pesto and hot pepper sauce in a small bowl. Set aside.

To serve, pipe or spoon about 2 teaspoons of the cream cheese mixture onto each potato slice and top with chopped red peppers and basil leaves, if desired. Makes 8 servings.

Pineapple Salsa and Fresh Mozzarella Bruschetta

Ready Pac

4 cups diced (¼ inch) Ready Pac Sliced Gold Pineapple

1½ cups diced red onion

1 cup diced red bell pepper

¼ cup chopped fresh cilantro

¼ cup minced jalapeños, seeds removed

½ cup extra-virgin olive oil, divided

¼ cup fresh lemon juice

1½ teaspoons grated lemon zest

½ teaspoon coarse sea salt, plus more to taste

1 French baguette, sliced diagonally into ¼-inch-thick slices (32 slices)

1 pound fresh mozzarella cheese

Coarsely ground black pepper

In a mixing bowl, combine pineapple, red onions, bell pepper, cilantro and jalapeños. Toss lightly with spatulas to mix. Set aside.

In a small bowl, whisk together ¼ cup olive oil, lemon juice, lemon zest and ½ teaspoon salt. Drizzle over the pineapple mixture. Mix well. Cover with plastic wrap and refrigerate for 30 minutes to 2 hours.

Meanwhile, preheat oven to 400°F. Arrange bread slices on a large baking sheet. Brush lightly with the remaining olive oil. Bake until lightly golden brown, 8-10 minutes. Cut mozzarella into 16 slices, then cut each slice in half.

To serve, arrange the toasted bread slices on a serving platter. Top each bread slice with a mozzarella slice. Sprinkle lightly with salt and pepper. Spoon equal portions of the pineapple mixture over the mozzarella slices. Makes 8-10 servings.

Grape and Goat Cheese Bruschetta

Stevco

1 cup chopped seedless grapes
⅔ cup goat cheese crumbles
12 slices (½ inch thick)
  whole- wheat baguette

Extra-virgin olive oil
Balsamic vinegar

Preheat the oven broiler. In a medium bowl, lightly toss together grapes and goat cheese. Set aside. Place baguette slices on a baking sheet and broil for

30-45 seconds. Remove from the oven and turn the slices over. Lightly brush the tops with olive oil. Place a small spoonful of the grape and goat cheese mixture on top of each baguette slice. Broil for about 3-4 minutes, or until golden brown. Drizzle with vinegar and serve. Makes 12 servings.

Broccoli Rabe Pesto
Andy Boy

2 cups Andy Boy iceless premium-cut broccoli rabe

½ cup extra-virgin olive oil, plus more for sautéing

1 garlic clove, peeled

¾ cup walnuts or pignoli (pine nuts)

½ teaspoon salt

Blanch broccoli rabe in boiling water for 2 minutes; drain. Sauté broccoli rabe in olive oil over medium heat for 4 minutes, or until tender but not soft. Remove from the heat and let cool.

In a small food processor, puree garlic. Add nuts and process to a fine consistency. Add the cooled broccoli rabe and process until smooth. Add salt and olive oil; process until the oil is fully incorporated.

Spread the pesto over your favorite grilled bread or sandwich or use as a dip with your favorite chips. Makes 4-6 servings.

Recipe courtesy of Angela Gismondi.

Parmesan Herb Crackers
Kirkland Signature/Olde Thompson

½ cup (1 stick) unsalted butter, at room temperature

1 cup grated Parmesan cheese

2½ teaspoons Kirkland Signature Organic No-Salt Seasoning ⬤Organic

1 cup all-purpose flour

Kirkland Signature parchment paper

In a medium bowl, beat butter and Parmesan together with a hand mixer. Add no-salt seasoning and beat until combined. Slowly add flour and beat just until combined (the mixture will be crumbly).

Pour the mixture onto a clean surface and firmly press into a 1½-inch-thick log. Wrap tightly in plastic wrap and refrigerate for a minimum of 45 minutes.

Preheat oven to 350°F. Line a baking sheet with parchment paper.

Cut the log into slices about ⅜ inch thick and place on the lined baking sheet. Bake for 15-20 minutes, or until golden around the edges. Let cool on the pan for 10 minutes before serving. Makes 24-30 crackers.

KIRKLAND *Signature*

Raspberry Salsa
Naturipe Farms

1½ cups raspberries,
  1 cup diced

½ cup seeded and
  diced tomatoes

½ cup diced fresh jicama

½ cup diced fresh mango

3 tablespoons chopped
  fresh cilantro

1 tablespoon minced
  jalapeño

Juice of 1 lime
  (2 tablespoons)

1 tablespoon honey

¼ teaspoon salt

In a bowl, combine all ingredients and stir to blend.

Serve with chips or on top of cream cheese. Makes 2 cups.

Tip: This can also be served with fish as an entrée.

Avocado Fruit Salsa
Nature's Partner/Mulholland Citrus/Sequoia Orange

3 medium-sized ripe
  avocados, pitted, peeled
  and diced

3 tablespoons lemon juice

½ cup plain Greek yogurt

2 tablespoons agave nectar

2 California-grown
  mandarins, peeled
  and segmented

2 navel oranges, peeled,
  segmented and diced

2 nectarines, pitted
  and diced

2 kiwifruit, peeled
  and diced

1 cup diced seedless
  watermelon

1 cup blueberries

1 cup red or green seedless
  grapes, halved

Cinnamon sugar pita chips,
  for serving

In a large bowl, mix avocados and lemon juice. Drain off excess lemon juice and save it. Set the avocados aside.

In a small bowl, thoroughly whisk the reserved lemon juice, yogurt and agave nectar.

Add mandarins, oranges, nectarines, kiwifruit, watermelon, blueberries and grapes to the avocados in the large bowl. Gently mix to combine. Fold in the dressing.

Serve with cinnamon sugar pita chips. Makes 8-10 servings.

Sweet and Spicy Watermelon Salsa

Dulcinea Farms

3 cups finely diced
   Dulcinea PureHeart mini
   seedless watermelon

1 jalapeño, seeded
   and diced

½ cup finely diced
   red onion

¼ cup chopped fresh
   cilantro, plus sprigs
   for garnish

2 tablespoons fresh
   lime juice

1 tablespoon agave nectar

½ teaspoon garlic salt

Tortilla chips, for serving

In a medium bowl, combine watermelon, jalapeño, onion, cilantro, lime juice, agave nectar and garlic salt. Mix well.

Cover and refrigerate for 1 hour.

When the salsa is chilled, scoop into a serving dish and garnish with cilantro sprigs. Serve with tortilla chips. Makes 6 servings.

Blueberry Corn Salsa

HBF International

1 pint HBF International
   blueberries, chopped

1 cup frozen corn

1 cucumber, diced

1 yellow bell pepper, diced

1 bunch of cilantro, chopped

1 red onion, diced

1 jalapeño or serrano
   pepper, seeded and diced

¼ cup honey

Juice of 1 lime

1 tablespoon grated
   fresh ginger

1 tablespoon ground cumin

½ teaspoon kosher salt

In a bowl, combine all ingredients and stir to blend.

Chill for 1 hour.

Serve with pita chips or tortilla chips. Makes 8-10 servings.

Naturally Aged Queso
Tillamook

2 cups (8 ounces) cubed Tillamook Monterey Jack Cheese

1 cup (4 ounces) cubed Tillamook Medium Cheddar Cheese

2 jalapeños, stems and seeds removed, finely chopped

¼ red onion, diced

1 tablespoon chopped fresh cilantro

1 Roma tomato, chopped

1 dash of cayenne pepper

3 dashes of Tabasco sauce

Preheat oven to 450°F.

Mix all ingredients in a medium-sized bowl, then arrange in a terra-cotta baking dish. Bake until the cheese is thoroughly melted, about 10-12 minutes.

Remove from the oven and let cool for 2-3 minutes, then enjoy immediately.

Gather friends and family and serve as a dip with your favorite tortilla chips. Makes 4 servings.

Recipe courtesy of Chef Hosea Rosenberg, owner, Blackbelly Catering in Boulder, Colorado, and Bravo's Top Chef Season Five Winner. www.blackbellycatering.com, 303.247.1000

Tillamook

Marinated Tomato, Fresh Fig and Feta Cheese Pizza
Stellar Distributing

3 cups seeded, cubed vine-ripe tomatoes

1 tablespoon chopped fresh garlic

¼ cup shredded fresh basil

¼ cup chopped green or black olives

¼ cup olive oil

Pinch of salt

3 balls of pizza dough (8 ounces each)

1 pound (about 16) fresh California figs, sliced

12 ounces feta cheese

In a large bowl, combine tomatoes, garlic, basil, olives, olive oil and salt. Let stand for 30-45 minutes.

Preheat oven to 500°F.

Roll out each pizza dough ball into a circle about ½ inch thick and 10 inches in diameter. Place on a baking sheet. Spread with marinated tomatoes. Top with sliced figs and sprinkle with cheese.

Bake until the cheese is melted and the crust is browned, about 8-10 minutes. Cut each pizza into 8 wedges and serve hot. Makes 24 servings.

Nutritional information: Each serving has 150 calories (38% from fat), 5 g protein, 19 g carbohydrates, 7 g fat (3 g saturated), 15 mg cholesterol, 1 g fiber, 330 mg sodium, 5 g sugar, 100 mg potassium.

Recipe courtesy of De Angelo's Restaurant, Merced, California.

Beef Filet Pretzel Sliders with Horseradish Sour Cream Sauce

Daisy Brand/Labriola Baking Company

4 2-ounce beef filet tenders, USDA Choice or better

Kosher salt

Coarsely ground black pepper

4 Labriola Pretzel Slider Buns

CARAMELIZED ONIONS

2 tablespoons unsalted butter

1 Spanish onion, julienne cut

1 tablespoon brown sugar

Pinch of salt

Pinch of pepper

HORSERADISH SOUR CREAM SAUCE

8 ounces Daisy Brand Sour Cream

2 tablespoons prepared horseradish

2 teaspoons finely chopped chives

Pinch of salt and pepper

Prepare the onions: In a sauté pan over medium-high heat, combine butter, onions, brown sugar, salt and pepper. Toss until the butter is melted and the onions are coated with the sugar, salt and pepper. Continue to cook, tossing every 90 seconds, until the onions are dark brown and caramelized. Set aside.

Prepare the sauce: In a medium mixing bowl, combine all ingredients. Fold until all ingredients are incorporated. Let stand.

Season both sides of beef filet tenders with salt and pepper. Heat a sauté pan over medium-high heat. Place the seasoned filets in the middle and leave for 2 minutes. Turn and cook for an additional 2 minutes. (Add or subtract time according to taste.) Remove from the pan and let rest for 2 minutes. Slice each tender into 4 strips.

Slice buns in half. On each bottom half, layer caramelized onions, filet slices and horseradish sour cream sauce. Add the top half. Makes 4 servings.

Chocolate Malt-Cherry Snack Mix
General Mills

2 cups Corn Chex cereal

2 cups Rice Chex cereal

2 cups Wheat Chex cereal

1 cup dry-roasted peanuts

1 cup semisweet chocolate chips

¼ cup butter or margarine

1 cup natural-flavored malted milk powder

2 cups miniature marshmallows

1½ cups coarsely chopped malted milk balls

½ cup dried cherries, chopped

In a large bowl, mix cereals and peanuts.

In a 1-quart microwavable bowl, microwave chocolate chips and butter on high for 1 minute; stir. Microwave about 30 seconds longer, or until the mixture can be stirred smooth. Pour over the cereal mixture, stirring until evenly coated.

Gradually stir in malted milk powder until evenly coated. Stir in remaining ingredients. Spread on waxed paper to cool. Store in an airtight container. Makes 26 servings (½ cup each).

Nutritional information: Each ½-cup serving has 190 calories (70 calories from fat), 3 g protein, 25 g carbohydrates, 8 g fat (4 g saturated, 0 g trans fat), 5 mg cholesterol, 2 g fiber, 170 mg sodium, 14 g sugar.

Green Tea Mango Spritzer
Kirkland Signature/Ito En

2 cups water

4 Kirkland Signature/ Ito En green tea bags

⅓ cup honey or sugar

2 cups mango nectar

2 cups chilled seltzer

Ice cubes

6 fresh mango spears

¼ cup fresh blueberries

Mint sprigs, for garnish (optional)

Heat water to 175°F. Add teabags and steep for 30 seconds. Remove the teabags and add honey or sugar to the brewed tea. Let cool, then refrigerate until chilled.

Add mango nectar and seltzer to the chilled tea.

Pour over ice cubes into individual glasses. Add mango spears and a sprinkling of blueberries.

Garnish with a fresh mint sprig. Makes 6 servings.

Variation: Add a splash of vodka to each glass for a Tipsy Spritzer.

Apple Sangria
Borton & Sons

3½ cups chopped Borton & Sons Honeycrisp or Pink Lady apples (about 2 pounds)

½ cup apple schnapps

½ cup honey

4 whole cloves

2 3-inch cinnamon sticks

2 ¼-inch slices peeled fresh ginger

1 large navel orange, quartered

1 750-milliliter bottle fruity red wine (such as Beaujolais)

¼ cup club soda, chilled

4 thin horizontal slices Honeycrisp or Pink Lady apples

In a large bowl, combine first 8 ingredients; stir well. Refrigerate for 4 hours, or until thoroughly chilled.

Strain the wine mixture through a sieve into a bowl. Discard the solids.

Pour about ⅔ cup sangria over ice into each of 4 glasses. Top with 1 tablespoon club soda and 1 apple slice. Makes 4 servings.

South African Sundowners
Seald Sweet

2 cups sugar

2 cups water

Ice cubes

3 South African oranges, divided

1 lemon

1½-2 ounces vodka

To prepare simple syrup, combine sugar and water in a saucepan. Bring to a quick boil, stirring with a wooden spoon until the sugar dissolves. Cool completely.

To prepare the drinks, fill a 32-ounce cocktail shaker half full with ice cubes. Squeeze the juice from 2 oranges and 1 lemon into the shaker. Add ¼ cup of the simple syrup; save extra simple syrup in a covered plastic container and refrigerate for future use. Add vodka.

Shake vigorously and pour into chilled martini glasses. Garnish with orange slices. Makes 2 servings.

Creamy Citrus Shake
Sunny Delight

½ cup milk

¾ cup SunnyD Tangy Original

4 large scoops vanilla ice cream or frozen yogurt

Orange slices, for garnish

In a blender, combine milk, SunnyD and ice cream; blend until smooth.

Pour into glasses and garnish with orange slices. Makes 2 servings.

Coffee Smoothie
Starbucks Coffee

¾ cup low-fat vanilla frozen yogurt

¼ cup cold nonfat milk

1 stick Starbucks VIA Ready Brew

1 banana

1 cup ice

In a blender, combine frozen yogurt, milk, Starbucks VIA Ready Brew, banana and ice.

Blend and serve. Makes 1 serving.

Tip: Try a scoop of protein powder in this afternoon pick-me-up.

Apple and Carrot Smoothie with Ginger

Stemilt Growers

¾ cup ice cubes

2 Stemilt apples, quartered and cored

2 medium carrots, ends trimmed, cut into 1-inch lengths

½- to 1-inch-square knob of peeled fresh ginger

½ navel orange, peel and pith removed

½ small banana, peeled

1 tablespoon golden flaxseed meal (optional)

½-1 cup water (depending on preferred consistency)

Place ice cubes in a blender, followed by apples, carrots, ginger, orange, banana and flax meal. Add ½ cup water.

Blend on high (or on "whole juice," or "smoothie," as applicable on blender settings) for designated time, or about 1 minute, until the ingredients are completely broken down/puréed.

Blend in additional water to thin out, if desired. Serve immediately. Makes about 3 servings.

Blueberry Cranberry Smoothie

Kirkland Signature/Cott

1¼ cups Kirkland Signature cranberry juice cocktail, chilled

2 cups frozen blueberries

½ cup almond milk

¼ cup orange juice

2 tablespoons honey

¼ cup ice cubes

Combine cranberry juice, blueberries, almond milk, orange juice, honey and ice cubes in a blender.

Spin on the highest setting, blending until smooth.

Pour into glasses. Serve immediately. Makes 2-3 servings.

Tip: For a tropical twist, add ½ cup pineapple chunks.

Soups & Sides

Orzo Risotto
Kirkland Signature/Kerry

- 2 tablespoons Kirkland Signature extra virgin olive oil
- 2 tablespoons Kirkland Signature salted butter
- 2 cups uncooked orzo pasta
- ½ cup finely diced onion
- 1½ teaspoons minced garlic
- ½ cup dry white wine
- 4 cups Kirkland Signature organic chicken stock, divided
- ¼ teaspoon ground white pepper
- ⅓ cup chopped fresh parsley
- 1 cup grated Parmesan cheese
- 1 pound Kirkland Signature shrimp, cooked (optional)

In a 2-quart saucepan, heat olive oil and butter over medium heat. When the oil is hot and the butter melted, add orzo and toast lightly, about 3 minutes.

Add onion and sauté until soft, about 3 minutes. Mix in garlic and sauté until fragrant, about 30 seconds.

Add wine and cook, stirring, until it has nearly evaporated. Add 2 cups of stock and cook, stirring constantly, until it has been absorbed by the orzo.

Add remaining 2 cups of stock and white pepper. Cook, stirring, until absorbed by the orzo.

Remove the saucepan from the heat. Stir in parsley, Parmesan and shrimp (if desired). Makes 6-8 servings.

Blueberry Quinoa Risotto
Frank Donio/Sunny Valley

- ¼ cup diced onion
- 3 tablespoons olive oil
- 1 cup quinoa
- ½ cup white wine (such as Pinot Grigio)
- 3 cups chicken broth, divided
- 1 cup fresh blueberries
- 1 tablespoon fresh thyme
- ½ teaspoon lemon juice
- Salt and pepper

In a large skillet, sauté onion in olive oil over medium heat until the onion is translucent.

Add quinoa, wine and ½ cup chicken broth; cook, stirring, for about 1 minute.

Add blueberries, thyme and ½ cup chicken broth; cover, lower the heat, and simmer, stirring occasionally. Continue adding chicken broth in ½-cup increments as it is absorbed.

When the broth is almost completely absorbed, remove from the heat and stir in lemon juice. Add salt and pepper to taste and serve hot. Makes 4 servings.

Broccoli and Pancetta Quinoa Patties

Taylor Farms

1 cup quinoa

4 cups Taylor Farms broccoli florets

2 ounces pancetta, cubed

3 garlic cloves, minced

3 green onions, finely chopped

½ cup bread crumbs

¾ cup grated Parmesan cheese

2 large eggs, beaten

¼ cup chopped fresh Italian parsley

¼ cup chopped fresh basil leaves

½ teaspoon salt and pepper to taste

Extra-virgin olive oil

Rinse quinoa in a mesh strainer. Cook in 2 cups of boiling water for 15 minutes. Set aside.

Meanwhile, steam broccoli florets until tender. Finely chop and set aside.

In a small frying pan, cook pancetta and garlic over medium heat for 6-8 minutes.

In a large bowl, combine pancetta and garlic, green onions, broccoli, bread crumbs, cheese, eggs, parsley, basil, quinoa, salt and pepper to taste. Mix well and form into patties (makes roughly 10-14 patties).

Heat oil in a nonstick frying pan over medium-low heat. Add patties and cook for 7-10 minutes, or until the bottoms are browned. With a spatula, carefully flip and cook for 7 minutes, until browned. Set the patties on paper-towel-lined plates to absorb excess oil. Makes 10-14 patties.

Easy Grilled Potato and Onion Packets

Basin Gold Cooperative

2 large Basin Gold russet potatoes, thinly sliced

1 large Basin Gold yellow onion, thinly sliced

½ red bell pepper, thinly sliced

½ green bell pepper, thinly sliced

½ cup shredded Parmesan cheese

Leaves from 2 sprigs of rosemary, coarsely chopped

Salt and pepper

4 tablespoons extra-virgin olive oil

Preheat grill for medium heat.

For each packet, measure out 2 squares of aluminum foil large enough to easily wrap the vegetables. Layer one piece of foil on top of the other. Place a quarter of the potatoes, onion and peppers in the center and sprinkle with some Parmesan, rosemary, and salt and pepper to taste. Drizzle with 1 tablespoon of olive oil. Wrap into a flattened square and seal the edges. Repeat with the remaining ingredients.

Place the aluminum-wrapped packages over indirect heat and cover the grill. Cook for approximately 30-40 minutes, turning once. The packets are ready when the potatoes are tender. Serve hot off the grill. Makes 4 servings.

Tip: For a little kick, add some red pepper flakes to the packets.

Basin Gold

Fiesta Potato Smashers
Top Brass Marketing/Farm Fresh Direct

5 small yellow potatoes
and 5 small red potatoes

1 pint sweet mini peppers

Cooking spray

4 tablespoons fat-free sour
cream or fat-free Greek
yogurt (optional)

8 sprigs cilantro

Salt, chili powder and
freshly ground pepper

Place whole potatoes (do not poke) in a microwave-safe covered dish. Microwave on high for 3-4 minutes, or until nearly tender.

While the potatoes are cooking, cut mini peppers into ¼-inch slices. Spray a nonstick pan with cooking spray and heat to medium. Add the peppers and sauté until they start to brown. Remove from the pan and set aside.

Remove the potatoes from the microwave. Using a layer of paper towels to cover each potato, smash them on a cutting board until 1¾ inches thick.

Spray the sauté pan with cooking spray, heat on high, and add the smashed potatoes. Cook for 1-2 minutes, or until the potatoes start to brown.

Place the potatoes on a plate and layer with sour cream or yogurt, peppers and cilantro. Dust with salt, chili powder and pepper to taste. Serve warm. Makes 8-10 servings.

Individual Red Potato and Onion Tartes Tatin
Wallace Farms/Skagit Valley's Best Produce/Valley Pride

3 sheets frozen puff
pastry, thawed

2 tablespoons olive oil

3 medium sweet onions,
thinly sliced, separated

¾ cup crumbled
Gorgonzola cheese

12 small Washington
red potatoes, thinly
sliced (unpeeled)

Salt and pepper

Special equipment:
6 4¼-by-1-inch metal
tart pans with
removable bottoms

With a rolling pin, roll out puff pastry to ⅛-inch thickness. Using the top edge of a tart pan, cut out 6 pastry circles. Prick each circle with a fork. Place on a cookie sheet. Refrigerate for 30 minutes.

Preheat oven to 400°F. Butter the tart pans.

Heat olive oil in a sauté pan over medium heat. Add onion slices and cook, stirring occasionally, until golden and caramelized.

Arrange some onion slices in each tart pan. Sprinkle with cheese. Add a layer of potato slices. Sprinkle with salt and pepper to taste. Repeat the layers. Place a circle of chilled puff pastry on top of each tart.

Bake until the tops are puffed and golden, about 20 minutes. Invert onto a plate and serve. Makes 6 servings.

Nutritional information: Each serving has 299 calories, 10 g protein, 31 g carbohydrates, 15 g fat (46% calories from fat), 21 mg cholesterol, 4 g fiber, 501 mg sodium.

Potato Salad
Kirschenman

5 pounds unpeeled new red potatoes (or peeled if you like), cut into 1-inch pieces

1 teaspoon salt

1½ cups mayonnaise

1 tablespoon distilled white vinegar

4 tablespoons milk

Coarse salt

Freshly ground pepper

¾ cup thinly sliced green onions

¾ cup diced yellow onion

1 cup diced celery

¼ cup chopped fresh dill

¾ cup diced (¼ inch) dill pickles

1 cup diced white Cheddar cheese

6 hard-boiled eggs, coarsely chopped

In a large pot, cover potatoes with cold water; add salt. Bring to a boil, then reduce the heat, cover, and simmer until the potatoes are tender when pierced with a fork, about 20 minutes. Drain, then rinse with cold water to stop the cooking. Let the potatoes cool before mixing with the other ingredients.

In a large bowl, whisk together mayonnaise, vinegar and milk. Add a little salt and pepper. Add the potatoes and gently combine with a rubber spatula. Add the remaining ingredients, again gently combining. Season to taste with salt and pepper. Makes 12-14 servings.

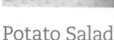

Grilled Potato Salad with Vegetables, Bacon and Balsamic Syrup
Rupari Foods

Serve as an accompaniment to Tony Roma's ribs.

1 pound mini new potatoes

1 large red onion, cut into 1½-inch chunks

4 ounces white mushrooms, cut in half

1 yellow bell pepper, cut into 1½-inch chunks

6 garlic cloves, minced

3 tablespoons olive oil

1 teaspoon chopped fresh oregano

Salt and pepper

6 slices thick-cut bacon, fried crisp and chopped

¼ cup grated Parmesan cheese

BALSAMIC SYRUP

½ cup balsamic vinegar

2 tablespoons brown sugar

Prepare the balsamic syrup: In a small saucepan, combine vinegar and sugar. Bring to a boil over medium-high heat, then lower the heat and simmer until reduced to ¼ cup, about 8-10 minutes. Let cool.

Boil potatoes for 10-15 minutes, until fork tender. Drain.

Preheat the grill to medium-high.

In a large bowl, combine potatoes, onion, mushrooms, pepper, garlic, olive oil, oregano, and salt and pepper to taste. Gently toss. Pour into a grill basket. Grill for 10-12 minutes per side, or until lightly charred and tender.

Arrange the grilled vegetables on a platter. Garnish with bacon and cheese. Drizzle with balsamic syrup. Makes 6-8 servings.

Ratatouille
BC Hot House Foods

4 BC Hot House
  mini eggplants

Salt

2 yellow onions

3 BC Hot House bell peppers

5 zucchini

4 BC Hot House
  beefsteak tomatoes

Olive oil

4 garlic cloves, minced

1 bay leaf

4 sprigs of thyme

¼ cup sliced basil, plus
  more for garnish

Pepper

Chop eggplants into bite-size cubes, toss with salt and strain.

Dice onions. Chop peppers, zucchini and tomatoes into bite-size pieces and keep separate.

Warm 1 teaspoon oil in a large pot over medium heat. Add onions and a pinch of salt. Sauté until softened. Add peppers and cook for 5 minutes. Transfer to a bowl.

Add 1 teaspoon oil and sauté zucchini with a pinch of salt for 5 minutes. Transfer to the bowl.

Warm 2 teaspoons oil and sauté eggplant for 10 minutes. Transfer to the bowl.

Warm 1 teaspoon oil and sauté garlic for 1 minute. Add tomatoes, bay leaf and thyme. Stir in the other vegetables. Simmer on low for 45 minutes.

Just before serving, stir in basil and pepper to taste. Sprinkle each serving with basil and a drizzle of olive oil. Makes 8-10 servings.

Oven-Roasted Baby Carrots and Potatoes with Garlic
Grimmway Farms

5-6 cups Bunny-Luv organic
  baby carrots ⬤Organic

2-3 pounds red potatoes,
  peeled and cut into
  about 2-inch pieces

⅓ cup olive oil

4-8 garlic cloves,
  finely chopped

2 tablespoons coarse salt

Freshly ground
  black pepper

Preheat oven to 400°F.

Dry carrots and potatoes well with a paper towel and place in a large bowl.

In a small bowl, combine olive oil, garlic, salt and pepper to taste; mix well to blend. Pour over the veggies and toss to coat with a wooden spoon or clean hands. Spread on a large nonstick baking sheet or a pan lined with foil and sprayed liberally with cooking spray.

Roast for about 30 minutes, or until the potatoes are fork-tender, tossing occasionally.

Makes 4-6 servings.

Asparagus with Cherry and Honey Vinaigrette

Gourmet Trading/Jacobs Malcolm & Burtt/Grower Direct

1 pound fresh asparagus spears
1 teaspoon salt
½ cup walnut halves
¼ teaspoon finely grated
   lemon zest

CHERRY AND HONEY VINAIGRETTE
1 cup extra-virgin olive oil
⅓ cup red wine vinegar
2½ tablespoons Dijon mustard
2½ tablespoons honey
⅔ cup chopped California cherries
Salt and pepper

Prepare the vinaigrette: In a small bowl, whisk olive oil, vinegar, mustard and honey. Add cherries and salt and pepper to taste. The vinaigrette can be stored, covered, for up to a week in the refrigerator. Let it warm to room temperature before using.

Break the woody ends off the asparagus. Soak in cold water for a few minutes. Bring a large pot of water to a boil. Add salt to the boiling water. Have a large pan of iced water ready.

Add asparagus to the boiling salted water. Cook until just tender, 3-7 minutes. Quickly remove the spears with tongs and drop in the iced water. Drain, then pat the spears dry.

Arrange the asparagus on a large platter and drizzle with the vinaigrette. Sprinkle with walnuts and lemon zest. Makes 4 servings.

  JACOBS MALCOLM & BURTT

Grape Tomato Biscuits
Houweling's Tomatoes

2 cups Houweling's grape tomatoes, washed and sliced in half

3 cups all-purpose flour

1 tablespoon baking powder

½ teaspoon baking soda

½ teaspoon salt

¾ cup cold butter, cut into cubes

1 large egg

¾ cup cold buttermilk

¾ cup ricotta cheese

1 egg, lightly beaten, for egg wash

Preheat oven to 225°F.

Place tomatoes cut side up on a baking tray lined with parchment paper. Bake for 3 hours, or until shriveled and dried up. Remove and let cool.

Preheat oven to 400°F.

In a bowl, sift together flour, baking powder, baking soda and salt. Cut in butter until the mixture resembles coarse meal. In a separate bowl, lightly beat egg and buttermilk. Add to the flour mixture all at once and stir just enough for the dough to come together. Add the cooled tomatoes and ricotta, gently blending.

Place the dough on a floured board and roll or pat into a 1-inch thickness. Cut into biscuits using a 2-inch cookie cutter. Reshape and roll out excess dough to create more biscuits. Place on a parchment-lined baking sheet and brush with egg wash. Bake for 12-15 minutes. Serve warm or at room temperature. Makes 12 biscuits.

Mango and Avocado Salsa
Freska Produce/Amazon Produce Network

2 firm but ripe mangoes, peeled, pitted and diced

2 firm but ripe avocados, peeled, pitted and diced

2 tablespoons minced, seeded serrano pepper

¼ cup diced red onion

¼ cup diced red bell pepper

2 tablespoons chopped fresh cilantro leaves

Grated zest and juice of 1 lime

1 teaspoon chili powder

1 tablespoon extra-virgin olive oil

In a bowl, combine all ingredients.

Let sit at room temperature for 10 minutes before serving to allow the flavors to blend.

Serve with grilled chicken or grilled fish such as tuna or mahi-mahi. Makes 8 servings.

Recipe courtesy of the National Mango Board, 2013.

Southwest Chicken Vegetable Soup

Better Than Bouillon

1 tablespoon extra-virgin olive oil

1 medium yellow onion

4 cups water

2 tablespoons Better Than Bouillon All-Natural Reduced Sodium Chicken Base

1 (14.5-ounce) can petite cut tomatoes, undrained

2 (5.5-ounce) cans spicy tomato juice

⅓ cup prepared salsa

2 medium carrots, peeled and sliced

1 celery rib, sliced

2 tablespoons freshly squeezed lime juice

1 cup frozen corn

2 teaspoons ground cumin

1 teaspoon chili powder

½ teaspoon ground oregano

½ teaspoon garlic powder

½ teaspoon salt

1 (15-ounce) can black beans

2 cups cooked, chopped chicken

¼ cup chopped cilantro

Heat olive oil in a soup pot over medium-high heat. Chop onion, add to the pot, and cook, stirring, until tender.

Reduce the heat to medium. Add water, then stir in chicken base until dissolved. Add tomatoes, tomato juice, salsa, carrots, celery, lime juice, corn, cumin, chili powder, oregano, garlic powder and salt. Stir and bring to a boil.

Reduce the heat, cover, and simmer for 15 minutes, stirring occasionally. Rinse and drain beans; add to the soup with chicken and cilantro. Stir and heat through. Makes 8 servings.

SOUTHEASTERN *Mills.*

Organic Chicken Chipotle Tortilla Soup

Kirkland Signature

8 cups organic chicken broth

2 tablespoons canola or vegetable oil, divided

1 cup diced yellow onion

½ bunch cilantro, chopped

30 Kirkland Signature organic tortilla chips ❂Organic

1 canned chipotle pepper

½ teaspoon ground cumin

1 teaspoon sugar

2 boneless, skinless organic chicken breasts ❂Organic

1 zucchini

1 ear white corn

1 tablespoon fresh-squeezed lime juice

Queso fresco, for serving

Place chicken broth in a pot and bring to a simmer over medium-high heat.

In a saucepan, heat 1 tablespoon oil over medium-high heat. Add onion, cover, and cook until translucent. Add cilantro and tortilla chips, then ladle in enough broth to cover. Simmer, covered, for 20 minutes, or until soft. Add chipotle, cumin and sugar. Puree with a mixing wand or blender. Add to the chicken broth. Simmer for 15 minutes.

Grill chicken until lightly browned. Coat zucchini and corn with 1 tablespoon oil and grill until you see char marks.

Dice the chicken and zucchini. Cut corn kernels off the cob. Add to the soup. Add lime juice. Crumble cheese on top. Makes about 6 servings.

Garlic and Potato Soup
Christopher Ranch/MountainKing Potatoes

1½ cups peeled Christopher Ranch garlic cloves

1½ teaspoons extra-virgin olive oil, divided

¾ teaspoon salt, divided

¼ teaspoon ground black pepper

2 cups sliced onions

3 cups peeled and diced MountainKing Butter Gold potatoes

1 bay leaf

4¾ cups vegetable stock

1 teaspoon chopped fresh thyme

¾ cup heavy cream

¼ teaspoon ground white pepper

1½ teaspoons chopped fresh chives, parsley or basil, for garnish

Shredded Parmesan cheese, for garnish

Preheat oven to 325°F. Place garlic cloves on a baking sheet. Sprinkle with ½ teaspoon olive oil, ¼ teaspoon salt and black pepper, coating evenly. Roast in the oven for 25-30 minutes, or until the cloves are light brown and soft.

Heat 1 teaspoon olive oil in a large saucepan over medium heat. Add onions and potatoes; sauté, stirring continuously, for 2 minutes. Stir in the roasted garlic, bay leaf and vegetable stock. Bring to a boil, then reduce the heat and stir in thyme. Simmer, uncovered, for 15-20 minutes, or until the potatoes are cooked.

Stir in heavy cream, ½ teaspoon salt and white pepper. Remove and discard the bay leaf. Carefully pour the soup into a blender and puree.

Garnish each bowl of soup with chopped chives, parsley or basil and/or shredded Parmesan. Makes about 10 servings.

Salads

Firecracker Salad

NatureSweet

8 ounces thin yellow or green beans, trimmed

5 tablespoons olive oil

3 tablespoons fresh lime juice (from 1 medium-size lime)

1 tablespoon Dijon mustard

1 tablespoon crushed red pepper flakes, or to taste

Salt and freshly ground pepper

⅓ cup chopped fresh basil leaves

1 cup NatureSweet Cherubs tomatoes

½ cup sliced red onion

1 10-ounce package torn leaf lettuce

Cook beans in boiling water until crisp-tender, about 5 minutes. Quickly drain and cool the beans under cold water. Pat dry.

In a large bowl, whisk together olive oil, lime juice, mustard, red pepper flakes, and salt and pepper to taste.

Stir in basil, beans, tomatoes and onion, tossing to coat. Taste and adjust the seasoning.

Add lettuce and toss to coat. Makes 4 servings.

Baby Spinach Quinoa Salad

Boskovich Farms

⅓ cup quinoa

½ pound Boskovich Farms Fresh 'N' Natural organic baby spinach

½ cup sliced almonds (can be toasted if desired)

½ red onion, chopped

¾ cup crumbled feta cheese

½ cup pomegranate arils

3 tablespoons red wine vinegar

2 tablespoons extra-virgin olive oil

2 teaspoons honey

1 teaspoon Dijon mustard

Salt and pepper

Cook quinoa according to package directions and let cool.

In a large bowl, combine spinach, cooled quinoa, almonds, red onion, feta and pomegranate arils.

In a small bowl, whisk together vinegar, olive oil, honey, mustard, and salt and pepper to taste. Pour over the salad and toss until the spinach is coated.

Serve immediately. Makes 4 servings.

Orange Salad with Fennel and Spinach
Kings River Packing

3 navel oranges
1 fennel bulb
2 tablespoons fresh lemon juice
3 tablespoons red wine vinegar
Salt and pepper
¼ cup olive oil
9 cups fresh spinach

Cut peel, including all the white pith, from the oranges. With a sharp knife cut ¼-inch slices from between the membranes and transfer to a bowl with any juices (about 36 slices).

Cut fennel bulb in half and remove the core. Thinly slice the bulb lengthwise. Add to the orange slices and toss.

In a small bowl, whisk together lemon juice, vinegar, and salt and pepper to taste. Add olive oil in a steady stream, whisking the dressing until it is emulsified.

Drizzle a small amount of dressing on the orange/fennel mixture and toss. Let the mixture stand, stirring occasionally, until the fennel is slightly wilted, about 15 minutes.

In a large bowl, toss spinach with dressing. Divide the spinach among 6 plates and top with the orange/fennel mixture. Serve immediately. Makes 6 servings.

Fresh Citrus and Avocado Summer Salad
Earth Source Trading/Cecelia Packing

2 Cecelia Cara Cara oranges
2 Earth Source Trading limes
3 tablespoons olive oil
½ teaspoon salt
Pinch of cayenne pepper
1 large ripe avocado
16 ounces spring mix
2 thin slices red onion, separated into rings

SPICED SUGARED PECANS
½ cup unsalted pecan halves
3 tablespoons granulated sugar
2 teaspoons water
¼ teaspoon salt
Pinch of cayenne pepper

Prepare the pecans: In a small frying pan, combine all ingredients. Cook over medium heat, stirring, until the sugar is golden and coats the pecans, about 7 minutes. Turn onto a piece of foil and let cool.

Peel 1 orange and slice into thin rounds. With the other orange, grate 1 teaspoon zest and squeeze 2 tablespoons juice.

Squeeze the juice from the limes.

In a small bowl, combine orange zest and juice. Whisk in lime juice, olive oil, salt and cayenne pepper.

Cut avocado in half, peel, and slice into wedges.

Place salad greens on plates. Scatter avocado and orange slices on the greens. Top with red onion rings. Drizzle with dressing and sprinkle with pecans. Makes 4 servings.

Citus Trio Salad with Kale, Feta and Dates

Paramount Citrus

1 bunch kale, stemmed and thinly sliced, or sliced baby kale (6-8 cups)

¼ cup chopped fresh mint

1½ cups cooked couscous (Israeli or regular), cooled

½ cup crumbled feta cheese, plus more for garnish

½ cup sliced pitted dates

Salt

1 Paramount Citrus grapefruit, peeled, sliced in ¼-inch-thick rounds and quartered

2 Paramount Citrus navel oranges, peeled, sliced in ¼-inch-thick rounds and halved

1-2 avocados, sliced ¼ inch thick

¼ cup toasted sliced almonds

GINGER-LIME DRESSING

½ cup olive oil

¼ cup juice from a Paramount Citrus lime

¼ cup honey

2 tablespoons cider vinegar

2 teaspoons grated fresh ginger

1 teaspoon kosher salt

Prepare the dressing: Combine all ingredients in a jar with a lid and shake well, or whisk in a bowl. Refrigerate extra dressing for another use.

In a large bowl, combine kale, mint and 4 tablespoons dressing. Gently mix in couscous, feta and dates. Add more dressing to taste and season with salt if desired.

Divide the salad among 4-6 plates. Arrange alternating slices of grapefruit, orange and avocado on top. Garnish with almonds and additional feta. Makes 4-6 servings.

PARAMOUNT
CITRUS

Spinach Salad with Fennel, Oranges, Grapes and Kiwi

Castle Rock Vineyards/Unifrutti of America

3 South African
   navel oranges

48 Chilean or
   California grapes

3 Greek kiwifruit

1 fennel bulb

3 tablespoons white
   wine vinegar

2 tablespoons fresh
   orange juice

½ teaspoon Dijon mustard

Salt and pepper

¼ cup olive oil

7 cups fresh spinach

2 cups arugula

½ cup toasted
   chopped walnuts

Cut the peel, including all the white pith, from the oranges. With a sharp knife, cut into ¼-inch slices and transfer to a bowl.

Wash grapes and toss with the oranges.

Peel kiwifruit, slice crosswise, and toss with the oranges and grapes.

Cut fennel bulb in half and remove the core. Thinly slice the bulb lengthwise. Set aside.

In a small bowl, whisk vinegar, orange juice, mustard, and salt and pepper to taste. Add olive oil in a steady stream and whisk the dressing until it is emulsified.

In a large bowl, combine spinach, arugula, walnuts, half the fruit and the fennel. Toss with the dressing.

Divide the salad among 6 plates and garnish with the remaining fruit. Makes 6 servings.

Arugula Salad with Clementines, Goat Cheese and Toasted Pine Nuts

Duda Farm Fresh Foods

2 ounces pine nuts
   (scant ½ cup)

4 cups arugula

2 Citrine clementines,
   peeled and thinly sliced

4 ounces goat cheese,
   crumbled

2 tablespoons olive oil

2 tablespoons
   balsamic vinegar

½ teaspoon salt

¼ teaspoon pepper

In a small dry pan, toast pine nuts over medium-low heat until browned. Set aside to cool.

Scatter arugula on a large platter and top with clementine slices and crumbled goat cheese.

In a small bowl, whisk olive oil, vinegar, salt and pepper. Drizzle on top of the salad. Sprinkle with toasted pine nuts and serve immediately. Makes 4 servings.

Note: If you'll be serving the salad at a later time, store the vinaigrette in a separate container and pour over the greens just before serving.

Duda
farm fresh foods

Roasted Grape Salad

Anthony Vineyards

¾ **pound red seedless grapes, stemmed**

½ **cup plus 2 teaspoons extra-virgin olive oil, divided**

2 **shallots, peeled**

4 **tablespoons balsamic vinegar**

1 **tablespoon honey (optional)**

1 **ripe pear**

6 **ounces arugula**

Freshly ground black pepper

Preheat oven to 250°F. Line a baking sheet with nonstick foil. Arrange grapes in a single layer on the pan. Drizzle with 1½ teaspoons olive oil and toss to coat. Bake for 2½ hours, or until the grapes are shriveled and lightly caramelized.

After the grapes have been cooking for an hour, place shallots on a piece of foil. Drizzle with ½ teaspoon olive oil. Wrap the foil around the shallots and seal. Place on a small baking sheet and bake in the oven for 1½ hours, or until tender. When the grapes are done, remove them from the baking sheet and reserve any of the remaining juices in a small bowl. Mince the shallots and add with their juices to the bowl, along with vinegar and ½ cup olive oil. Stir well to combine. Taste the dressing and add honey if you want a sweeter dressing. Quarter and core the pear. Cut into thin slices. Place arugula on a large plate and top with roasted grapes and pear slices. Drizzle with dressing and add pepper to taste. Makes 3 servings.

Tips: The dressing can be processed in a blender for a smoother texture. It can also be made a day ahead and refrigerated, covered. Bring the dressing to room temperature before using.

ANTHONY
VINEYARDS

Bosc Pear and Goat Cheese Salad
Wawona Packing Company

2 tablespoons sherry vinegar

1 small shallot, roughly chopped

Grated zest and juice of 1 lemon

4 tablespoons extra-virgin olive oil

Kosher salt and freshly ground black pepper

2 ripe Bosc pears

6 cups baby arugula or mâche salad greens (or a mix)

4 ounces young goat cheese, such as Laura Chenel, crumbled

In a food processor, combine vinegar, shallot, and lemon zest and juice. Process while slowly adding olive oil in a thin stream until emulsified. Season to taste with salt and pepper. Set aside.

Quarter the pears and remove the core and seeds. Uniformly slice the pear wedges. This should be done shortly before serving to avoid oxidation.

When ready to serve, place greens in a mixing bowl and add the dressing, reserving 2 tablespoons. Toss the greens and transfer to a serving platter (or 4 salad plates). Toss the pear slices in the same bowl with the reserved dressing.

Garnish the greens with the pear slices and crumbled goat cheese. Serve immediately. Makes 4 servings.

Avocado Pineapple Blueberry Salad
Naturipe Farms

6 cups mixed greens

¾ cup prepared citrus vinaigrette, divided

¾ cup grilled pineapple chunks

¾ cup diced avocado

¾ cup blueberries

¼ cup thinly sliced red onion

Place mixed greens in a large bowl.

Reserve 3 tablespoons of vinaigrette. Add the remaining vinaigrette to the greens and toss to coat.

Divide the greens among 6 plates.

Using the same bowl, combine pineapple chunks, avocado, blueberries, red onion and the remaining vinaigrette; toss to coat.

Arrange the fruit mixture evenly over the greens. Serve immediately. Makes 6 servings.

Kale and Spinach Chop Salad with Apples

Stemilt Growers

6 cups loosely packed, roughly chopped fresh kale, center ribs removed (about 5-6 large leaves)

2 Stemilt apples, cored, cut into 8 wedges and thinly sliced (about 3 cups)

1 navel orange

4 cups loosely packed, roughly chopped fresh baby spinach (about 4 ounces)

2 cups shredded carrots

½ cup thinly sliced green onions

1 cup thinly sliced celery

½ cup thinly sliced halved radishes

2 cups roughly chopped dry-roasted, unsalted almonds

1 cup dried cranberries

VINAIGRETTE

¼ cup good balsamic vinegar

¼ cup freshly squeezed orange juice

2 teaspoons apricot jam

½ teaspoon tamari soy sauce

2 teaspoons honey

¼ cup extra-virgin olive oil

Prepare the vinaigrette: In a bowl, combine vinegar, orange juice, jam, tamari and honey; whisk until just combined. Whisk in olive oil.

Place chopped kale in a large bowl. Add 2-3 tablespoons of vinaigrette and "massage" it into the greens with clean hands for 1 minute. (This will help "tame" and soften the kale.) Place sliced apples in a small bowl and squeeze juice from the orange over them; toss to coat. (A touch of citrus keeps the apple flesh white.) Set aside. Add spinach, apples (drained), carrots, green onions, celery and radishes to the kale. Lightly dress the salad with vinaigrette and toss to fully coat. Add almonds and cranberries; toss a few more times to just incorporate. Serve immediately. Makes 4 servings.

White Peach Butterleaf Salad

Kingsburg Orchards

6 cups butterleaf (or butter) lettuce

3 Kingsburg Orchards white peaches

¼ cup sunflower seed kernels

½ cup crumbled cooked bacon

Prepared poppy seed dressing, to taste

Rinse the lettuce, pat dry, and chop.

Wash peaches, then slice them. Discard the pits.

Toss together the lettuce, peaches, sunflower seeds, bacon and dressing.

Serve immediately. Makes 4-6 servings.

Grilled Peach and Arugula Salad

I.M. Ripe

GRILLED PEACHES

3 I.M. Ripe peaches, halved and pitted

1-2 tablespoons olive oil

NECTARINE DRESSING

1 I.M. Ripe nectarine, quartered and pitted

1½ tablespoons champagne vinegar

1½ tablespoons sherry vinegar

2 tablespoons blue agave nectar or honey

1 tablespoon fresh lemon juice

½ teaspoon salt

⅛ teaspoon cayenne pepper

4 tablespoons extra-virgin olive oil

SALAD

3 ounces pancetta, cooked until crisp and crumbled

½ cup pecans

5 ounces arugula

½ cup dried cranberries or raisins

4 ounces crumbled goat cheese

Salt and freshly ground pepper to taste

Prepare the grilled peaches: Preheat the grill to high. Brush the flesh of each peach half with olive oil and grill flesh side down for 2-5 minutes, or until black grill marks appear. Set aside.

Prepare the dressing: Place all ingredients in a blender and puree.

Assemble the salad: In a large bowl combine all ingredients and toss with the dressing.

Divide the salad among 6 plates and place a grilled peach on each plate. Makes 6 servings.

Asian Plum Salad
with Ginger Dressing
Rivermaid Trading Company

8 cups baby spinach

1 cup water chestnuts cut
in thin julienne strips

2 ripe plums, pitted and
thinly sliced

2 green onions, thinly sliced

¼ cup torn cilantro leaves

Crispy wonton strips
(optional)

GINGER DRESSING

¼ cup thick teriyaki sauce

2 tablespoons rice vinegar

1 tablespoon vegetable oil

1 teaspoon toasted
sesame oil

1 teaspoon grated
fresh ginger

½ teaspoon sugar

In a medium salad bowl, combine spinach, water chestnuts, plums, green onions and cilantro.

Prepare the dressing: Whisk together all ingredients and pour over the salad. Toss well to coat.

Top with wonton strips. Makes 4-6 servings.

Mango Salad
Freska Produce/Amazon Produce Network

1 Freska mango, peeled
and sliced

1 head leaf lettuce, rinsed,
dried and chopped into
bite-size pieces

½ pound fresh strawberries

½ pound fresh blueberries

1 cup cherry tomatoes

½ cup fresh grapes

1 medium avocado,
cut in bite-size pieces

¼ cup chopped toasted
slivered almonds

¼ cup chopped red onion

4 slices of cooked bacon,
crumbled into bits

Your favorite dressing

In a large salad bowl, toss together mango slices, lettuce, strawberries, blueberries, tomatoes, grapes, avocado, almonds and onion.

Cover and refrigerate for 30 minutes to let the flavors blend. Do not leave in the refrigerator for more than 3 hours.

Sprinkle with bacon. Serve with dressing to taste. Makes 6-8 servings.

Apple, Cranberry and Blue Cheese Salad
Cuizina Food Company

Serve as an accompaniment to Kirkland Signature Chicken Penne Alfredo.

2 ounces Bibb lettuce

9 ounces romaine lettuce

2 Granny Smith apples

½ cup cherry tomatoes

3 ounces mixed spring greens

¼ cup julienned jicama

½ avocado, diced

3 ounces Oregon blue cheese crumbles

¼ cup dried cranberries

Cracked black pepper

APPLE RIESLING VINAIGRETTE

3 fresh basil leaves, chopped

¼ cup chopped fresh cilantro

2 tablespoons Washington state Riesling

2 tablespoons apple cider vinegar

2 tablespoons honey

2 tablespoons apple juice

¼ cup Dijon mustard

⅛ teaspoon cinnamon

½ cup extra-virgin olive oil

Pinch of kosher salt

Cut Bibb and romaine lettuce into 1-inch pieces. Core and slice the apples. Cut cherry tomatoes in half.

In a salad bowl, combine the greens, apples, jicama, tomatoes and avocado.

Prepare the vinaigrette: In a bowl, combine basil, cilantro, wine, vinegar, honey, apple juice, mustard and cinnamon. Slowly whisk in olive oil. Add salt to taste.

Drizzle the vinaigrette on the salad and gently toss. Top with a garnish of blue cheese and cranberries. Add black pepper to taste. Makes 6 servings.

Grape and Cranberry Salad
Pandol Bros., Inc.

1 16-ounce container frozen whipped dessert topping, thawed

1 14-ounce can sweetened condensed milk

1 20-ounce can crushed pineapple, drained

2 14-ounce cans whole cranberry sauce

2 cups quartered Pandol red seedless grapes

1 cup chopped walnuts

Grapes and walnuts, for garnish (optional)

In a large bowl, combine whipped topping and condensed milk. Stir until well blended.

Fold in pineapple, cranberry sauce, grapes and walnuts.

Chill for at least 3 hours and up to overnight.

To serve, garnish with grapes and walnuts. Makes 16 servings.

Southwest Watermelon Salad

Keystone

½ watermelon, sliced or diced, rind removed

1 tablespoon fruit seasoning, or more to taste (see note)

1 certified sweet onion, thinly sliced

2 apples, diced

1 fennel bulb, thinly sliced

1 yellow bell pepper, diced

1 teaspoon extra-virgin olive oil

¼ cup chopped cilantro, or more to taste

Grated zest of 1 lemon and 1 lime

Juice of 1 lemon and 1 lime

On a large platter, shingle sliced watermelon or arrange diced watermelon. Sprinkle with fruit seasoning.

In a bowl, combine all other ingredients and mix well. Place the mixture on top of the watermelon. Makes 10-12 servings.

Note: Fruit seasoning is a specialty product found in most Mexican food stores. If unavailable, use chili powder, salt and black pepper to taste.

Keystone

Watermelon Grape Mint Salad

Quick & Easy

Kirschenman

10 cups cubed seedless watermelon

10 cups red seedless grapes

1¼ cups white grape juice

5 teaspoons minced fresh mint

5 teaspoons honey

In several large bowls, combine watermelon and grapes.

In a small bowl, combine grape juice, mint and honey. Whisk to blend.

Pour the dressing over the fruit and toss to coat. Serve immediately in a watermelon boat or large bowl. Makes 20 servings.

Summer Fruit Salad with Citrus/Champagne Vinaigrette and Feta Cheese

Oppenheimer Group/Fillmore-Piru Citrus/
Mas Melons & Grapes

¼ cup honey

¼ cup fresh lemon juice

3 tablespoons champagne vinegar

½ cup olive oil

2 cups honeydew melon balls

2 cups watermelon balls

2 cups Flame grapes

1½ cups easy-peel orange segments

Grated zest of 1 lemon

Grated zest of ½ orange

5 mint sprigs, finely chopped

½ cup feta cheese

In a blender or food processor, pulse honey and lemon juice. Blend in vinegar 1 tablespoon at a time. With the machine running, slowly add olive oil, blending until emulsified.

In a bowl with a tight-fitting lid, combine fruit, citrus zests and mint. Gently mix in the vinaigrette. Cover and chill for at least 1 hour and up to 4 hours.

To serve, top the salad with feta and drizzle with vinaigrette from the bowl. Makes 6-8 servings.

Summer Fruit Salad with Lemon and Honey Syrup

Western Fresh Marketing/Sun World/
Blossom Hill-Lucich-Santos Farms

3 cups chopped cantaloupe

2 cups Sun World Scarlotta Seedless red grapes

1½ cups sweet cherries, pitted and halved (about ½ pound)

1½ cups peeled and chopped peaches (about 2 peaches)

6 Western Fresh Marketing fresh figs, quartered

4 Blossom Hill apricots, quartered and pitted (about ½ pound)

½ cup chopped fresh mint

LEMON AND HONEY SYRUP

1 cup water

⅓ cup honey

2 tablespoons fresh lemon juice

½ teaspoon vanilla extract

Prepare the syrup: In a small saucepan, combine all ingredients. Bring to a boil, then lower the heat to medium and simmer until the mixture is reduced to ¼ cup (about 15 minutes). Let cool.

In a large bowl, combine cantaloupe, grapes, cherries, peaches, figs and apricots. Pour the syrup over the fruit and toss gently to coat. Cover and chill for 1 hour, stirring occasionally. Stir in mint just before serving. Makes 8 servings.

Melon and Pineapple Shrimp Salad
Del Monte Fresh Produce

2 pounds raw medium shrimp, peeled and deveined

Splash of lemon juice

Salt and pepper

1 cup extra-virgin olive oil, divided

½ Del Monte Gold Extra Sweet pineapple, diced into small chunks

1 large Del Monte fresh red bell pepper, diced into small chunks

1 Del Monte fresh MAG melon, diced into small chunks, divided

1 Del Monte fresh honeydew melon, diced into small chunks

1 cup fresh mint leaves, divided

Place shrimp, lemon juice and salt to taste in a large pot of water. Set over high heat and bring to a boil. Once the water starts boiling, remove from the heat and strain the shrimp. Rinse with cold water to stop the cooking. In a sauté pan, heat ¼ cup olive oil over medium heat. Add pineapple and red pepper chunks; sauté until the pineapple becomes somewhat transparent and the pepper is soft. Set aside to cool. Place 1 cup *each* of the melon chunks, ½ cup of mint leaves and ½ cup olive oil in a blender and blend until smooth. In a large bowl, combine the remaining melon chunks, shrimp, sautéed pineapple and peppers, and the blended mixture. Mix and season to taste with salt and pepper. Garnish with the remaining olive oil, mint leaves and pineapple leaves (optional). Makes 4 servings.

Shrimp Salad with Poached Pears, Toasted Pecans and Champagne Vinaigrette
Chicken of the Sea Frozen Foods

1 head Bibb lettuce

2 cups Champagne

½ cup sugar

2 tablespoons lemon juice

2 fresh pears

¼ cup pecans

1 pound cooked 31/40 shrimp, peeled and deveined

CHAMPAGNE VINAIGRETTE

½ cup chilled poaching liquid

¾ cup olive oil

¼ cup champagne vinegar

Salt and pepper to taste

Clean and quarter lettuce; place each quarter on a serving plate and refrigerate.

Combine Champagne, sugar and lemon juice in a saucepan and bring to a boil. Add pears, reduce the heat and simmer for 10-15 minutes, or until the pears are tender and easily pierced with a fork. Remove the pears with a slotted spoon and chill. Remove the poaching liquid from the pan and refrigerate until chilled.

Preheat oven to 350°F.

Place pecans on a baking sheet and bake for 5 minutes, or until aromatic. Set aside.

Prepare the vinaigrette: Combine all ingredients and whisk to blend.

Cut the pears in half, remove the core, and slice. Place the pear slices on the lettuce. Arrange shrimp on top. Add vinaigrette to taste. Garnish with toasted pecans. Makes 4 servings.

Tropical Shrimp Salad
Chestnut Hill Farms/Legend Produce

2 cups diced fresh Caribbean Sweet pineapple

3 cups diced fresh Chestnut Hill Farms or Legend Produce cantaloupe

1 red bell pepper, seeded and diced

½ red onion, diced

1½ tablespoons grated fresh ginger

¼ cup chopped fresh mint leaves, plus sprigs for garnish

1 small jalapeño, seeded and minced

2 tablespoons lime juice

½ 15-ounce can black beans, rinsed

2 pounds cooked, peeled and deveined shrimp

Salt and pepper (optional)

Lettuce leaves, for serving

Lime slices, for garnish

In a large bowl, mix pineapple, cantaloupe, bell pepper, onion, ginger, mint, jalapeño and lime juice. Stir well, then cover and refrigerate for at least 2 hours (best 4-6 hours).

Just before serving, stir in black beans, shrimp (save a few for garnish), and salt and pepper to taste.

To serve, line a large glass bowl or individual serving dishes with lettuce leaves. Scoop the chilled salad mixture on top. Garnish with a few shrimp, lime slices and mint sprigs. Makes 8 servings.

Grilled Lobster Salad with Orange-Tarragon Dressing

Sunkist Growers

3 tablespoons chopped fresh
  tarragon leaves

4 Sunkist oranges (navel,
  Valencia or Cara Cara), divided

2 tablespoons Dijon mustard

¼ cup sunflower or vegetable oil

Salt and white pepper

4 lobster tails (about ¼ pound each) in shells

1 head butter lettuce

1 medium avocado, cut into ½-inch cubes

1 pint cherry tomatoes, cut into quarters

1 yellow bell pepper, coarsely chopped

1 red onion, coarsely chopped

Prepare dressing by whisking tarragon, juice and grated zest of 2 oranges, mustard and oil in a medium bowl. Season to taste with salt and pepper. Set aside ½ cup for marinade.

Preheat the grill to medium-high. Spoon some marinade on the meat of the lobster tails and place meat side down on the grill. Grill for 8-10 minutes on each side, or until the meat is opaque (white/pink color) and can be pulled easily from the shell. Remove the meat from the shells and cut in half lengthwise.

On 4 serving plates, make a bed of lettuce leaves. Top the lettuce with lobster, avocado, tomatoes, bell pepper, onion and segments of the remaining 2 oranges.

Drizzle the salads with dressing and pass additional dressing on the side. Makes 4 servings.

Tip: 1½ pounds of large peeled, deveined uncooked shrimp can be used in place of lobster. Marinate the shrimp in ¼ cup dressing for 10-15 minutes, then grill for about 3 minutes on each side, or until firm and pink in color.

Sunkist

Lobster and Shrimp Mediterranean Salad
Pescanova

2 Pescanova frozen Warm Water Brazilian Lobster Tails

3 tablespoons salt

1 pound Kirkland Signature cooked peeled shrimp (50-70), thawed

2 cups diced bell peppers (yellow, green and/or red)

½ cup chopped fresh parsley

½ cup chopped fresh chives

2 hard-boiled eggs, chopped (optional)

DRESSING

½ cup lemon juice

1 cup olive oil

1 cup light, crisp white wine (e.g., Albariño)

2 tablespoons Dijon mustard

½ teaspoon salt, plus more to taste

Thaw lobsters in cold running water. Add salt to a large pot of water and bring to a boil. Drop the lobsters into the boiling water. When the water returns to a boil, cook for 3 minutes. Transfer the lobsters to a bowl filled with iced water for 3 minutes. Remove the shells and cut the meat into large bite-size pieces.

Prepare the dressing: Mix all the ingredients until well blended. Refrigerate for a few minutes.

In a chilled mixing bowl, combine lobster, shrimp, bell peppers, parsley, chives and eggs. Add dressing and stir until lightly coated. Season to taste with salt. Makes 6 servings.

PESCANOVA

Grilled Salmon Salad with Sunshine Citrus Dressing
Blumar

2 8-ounce salmon fillets

Olive oil

Romaine lettuce

Spinach leaves

Toasted sliced almonds

Dried cranberries

Feta cheese, crumbled

CITRUS DRESSING

¼ cup olive oil

3 tablespoons orange juice

1 teaspoon lemon juice

1 teaspoon honey

2 tablespoons chopped fresh basil

Dash of salt

Freshly ground black pepper to taste

Preheat the grill to medium-high.

Prepare the dressing: In a bowl, combine all ingredients and blend with a small whisk.

Brush salmon with olive oil to prevent sticking. Grill for 5 minutes per side, or until the fish flakes with a fork.

Slice the grilled salmon and serve on a bed of lettuce and spinach. Top with almonds, cranberries and feta. Drizzle with dressing. Makes 2 servings.

BLUMAR SEAFOODS

Spinach-Stuffed Salmon over Citrus Salad
Babé Farms/Gold Coast Packing

SALMON

2 garlic cloves, minced

1 tablespoon olive oil

6 cups Gold Coast spinach

½ teaspoon garlic salt

½ teaspoon ground black pepper

1 pound salmon fillet, divided into 4 pieces

1 teaspoon Dijon mustard

SALAD

¼ cup olive oil

¼ cup orange juice

1 tablespoon white wine vinegar

1 tablespoon Dijon mustard

2 tablespoons rice wine vinegar

¼ cup balsamic vinegar

8 cups Babé Farms Organic Spring Mix ♥Organic

½ red onion, thinly sliced

¼ cup feta cheese

4 tangerines, peeled and cut in bite-size pieces

Prepare the salmon: Preheat oven to 350°F. Sauté garlic with oil over medium heat until aromatic. Add spinach, garlic salt and pepper; sauté until wilted. Strain.

Cut a 2-inch horizontal pocket in each salmon piece. Stuff with the spinach mixture. Spread mustard evenly on the salmon. Bake for 18 minutes, or until cooked to taste.

Prepare the salad: Combine the first 6 ingredients and whisk until emulsified. Reserve ¼ cup dressing. Toss the remaining dressing with spring mix, onion, feta and tangerines.

Arrange the salad on 4 plates. Top with salmon and drizzle with reserved dressing. Makes 4 servings.

Mexican Chopped Tuna Salad
Quick & Easy

Chicken of the Sea

2 7-ounce cans Chicken of the Sea chunk light tuna in water, drained

1 5-ounce bag mixed salad greens

1 15-ounce can garbanzo beans, drained

1 15-ounce can kidney beans, drained

1 2.25-ounce can sliced black olives, drained

½ cup shredded Mexican cheese blend

1 medium ripe avocado, peeled, pitted and diced

½ cup homemade or deli fresh pico de gallo

Homemade or prepared creamy cilantro dressing

Tortilla chips, for serving

In a medium bowl, flake tuna. Gently fold in salad greens, beans, olives, cheese, avocado, pico de gallo and dressing to taste.

Serve immediately or chill until ready to serve. Serve with tortilla chips. Makes 4-6 servings.

Country Dijon Tuna Pasta Salad
Chicken of the Sea

1 pound elbow or any round-shaped pasta
1 cup nonfat plain yogurt
¼ cup whole-grain Dijon-style mustard
1 cup diced celery
½ cup diced green bell pepper
½ cup diced red bell pepper
½ cup diced red onion
2 7-ounce cans Chicken of the Sea Chunk Light Tuna in water, drained
Garlic salt and pepper

Cook pasta according to package directions. Drain and rinse in cold water. Set aside.

In a large bowl, mix yogurt and mustard until well blended.

Add celery, bell peppers, onion and pasta to the dressing mixture; blend well. Gently fold in Chicken of the Sea Chunk Light Tuna. Add garlic salt and pepper to taste if necessary.

Serve immediately or chill until ready to serve. Makes 10 servings.

Walnut, Chicken and Cherry Quinoa Salad
California Walnut Board

1 cup quinoa
1⅓ cups water
1½ cups diced grilled chicken
½ cup dried cherries
½ cup diced celery
¼ cup minced red onion
½ cup coarsely chopped Kirkland Signature walnuts, toasted
Chopped fresh thyme (optional)

DRESSING
⅓ cup extra-virgin olive oil
¼ cup white wine vinegar
1 teaspoon sugar
½ teaspoon salt, or to taste
1 garlic clove, minced
Freshly ground pepper, to taste

Rinse quinoa in a fine-mesh strainer; drain well. Bring water and quinoa to a boil in a medium saucepan; reduce the heat and simmer, covered, for 12 minutes. Let stand for 10 minutes, then fluff with a fork and let cool.

Place the cooled quinoa in a large bowl with the chicken, cherries, celery and onion.

Prepare the dressing: Whisk together all ingredients and pour over the salad; toss well to coat. Cover and chill for at least 1 hour.

Add walnuts and thyme to the salad just before serving. Makes 6 servings.

Tip: Replace the dried cherries with halved and pitted fresh cherries when they're in season.

Grape and Chicken Salad
Four Star Fruit

1 teaspoon curry powder

1 teaspoon smoked paprika

½ teaspoon salt

2 boneless, skinless chicken breasts, about 6 ounces each (see note)

2 cups Four Star Fruit red seedless grapes, rinsed, drained and cut in half

¼ cup chopped green onions (save some tops for garnish)

⅔ cup diced celery

¼ cup slivered almonds, toasted

4 cups shredded Napa cabbage

DRESSING

1 cup plain Greek yogurt

½ cup finely chopped unpeeled, seeded cucumber

2 teaspoons honey

½ teaspoon salt

⅛ teaspoon pepper, or to taste

In a small ramekin, combine curry powder, paprika and salt. Rub the mixture into the chicken breasts and set aside.

Prepare the dressing: In a small bowl, whisk together yogurt, cucumber, honey, salt and pepper. Refrigerate while preparing the chicken.

Preheat the grill to medium-high. Grill the chicken until cooked through (varies according to thickness). Let cool, then slice into strips. In a bowl, combine grapes, green onions, celery and almonds. On 4 plates, arrange a bed of cabbage. Top each with ¼ of the grape mixture, then ¼ of the grilled chicken breast slices. Drizzle with dressing. Makes 4 servings.

Note: For faster and more even cooking, before rubbing with seasonings, pound the chicken breasts between 2 pieces of plastic wrap to an even thickness.

Recipe developed by Christine W. Jackson, food stylist.

Chicken Waldorf Salad

Ready Pac

1 16-ounce bag Ready Pac Grand Parisian Complete Salad Kit (includes salad greens, frosted almonds, dried cranberries, feta cheese and white balsamic vinaigrette dressing)

⅓ cup freshly squeezed lemon juice

1½ teaspoons grated lemon zest

½ teaspoon ground cumin

1½ cups small red seedless grapes

2 celery stalks, sliced

1 large Fuji apple, diced

1 large Asian pear, diced

⅓ cup thinly sliced green onions

3-4 cups diced rotisserie chicken or cooked chicken

½ cup walnuts, toasted (optional)

Coarse sea salt

Coarsely ground pepper

In a small mixing bowl, combine vinaigrette dressing from the salad kit, lemon juice, lemon zest and cumin. Gradually whisk together until well blended. Set aside.

In a chilled large salad bowl, combine salad greens, grapes, celery, apple, Asian pear, green onions, chicken, walnuts, frosted almonds, dried cranberries, feta, and salt and pepper to taste. Toss lightly.

Drizzle half of the vinaigrette mixture over the salad. Toss lightly. Drizzle the remaining vinaigrette mixture over the salad. Toss lightly to coat all ingredients evenly. Makes 6-8 servings.

Chicken Salad on the Half Shell

California Avocado Commission/Calavo Growers/Del Rey Avocado/Eco Farms/Giumarra Escondido/Index Fresh/ McDaniel Fruit Co./Mission Produce/West Pak Avocado, Inc.

2 pounds cooked shredded chicken (rotisserie chicken works well)

2½ tablespoons fresh lemon juice, divided

1 cup sliced celery

1 cup chopped green onions

1 cup chopped red bell pepper

⅔ cup chopped fresh cilantro (optional)

1 cup mayonnaise or reduced-fat mayonnaise

Salt and freshly ground black pepper

4 large ripe fresh California Avocados (see note)

In a large bowl, toss chicken with 2 tablespoons lemon juice. Stir in celery, green onions, bell pepper, cilantro, mayonnaise, and salt and pepper to taste.

Cover and refrigerate for at least 1 hour.

Cut avocados in half and remove the seeds. Brush the insides with the remaining lemon juice. Mound scoops of the chicken salad onto the avocado halves and serve immediately. Makes 8 servings.

Note: As with all fruits and vegetables, wash avocados before cutting.

© 2013 California Avocado Commission

Spicy Broccoli Salad
Mann's

6 cups broccoli florets

½ cup julienned red
   bell pepper

¼ cup julienned white onion

Salt and pepper

¼ cup toasted pepitas
   (shelled pumpkin seeds)

½ cup crumbled Cotija cheese

DRESSING

¾ cup crema fresca casera
   (Mexican-style sour cream)

2 tablespoons Sriracha
   sauce (or your favorite
   hot sauce)

1 tablespoon honey

Juice of ½ lime

Prepare the dressing: Combine all ingredients in a bowl and whisk to blend.

Place broccoli in a large mixing bowl. Cut any larger florets into bite-size pieces. Add bell pepper and onion. Pour the dressing over the broccoli and toss to coat. Season to taste with salt and pepper. This can be prepared ahead of time and kept in the refrigerator, covered, for 1 day.

Before serving, sprinkle the salad with pepitas and cheese crumbles. Makes 8 servings.

Tip: Serve with grilled chicken or steak.

Cashew Cluster Broccoli Salad
Kirkland Signature

5-6 cups broccoli florets
   cut in bite-size pieces

½ cup dried cranberries

½ cup coarsely chopped
   Kirkland Signature
   cashew clusters

½ cup crumbled
   cooked bacon

1 hard-boiled egg, sliced,
   for garnish

SAUCE

½ cup mayonnaise

½ cup plain yogurt

1 teaspoon white vinegar

2 tablespoons sugar

Prepare the sauce: In a small bowl, combine all ingredients. Cover and refrigerate for about 2 hours.

In a large bowl, combine broccoli, cranberries, cashew clusters and bacon; toss lightly. Add the sauce and mix until well coated. Arrange sliced eggs on top.

Refrigerate until ready to serve. Makes about 5 servings.

Antipasto Salad with Pickled Red Onions

Tanimura & Antle

1 Tanimura & Antle Artisan Sweet
  Italian Red Onion

1 cup rice wine vinegar

½ tablespoon black peppercorns

1 teaspoon fennel seeds

1 tablespoon sugar

½ cup water

2 heads Tanimura & Antle
  Artisan Romaine

1 head Tanimura & Antle Lettuce
  (Green and Red Petite Tango variety)

4 ounces salami, thinly slivered

4 ounces provolone cheese,
  thinly slivered

½ cup sliced black olives

½ cup diced Roma tomato

½ cup garlic croutons

¼ cup prepared Italian dressing

Peel red onion and thinly slice. Place in a glass bowl. In a nonreactive saucepan, combine vinegar, peppercorns, fennel, sugar and water. Bring to a simmer, then lightly simmer for 5 minutes. Let cool for 30 minutes. Strain the liquid into the sliced onions and stir to coat. Refrigerate for 2 hours.

Cut the core end off the romaine, separate the leaves and rinse under warm water. Towel-dry the individual leaves. Cut the core end off the Tango lettuce to release the leaves; cut the leaves crosswise into small pieces. Rinse and drain well. For extra crunch, crisp the washed lettuce in the fridge for 30 minutes.

In a bowl, combine salami, cheese, olives, tomato, croutons and Tango lettuce; carefully mix the ingredients.

Right before serving, add the dressing and toss to coat. Place the salad mixture on the romaine leaves and garnish with pickled red onion. Makes about 16 servings.

Greek Salad-Stuffed Campari
Village Farms

15 Village Farms Sinfully Sweet Campari tomatoes

2 Village Farms Luscious Seedless Long English Cucumbers, diced

1 Village Farms Yellow Sweet Bell Pepper, seeded and diced

½ small red onion, diced

⅓ cup Kalamata olives (pitted), diced

1 tablespoon chopped fresh parsley

5 ounces feta cheese, divided

DRESSING

⅓ cup lemon juice

⅔ cup extra-virgin olive oil

Pinch of dried oregano

Salt and pepper to taste

Prepare the dressing: Whisk together all ingredients.

Cut the top off each tomato and hollow out the center.

In a large bowl, toss together cucumbers, bell pepper, red onion, olives, parsley and half of the feta. Add about 2 tablespoons of dressing and toss. Season to taste.

Stuff the tomatoes with the salad mixture and top with the remaining feta. Drizzle with the remaining dressing. Makes 4-6 servings.

Recipe created by Chef Darren Brown, Oru Restaurant, Fairmont Pacific Rim Hotel, Vancouver, B.C., exclusively for Village Farms.

Holiday Tree
Chilean Avocado Importers

3 large ripe Hass avocados from Chile

2 tablespoons lemon juice

¼ cup crumbled feta cheese

¼ orange or yellow bell pepper, diced

Grape or small cherry tomatoes

Pomegranate seeds (optional)

1 bag (5 ounces) mixed baby salad greens

CITRUS VINAIGRETTE

1 small grapefruit, halved

1 orange, halved

1 lime, halved

1 tablespoon Dijon mustard

½ teaspoon salt

Pepper

¼ cup avocado or olive oil

Cut avocados in half, remove the pit and peel. Cut each avocado half lengthwise into 4-5 slices. Sprinkle the slices with lemon juice.

On a large plate or platter, arrange the largest avocado slices to form the branches of the tree. Scatter with cheese, diced pepper, tomatoes and pomegranate seeds.

Prepare the vinaigrette: Squeeze the juice from the grapefruit, orange and lime into a small bowl. Whisk in mustard, salt and pepper to taste, and avocado or olive oil.

In a salad bowl, toss the smaller avocado slices with baby greens and vinaigrette. Makes 6 servings.

Nutritional information: Each serving has 326 calories, 4 g protein, 14 g carbohydrates, 18.5 g fat (3 g saturated), 14 mg cholesterol, 3 g fiber, 337 mg sodium.

Chef's Choice

Top chefs are known for their ability to create delicious recipes that showcase not only fresh ingredients but also the cook's personality. We asked several of the best chefs around to work their magic with products from these great companies:

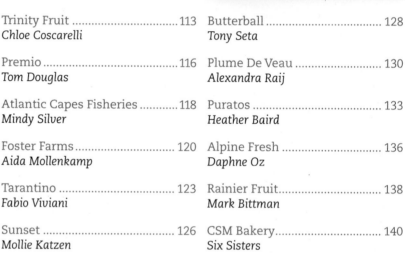

DELANO FARMS

DOUGLAS LYLE THOMPSON

Susan Spungen

Susan Spungen is the culinary consultant and food stylist behind the feature films Julie & Julia, It's Complicated and Eat Pray Love. Spungen, the founding food editor of Martha Stewart Living Omnimedia, is also a cook, recipe developer and editor whose work appears frequently in Bon Appétit, Food & Wine and More. Her latest book is What's a Hostess to Do? 313 Ideas and Inspirations for Effortless Entertaining (Artisan Books, 2013).

Chicken Tartines with Grapes recipe on page 86.

Chicken Tartines with Grapes
Delano Farms

Recipes developed by Susan Spungen

3 ounces cream cheese, softened

2 ounces blue cheese,
 any type, crumbled

Milk, for thinning

4 thin slices country bread
 (with a thick, chewy texture)

1½ cups baby arugula or frisée

12 ounces sliced cooked chicken
 breast (roasted, grilled or rotisserie)

1 cup Delano Farms green
 seedless grapes

In a small bowl, stir cream cheese until smooth. Stir in blue cheese, breaking it up as little as possible. Add a little milk to make it spreadable.

Spread each slice of bread with some of the blue cheese spread. Top with arugula or frisée, letting some of it hang over the edges. Arrange overlapping slices of chicken on top.

Thinly slice the grapes and scatter them over the tartines. Serve immediately. Makes 4 servings.

Chicken Tartines with Grapes photo on page 85.

Roasted Grape Chutney
Delano Farms

4 cups Delano Farms red
 seedless grapes

1 large shallot, sliced
 lengthwise (about ½ cup)

1 tablespoon chopped fresh rosemary

1 tablespoon extra-virgin olive oil

½ teaspoon coarse salt

Freshly ground black pepper

Preheat oven to 425°F.

Wash grapes well and shake off any excess moisture.

In a large bowl, combine all ingredients, tossing to combine well. Spread out on a rimmed baking sheet and place in the oven. After 10 minutes, stir once. Continue roasting for another 6-8 minutes, or until the liquid thickens and the grapes have mostly burst, watching carefully to make sure the juices don't burn.

Scrape into a bowl and cool to room temperature. Serve right away, or refrigerate, covered, for 2-3 days. Makes about 2 cups.

Tip: Serve with soft creamy cheeses or with grilled or roasted meats—especially pork.

Grape Schiacciata
Delano Farms

Extra-virgin olive oil
1 pound frozen pizza dough, thawed
Kosher salt

1 tablespoon chopped fresh rosemary
¾ cup halved Delano Farms black or red seedless grapes

Oil a baking sheet with olive oil. Stretch pizza dough into a rough oval about 10 by 13 inches. If the dough is too springy, let it rest for a few minutes and then try again. Place the dough on the baking sheet and drizzle with olive oil.

Let it rest for 15 minutes. Preheat oven to 400°F. Press your fingertips into the dough to make dimples all over the surface. Sprinkle with kosher salt and rosemary. Scatter grapes evenly over the surface. Bake for 30 minutes, or until the top is evenly golden and the bottom is browned and crisp. Cut into small pieces. Serves 6-8 as an appetizer.

Excerpted from What's a Hostess to Do?, *by Susan Spungen (Artisan Books, 2013).*

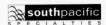

COURTESY OF ALICE CURRAH

Alice Currah

Alice Currah is the author of Savory Sweet Life and creator of the popular website SavorySweetLife.com, part of the Martha's Circle blog network. A contributor to PBS Parents and the Pioneer Woman's Tasty Kitchen, Currah has been named one of "Eight of the Very Best Food Bloggers" on Forbes.com and "Best of the Web" by Williams-Sonoma. One of her photographs won Saveur magazine's cover contest. She lives in Seattle.

Sesame Ginger King Salmon Fillets
South Pacific Specialties

Recipes developed by Alice Currah

¼ cup plus 2 tablespoons firmly packed dark brown sugar

¼ cup Asian sesame oil

3 tablespoons rice vinegar

2 tablespoons soy sauce

1 tablespoon minced fresh ginger

1 garlic clove

4 center-cut True Nature Seafood king salmon fillets (6-8 ounces each)

Kosher salt and freshly ground black pepper

2 tablespoons toasted black sesame seeds

Preheat oven to 450°F. Line a rimmed baking sheet with parchment paper or aluminum foil.

In a blender, combine brown sugar, sesame oil, vinegar, soy sauce, ginger and garlic. Blend until emulsified. Divide between 2 bowls.

Place salmon skin-side down on the baking sheet. Season to taste with salt and pepper. Brush each fillet with sauce from 1 bowl.

Bake for 15 minutes, or until opaque. Transfer to serving plates and pour the remaining sauce over the fillets. Sprinkle with sesame seeds. Makes 4 servings.

Tip: Leftover salmon? Add the salmon and sauce to fresh pasta and toss with cooked broccoli, asparagus or spinach.

Baked Spiced Yogurt-Coated Steelhead
South Pacific Specialties

1½-2 pounds boneless skin-on True Nature Seafood steelhead fillet

Kosher salt

Freshly ground pepper

¼ cup mayonnaise

¼ cup nonfat plain Greek yogurt

2 teaspoons curry powder

1 teaspoon garam masala

½ teaspoon ground cumin

½ teaspoon chili powder

½ teaspoon smoked paprika

Preheat oven to 375°F. Cover a large rimmed baking sheet with aluminum foil and lightly coat with nonstick spray.

Rinse steelhead under cold water and pat dry. Place on the baking sheet and season to taste with salt and pepper.

In a small bowl, mix mayonnaise, yogurt, curry powder, garam masala, cumin, chili powder and smoked paprika.

Generously coat the fish with the yogurt sauce, using a flexible spatula or the back of a spoon.

Bake, uncovered, for 15-20 minutes, or until the center is opaque (generally 10 minutes per pound). Let the fish rest for 10 minutes before serving. Makes 6-8 servings.

SHANE BEVEL

Ree Drummond

Ree Drummond is the #1 New York Times best-selling author of The Pioneer Woman Cooks: Recipes from an Accidental Country Girl, The Pioneer Woman Cooks: Food from My Frontier *and other books. Her website,* www.thepioneer woman.com, *showcases her cooking, photography and anecdotes about country life, and her hit cooking show,* The Pioneer Woman, *premiered on Food Network in 2011.*

Spicy Pulled Pork
JBS/Swift Premium

Recipes developed by Ree Drummond

1 whole onion, cut into quarters
1 tablespoon chili powder
½ cup packed brown sugar (light or dark)
4 garlic cloves, peeled
1 teaspoon dried oregano
2 teaspoons ground cumin

1-2 tablespoons salt, to taste
Freshly ground black pepper
3 tablespoons olive oil
2 tablespoons white wine vinegar
1 5- to 7-pound Swift Premium pork butt
Lime wedges, for serving
Flour tortillas, for serving

Preheat oven to 350°F. In a food processor, combine onion, chili powder, brown sugar, garlic, oregano, cumin, salt, pepper to taste, olive oil and vinegar. Pulse until combined.

Pour the mixture over the pork. Rub it into every nook and cranny of the meat, tucking it under folds and crevices. Place the pork in a roasting pan or Dutch oven and add 2 cups of water. Cover tightly and roast for 6-7 hours, turning once every hour. Make sure it's fork tender.

Increase the heat to 425°F and roast, uncovered, for 20 minutes, or until the skin gets crispy. Remove from the oven and let rest for 15 minutes.

Shred the meat with 2 forks and place on a large, lime-lined platter. Pour the pan juices over the shredded meat. Serve with warm tortillas. Makes 8 servings.

Herb-Roasted Pork Tenderloin
JBS/Swift Premium

2 whole Swift Premium pork tenderloins
Salt and pepper
8 tablespoons herbes de Provence (more if needed)

1 cup fruit preserves (fig, peach, plum)
1 cup water
1 tablespoon apple cider vinegar (or your preference)

Preheat oven to 425°F.

Season pork tenderloins liberally with salt and pepper, then with herbes de Provence, pressing to get the herbs to adhere to the pork.

Place the pork on a rack in a roasting pan or in a large oven-safe skillet and roast in the oven for 12-15 minutes, or until the internal temperature reaches 145°F. Remove from the oven and let it rest for 10 minutes.

While the pork is resting, combine preserves, water and vinegar in a small pan and bring to a simmer.

Slice the pork into thick pieces, then spoon the sauce/glaze over the slices. Makes 12 servings.

Rib-Eye Steaks with Whiskey Cream Sauce
JBS USA

5 tablespoons butter, divided
3 tablespoons diced onion
¼ cup whiskey
¼ cup beef stock or broth

Salt
Freshly ground black pepper
¼ cup light cream
2 JBS rib-eye steaks

Melt 2 tablespoons butter in a small skillet over medium heat. Add onion and cook until browned, about 4 minutes. Turn off the burner temporarily and pour in whiskey. As soon as the whiskey evaporates, turn the burner on to medium and pour in beef stock or broth. Add a dash of salt and pepper to taste.

Whisk in another tablespoon of butter. Let the mixture bubble for 30 seconds, then reduce the heat to low. Add cream and whisk, adding more cream if the mixture looks too brothy. Simmer on low heat.

Melt 2 tablespoons butter in a large skillet over medium-high heat. Generously salt and pepper each steak and add to the skillet. For medium-rare, cook 2 minutes on each side. For a thicker steak, cook 3-4 minutes per side. Generously spoon the sauce over each steak. Makes 2 servings.

Ginger Steak Salad
JBS USA

2 tablespoons soy sauce
1 tablespoon sherry
2 garlic cloves, minced
2 teaspoons brown sugar
1 JBS rib-eye or strip steak
2 tablespoons olive oil
8 ounces salad greens
2 whole green onions, sliced
Cherry tomatoes (optional)

SALAD DRESSING
2 tablespoons olive oil
2 tablespoons soy sauce
2 tablespoons white sugar
1 tablespoon lime juice
2 garlic cloves, finely diced
1 tablespoon minced fresh ginger
½ jalapeño, seeded and diced

In a ziplock bag, combine soy sauce, sherry, garlic and brown sugar; mix to blend. Add steak and marinate in the refrigerator, turning occasionally, for 30 minutes-2 hours.

Prepare the salad dressing: Combine all ingredients and whisk to blend.

When the steak is finished marinating, add olive oil to a hot skillet. Cook the steak about 1½-2 minutes per side, or until medium-rare. Remove from the skillet and let rest on a plate, allowing to cool slightly. Toss salad greens with ¾ of the salad dressing. Place the steak on a cutting board and slice thinly, then pour the juices from the plate over the top. Mound the tossed salad on a plate, then place sliced steak on top. Pour the remaining dressing over the top. Sprinkle green onions over the salad, and add cherry tomatoes if that makes your skirt fly up. Makes 4 servings.

White Rotisserie Chicken Enchiladas

Pilgrim's/Gold Kist

3 tablespoons canola oil, divided

12 corn tortillas

1 large onion, diced

1 jalapeño, seeded and minced

2½ cups shredded cooked Pilgrim's rotisserie chicken

3 4-ounce cans whole green chiles, diced, divided

1 teaspoon paprika, divided

2 cups chicken broth, divided

½ cup heavy cream

2 tablespoons butter

2 tablespoons flour

1 cup sour cream

2½ cups grated Monterey Jack cheese, divided

Salt and pepper

Cilantro, chopped

Picante sauce, for serving (optional)

Heat 2 tablespoons canola oil in a small skillet over medium-high heat. Fry tortillas for no longer than 20 seconds, just to soften (do not allow to become crisp). Place on a towel or stack of paper towels to drain.

Heat 1 tablespoon canola oil in a separate skillet over medium heat. Add onion and jalapeño; sauté for 1 minute. Add chicken, half of the green chiles and ½ teaspoon paprika. Stir together. Stir in ½ cup chicken broth. Add cream and stir, letting the mixture bubble and get hot. Remove from the heat and set aside.

In a separate large skillet, melt butter over medium heat. Sprinkle in flour, whisk together, and cook for 1 minute. Whisk in 1½ cups chicken broth and cook for 1-2 minutes. Stir in the remaining chiles. Reduce the heat, then stir in sour cream. Add 1½ cups grated cheese and stir to melt. Add ½ teaspoon paprika. Check seasoning and add salt and pepper to taste.

Preheat oven to 350°F.

To assemble, spoon some chicken mixture onto each tortilla. Top with plenty of grated cheese and roll up. Place seam-side down in a 13-by-9-inch casserole dish. Pour the cheese sauce evenly over the tortillas. Top with extra cheese if you like. Bake for 30 minutes, or until heated through. Sprinkle generously with chopped cilantro. Serve with picante sauce. Makes 6 servings.

Chicken Apricot Panini

Pilgrim's/Gold Kist

2 Pilgrim's boneless, skinless chicken breasts

Salt and pepper

3 tablespoons canola oil

6 tablespoons butter, divided

12-16 fresh sage leaves

¼ cup apricot preserves

¼ cup mayonnaise

8 thick slices crusty bread

½ red onion, thinly sliced

Cut chicken breasts in half and season to taste with salt and pepper. In a large skillet over medium-high heat, heat canola oil and 2 tablespoons butter. Add the chicken and brown on one side, about 3 minutes. Flip the chicken breasts and add some of the sage leaves to the hot oil. Flip them once and remove when they're starting to crisp. Repeat with the remaining sage. Remove the chicken when it's cooked through.

In a small bowl, stir together preserves and mayonnaise.

For each sandwich, spread a generous portion of the apricot/mayonnaise mixture on a slice of bread. Add some red onion. Place a piece of chicken on the onion and top with sage leaves. Top with another slice of bread. Butter both sides of the sandwich.

Grill in a panini press. Or grill in a skillet with a second heavy skillet on top to press the sandwich together, then flip and grill the other side. Makes 4 sandwiches.

Hidekazu Tojo

Since opening his restaurant, Tojo's, in 1988, Vancouver's Hidekazu Tojo has delighted dignitaries, Hollywood A-listers, rock stars and locals with his innovative adaptations of Japanese cuisine. A British Columbia Restaurant Hall of Fame member, Tojo is credited with creating the California Roll and the BBQ salmon skin BC Roll. Tojo-san has been featured on Martha Stewart *and in* The Washington Post *and* Gourmet *magazine.*

WINDSET FARMS

Tojo Windset Roll
Windset Farms

Recipes developed by Hidekazu Tojo

½ cup sushi rice (see recipe below)

1 nori sheet, 7 by 8 inches

1 Maestro sweet bell pepper, grilled whole, peeled, sliced into flat sheets

1 teaspoon mayonnaise

1 large (U/15) prawn, cooked tempura-style

1 yam stick, ⅞ by 4 inches, cooked tempura-style

1 pineapple slice, ⅜ by ⅜ by 4 inches

1 4-inch asparagus spear, blanched

3 avocado slices, ⅛ inch thick

1 slice peeled Fresco seedless cucumber – 4 by 8 inches, 3⁄16 inch thick, katsuramuki cut (see note)

Special equipment: bamboo sushi mat

Spread sushi rice evenly over nori, rough side up. Lay a sheet of grilled pepper on top of the rice. Spread with mayonnaise. Top with prawn and yam tempura, pineapple, asparagus and avocado. Roll widthwise using a bamboo sushi mat. Wrap the sushi roll with the cucumber slice. Cut into 4 pieces and serve. Makes 2 servings.

Note: To mimic a katsuramuki-style peel, take a potato peeler and peel around the cucumber in a spiral.

Sushi Rice
Windset Farms

½ cup rice vinegar

3 tablespoons sugar

1 tablespoon salt

1 2-inch piece dashi kombu (dried kelp)

4 cups Japanese short-grain rice

Combine vinegar, sugar and salt. Add kelp and store in an airtight container in a cool place. Rinse rice in cold water until the water runs clear. Cook the rice with 4½ cups cold water. Let sit for 10 minutes after cooking. Spread into a shallow, flat container.

Pour vinegar mixture over the warm rice and mix in using a wooden spatula in a "slicing" motion, fanning the rice continuously until it glistens. Let sit until the steaming stops, then repeat the slicing technique until cool. Place the rice in a container and cover with a damp towel. It will hold for up to 3 hours.

Prawn and Crab Cocktail Tojo-Style
Windset Farms

6-10 Symphony tomatoes

2 cooked tiger prawns, peeled and cut into ¾-inch pieces

1 ounce cooked crabmeat

3 Fresco cocktail cucumbers, halved and cut into ¾-inch chunks

¼ avocado, cut into ¾-inch cubes

¼ jalapeño, seeded and finely chopped

5 sprigs cilantro, chopped (leaves only)

Red onion slices and cilantro sprigs, for garnish

DRESSING

1 tablespoon rice vinegar

1 tablespoon freshly squeezed lemon juice

1 teaspoon olive oil

¼ teaspoon sugar

⅛ teaspoon salt

Plunge tomatoes into boiling water for 15 seconds, then immediately plunge into cold water. Peel the tomatoes. Cut any larger tomatoes into bite-size pieces.

Prepare the dressing: In a bowl, whisk together all ingredients.

In a large bowl, combine tomatoes, prawns, crab, cucumbers, avocado, jalapeño and cilantro. Add the dressing and toss lightly.

Spoon into martini glasses. Garnish with red onion slices and cilantro sprigs. Makes 2 servings.

GREG POWERS PHOTOGRAPHY

Carla Hall

Carla Hall attended L'Academie de Cuisine in Maryland and is owner and executive chef of Alchemy by Carla Hall, an artisan cookie company. She lives in Washington, D.C., and is a co-host on the talk show The Chew. *Hall is the author of* Cooking with Love: Comfort Food That Hugs You *(Atria, 2012) and the upcoming* Cooking with Carla: New Comfort Foods from Around the World *(Atria, 2014). Learn more at www.carlahall.com.*

Bacon, Blue Cheese and Apple Stacks
FirstFruits

Recipes developed by Carla Hall

1-2 FirstFruits Granny Smith apples

4 ounces blue cheese, crumbled (about 1 cup), divided

1 8-ounce block cream cheese, softened

3 tablespoons half-and-half

¼ teaspoon freshly ground black pepper

½ cup plus 2 tablespoons chopped toasted walnuts, divided

20 pieces crisp cooked bacon

Core 1 apple and cut it in half. Cut half of the apple into ¼-inch dice. Wrap the other half tightly in plastic wrap and refrigerate.

Reserve 2 tablespoons of the blue cheese. Place the remaining blue cheese in a food processor along with cream cheese, half-and-half and pepper. Process until well blended and smooth, stopping to scrape the sides and bottom of the bowl occasionally.

Transfer the blended cheese to a large bowl. Stir in the diced apple and ½ cup of the nuts. Cover and refrigerate for at least 30 minutes and up to 1 day.

If the cut side of the reserved apple has browned, slice off the brown part. Cut the apple into 40 very thin slices. Use a second apple if needed.

Divide the cream cheese blend among the bacon strips and spread evenly. Sandwich between 2 apple slices. Garnish with the remaining blue cheese and walnuts. Serve immediately. Makes 20 stacks.

Opal Apple Peanut Butter Dip
Quick & Easy

FirstFruits

1 cup creamy peanut butter

½ cup Greek yogurt

1 tablespoon honey

¼ teaspoon cinnamon

½ cup crunchy granola

3 FirstFruits Opal apples, sliced

In a large bowl, combine first 4 ingredients. Stir until smooth.

Transfer the dip to a serving bowl and top with granola.

Serve this healthy, kid-friendly dip with Opal apple slices. Makes 4-6 servings.

Garofalo

Ethan Stowell

Ethan Stowell is the executive chef and owner of Ethan Stowell Restaurants in Seattle. They include Tavolàta, How to Cook a Wolf, Anchovies & Olives, Staple & Fancy Mercantile, Rione XIII and Bar Cotto. In 2010, Stowell launched Lagana Foods, an artisan pasta line, and began consulting for the Seattle Mariners. To learn more about his food and book, visit www.ethanstowellrestaurants.com.

GEOFFREY SMITH

Spaghetti with Shrimp
Garofalo

Recipes developed by Ethan Stowell

Kosher salt

2 cups simple tomato sauce

¾ pound Garofalo spaghetti

1½ pounds fresh shell-on shrimp, 10-12 or 12-16 count

2 tablespoons chopped fresh Italian parsley

Freshly ground pepper

Extra-virgin olive oil, for drizzling

SHRIMP STOCK

2 tablespoons extra-virgin olive oil

Shells from 1 pound (or more) shrimp

3 garlic cloves

1 small onion, peeled and quartered

3 celery ribs, cleaned and chopped

½ cup white wine

Prepare the shrimp stock: In a medium saucepan, heat olive oil over medium heat. Add shrimp shells and garlic, and sauté for 2-3 minutes, or until the shells turn pink. Add onion, celery and wine, and bring to a boil. Add water to cover, bring to a boil, and simmer for 20-30 minutes to get the flavor out of the shells. Strain, pressing on the shells.

Set a pot of salted water to boil.

In a deep sauté pan, combine tomato sauce and 1 cup of shrimp stock. Bring to a simmer over medium heat. Cook for 10-15 minutes—not reducing the sauce, just mingling the flavors.

When the pot of water reaches a boil, add pasta and cook for 1 minute less than the package directions say, or until slightly firmer than al dente.

While the pasta cooks, add shrimp to the tomato sauce and simmer just until pink, 2-3 minutes.

When the pasta is ready, drain and add to the shrimp and sauce, along with the parsley. Season to taste with salt and pepper. Divide among 4 plates. Drizzle with olive oil and serve. Makes 4 servings.

Gemelli with Nettle Pesto
Garofalo

Kosher salt

12 ounces Garofalo gemelli

Grated Parmigiano-Reggiano, for serving

NETTLE PESTO

Kosher salt

4 ounces fresh nettle tips

3 garlic cloves

¾ cup pine nuts

1 cup extra-virgin olive oil

1 cup grated Parmigiano-Reggiano

Prepare the pesto: Bring a pot of salted water to a boil. Prepare an ice bath. Add nettles to the boiling water and cook for 3 minutes, then plunge immediately into the ice bath. Remove the nettles and squeeze very dry. Chop finely.

Combine the nettles with garlic, pine nuts and a pinch of salt in a food processor. Pulse to combine. Add oil in a steady stream until you have a uniform, thick paste. Transfer to a bowl and stir in cheese.

Set a pot of salted water to boil over high heat. Add gemelli and cook for 1 minute less than the package directions say. Drain, reserving the cooking liquid.

Toss the pasta with ½ cup of pesto and ¼ cup reserved pasta water. Divide among 4 bowls and top with grated Parmigiano-Reggiano. Serve hot or cold. Makes 4 servings.

Tip: Top the extra pesto with a sealing layer of olive oil, and it should last for 2-3 days in the fridge.

Radiatore with Pancetta, Chanterelles and Mint
Garofalo

Kosher salt

½ pound Garofalo radiatore

¾ pound fresh chanterelle mushrooms

2 tablespoons extra-virgin olive oil, plus more for drizzling

½ pound pancetta, cut into small dice

3 medium garlic cloves, thinly sliced

Pinch of chile flakes

Freshly ground pepper

2 tablespoons chopped fresh mint

2 tablespoons chopped fresh parsley

Parmigiano-Reggiano, for serving

Bring a large pot of lightly salted water to a rolling boil. Add pasta and cook for 1 minute less than the package directions say. While the pasta is cooking, clean mushrooms and slice off the tough end of each stem. Quarter the large mushrooms and halve the others. Set aside.

Heat olive oil in a sauté pan over medium heat. Add pancetta and sauté until some of the fat renders and the pancetta is golden, about 5 minutes. You don't want it to become too crisp. Add the mushrooms and sauté for 5-6 minutes, stirring occasionally. When the mushrooms are golden, add garlic and cook for 1 minute longer. Add chile flakes.

When the pasta is ready, drain and add to the mushroom-pancetta mixture, adding a couple of tablespoons of cooking water if the mixture seems dry. Season with salt and pepper. Add mint and parsley and toss.

Transfer to a serving bowl. Drizzle with olive oil. Shave Parmigiano-Reggiano on top. Makes 4 servings.

S·E·H·M·H·L·L

QUENTIN BACON

Ina Garten

Ina Garten, one of the country's most beloved culinary icons, is the author of eight best-selling cookbooks. She has twice been awarded the Emmy for Outstanding Culinary Lifestyle/Culinary Host for her show Barefoot Contessa Back to Basics. Her Sauté Dinners for Two and Skillet Dinners are available nationwide. She lives in East Hampton, New York, with her husband, Jeffrey. Visit her at www.BarefootContessa.com.

Salmon and Melting Cherry Tomatoes recipe on page 104.

Salmon and Melting Cherry Tomatoes
SeaMazz

Recipes developed by Ina Garten

Good olive oil

1 cup chopped sweet onion, such as Vidalia

2 teaspoons minced garlic (2 cloves)

2 cups (1 pint) cherry or grape tomatoes, halved through the stem

Kosher salt and freshly ground black pepper

1½ tablespoons good balsamic vinegar

1½ tablespoons julienned fresh basil leaves

4 SeaMazz frozen skinless salmon fillets, thawed

Preheat oven to 425°F.

Heat 3 tablespoons of olive oil in a medium (10-inch) sauté pan. Add onion and sauté over medium-low heat for 5 minutes, stirring occasionally, until very tender but not browned. Add garlic and sauté for 1 more minute. Stir in tomatoes, 1 teaspoon salt and ½ teaspoon pepper, and cook over medium-low heat for 10-15 minutes, stirring occasionally, until the liquid evaporates and the tomato sauce thickens slightly. Off the heat, stir in vinegar and basil.

Meanwhile, place a large (12-inch) cast-iron pan over high heat for 5 minutes. Brush salmon all over with olive oil, sprinkle liberally with salt and pepper, and place it skin side up in the pan. Cook the fish for 3-4 minutes without moving them, until browned. Turn the salmon skin side down with a small metal spatula and transfer the pan to the oven for 8 minutes. (The salmon will not be completely cooked through.) Remove the fish to a serving platter, cover with aluminum foil, and allow to rest for 5 minutes.

Reheat the tomatoes, season to taste, and serve hot, warm or at room temperature along with the salmon. Makes 4 servings.

All recipes adapted from Barefoot Contessa Foolproof. *Copyright © 2012 by Ina Garten. Published by Clarkson Potter, a division of Random House, Inc.*

Salmon and Melting Cherry Tomatoes photo on page 103.

Lobster and Potato Salad
SeaMazz

1½ pounds unpeeled small Yukon Gold potatoes (1½-inch diameter)

Kosher salt

3 tablespoons champagne or white wine vinegar

½ teaspoon Dijon mustard

½ teaspoon minced garlic

1 extra-large egg yolk, at room temperature (optional)

Freshly ground black pepper

½ cup good olive oil

¼ cup dry white wine

3 tablespoons drained capers

1 cup thinly sliced scallions (6-8)

½ cup (¼-inch) diced celery

½ cup (¼-inch) diced red onion

1¾ pounds SeaMazz lobster tails, cooked, shelled and cut in 1-inch dice

1 lemon

3 tablespoons chopped fresh tarragon

Place potatoes in a large pot and cover with water by 1 inch. Add 1 tablespoon salt and bring to a boil. Lower the heat and simmer for 15-25 minutes, depending on the size of the potatoes, until just tender. Drain in a colander, cover with a kitchen towel, and allow the potatoes to steam for 5-10 minutes. Cut them in quarters or halves, depending on their size, and place in a large bowl.

Meanwhile, whisk together the vinegar, mustard, garlic, egg yolk, 2 teaspoons salt and 1 teaspoon pepper. While whisking, slowly pour in the olive oil, making an emulsion. Stir in wine and capers.

While potatoes are still very warm, pour half the vinaigrette on the potatoes and toss them gently, allowing them to soak up the vinaigrette. Stir in scallions, celery, red onion, lobster and enough vinaigrette to moisten. Reserve any remaining vinaigrette. Add lemon zest and juice, tarragon, 2 teaspoons salt and 1 teaspoon pepper and toss carefully. Cover with plastic wrap and refrigerate for at least an hour to allow flavors to blend. Taste for seasonings and add more vinaigrette, if necessary. Serve at room temperature. Makes 6 servings.

Fennel and Garlic Shrimp
SeaMazz

6 tablespoons good olive oil

1 cup chopped fennel bulb, fronds reserved

3 tablespoons minced garlic (9 cloves)

¼ teaspoon crushed red pepper flakes

1 pound SeaMazz frozen jumbo (13- to 15-count) easy-peel shrimp, thawed and peeled with tails on

1 tablespoon chopped fresh flat-leaf parsley

1 tablespoon Pernod (optional)

1 teaspoon fleur de sel

½ teaspoon freshly ground black pepper

French bread, for serving

Heat olive oil in a large (12-inch) sauté pan over medium heat. Add fennel and sauté for 5 minutes, until tender but not browned. Turn the heat to medium-low, add garlic and red pepper flakes, and cook at a very low sizzle for 2-3 minutes, until the garlic just begins to color.

Pat shrimp dry with paper towels, add them to the pan, and toss together with the fennel and olive oil. Spread the shrimp in one layer and cook over medium heat for 2 minutes on one side. Turn the shrimp and cook for 2 minutes on the other side, until they're pink and just cooked through.

Off the heat, sprinkle with parsley, 1 tablespoon of chopped fennel fronds, Pernod (if using), fleur de sel and black pepper. Serve with bread to soak up all the pan juices. Makes 2-3 servings.

Food to live by.

Myra Goodman

EARTHBOUND FARM

Myra Goodman and her husband, Drew, founded Earthbound Farm in their backyard 29 years ago. Myra's cooking is inspired by the fresh, flavorful and healthful harvest of their organic farm, which led her to establish one of the country's first certified organic kitchens. Her third cookbook, Straight from the Earth: 100 Irresistible Vegan Recipes for Everyone *(Chronicle Books) is due out in early 2014.*

Spring Mix with Quinoa, Apples, Roasted Sweet Potatoes and Pecans
Earthbound Farm

Recipes developed by Myra Goodman

- 3 cups sweet potatoes, peeled and cut into ½-inch cubes
- 2 tablespoons olive oil, divided
- 1 teaspoon pure maple syrup
- Salt
- Pinch of cayenne pepper
- ½ cup quinoa (preferably tri-color), thoroughly rinsed
- 5 ounces (6 cups packed) Earthbound Farm spring mix, baby spinach or Half & Half (half of each)
- 1 large crisp apple, cored, thinly sliced and cut into bite-size pieces
- ¾ cup raw, unsalted pecans, toasted and coarsely chopped

SALAD DRESSING

- ¼ cup minced shallot
- 3 tablespoons white wine vinegar
- 1 teaspoon pure maple syrup
- ½ cup extra-virgin olive oil
- ¼ teaspoon salt
- Pinch of fresh ground black pepper

Preheat oven to 400°F. Place sweet potato cubes on a roasting pan, and sprinkle with 1 tablespoon plus 1 teaspoon olive oil, maple syrup, ½ teaspoon salt and cayenne pepper. Toss thoroughly with your hands, and spread out evenly on the pan. Bake for 20 minutes. Stir, then bake for 5-10 minutes, or until golden brown. Remove from the oven and cool to room temperature.

Heat 2 teaspoons olive oil in a small saucepan over medium heat. Add quinoa and cook for 4-5 minutes, stirring continuously. Add 1 cup of water and ¼ teaspoon salt. Bring to a boil, and then reduce heat to low. Simmer, covered, for 15 minutes, or until all the water is absorbed. Fluff with a fork, and then spread onto a cookie sheet to cool to room temperature.

Prepare the dressing: Combine all ingredients in a small jar. Cover and shake vigorously until thoroughly combined.

In a large bowl, combine salad greens and apple with about ⅔ of the dressing and toss. Add the quinoa and sweet potatoes and toss again. Taste and add more dressing and additional salt and pepper if desired. Top with toasted pecans. Makes 6 servings.

Garlicky Broccolette and Carrots
Earthbound Farm

- 2 tablespoons olive oil
- 4 large garlic cloves, minced
- 1 pound Earthbound Farm broccolette, ends trimmed, stems cut into 1-inch pieces and florets up to 2-inch lengths (6 cups)
- 1 small bunch carrots (peeling optional), sliced into bite-size pieces about ½ inch thick (2 cups)
- ½ cup hot water
- Salt and freshly ground black pepper

Place olive oil in a large skillet with a lid, and set over medium heat. Add garlic and cook for 1 minute, stirring continuously.

Add broccolette and carrots; sauté for 2 minutes, stirring frequently. Add water, cover the pan and raise the heat to medium-high. Cook, stirring once or twice, until the vegetables are crisp-tender, about 5 minutes. Season to taste with salt and pepper and serve hot. Makes 4 servings.

Chris Moyer

MICHAEL POHUSKI

Chef Chris Moyer is the Corporate Executive Chef for the Coleman Organic brand. He is responsible for keeping a close eye on emerging trends, new flavors and innovative products. As a graduate of the Culinary Institute of America in Hyde Park, New York, Moyer brings passion to the culinary arena with more than 15 years in the hotel restaurant industry. He's held top-tier positions in some of Maryland's best restaurants.

Barbecue Chicken and Tomato-Watermelon Salad
Coleman Organic

Recipes developed by Chris Moyer

¾ cup prepared barbecue sauce
¼ cup lemon juice
3 scallions, minced
1 Coleman Organic fresh
   whole chicken

TOMATO-WATERMELON SALAD
2½ cups chopped tomato
   (about 2 large tomatoes)
2 cups cubed watermelon
   (about 12 ounces)
3 scallions, chopped
3 tablespoons fresh lime juice
1 garlic clove, minced

Preheat a charcoal or gas grill to medium-high.

In a small bowl, whisk together barbecue sauce, lemon juice and scallions.

Split chicken in half through the breastbone and backbone. Rub with sauce.

When the grill is preheated, push coals to one side of the grill, using tongs. Replace the grill rack. (Or, if using a gas grill, turn off burners on one half of the grill.) Set chicken on the cool side of the grill—not over coals or burners. Close the lid, open the vents to maintain the fire, and cook the chicken for about 1½ hours, turning occasionally, or until a meat thermometer inserted in the thickest part of the thigh registers 180°F.

Prepare the salad: In a large bowl, stir together all ingredients.

Serve the chicken with the salad. Makes 4 servings.

Creamy Organic Chicken with Spinach and Mushroom Risotto
Coleman Organic

2 tablespoons olive oil
4 Coleman Organic boneless,
   skinless chicken breasts
2 tablespoons chopped shallots
1 cup sliced fresh mushrooms
1 cup chopped fresh spinach

1 9.9-ounce package Uncle Ben's
   Ready Risotto
¾ cup chicken broth
¼ cup grated Asiago cheese
Toasted focaccia bread, for serving

Preheat oven to 350°F.

Heat olive oil in a sauté pan over medium-high heat. Add chicken and brown on both sides. Transfer to a baking pan and bake in the oven for 15-18 minutes, or until the internal temperature is 170°F.

Add shallots, mushrooms and spinach to the pan and cook until wilted. Add risotto rice and mix in. Add broth and cook until the rice is tender.

Slice the chicken into bite-size pieces and add to the risotto. Add cheese and stir until it is melted.

Serve with focaccia. Makes 4 servings.

THE
AUSTRALIAN LAMB
COMPANY INC.

ANTHONYGARITOOFJACKSTUDIOS

David Burke

Blurring the lines between inventor, chef and entrepreneur, David Burke (www.davidburke.com) *is one of the pioneers in American cooking today. He is the innovator behind flavor-transfer spice sheets and more, his fascination with ingredients fueling a career marked by creativity and acclaim. He's written two books and publishes his own quarterly magazine, available in any of his restaurants.*

THE
AUSTRALIAN LAMB
COMPANY INC.

"Classic" Rack of Australian Lamb

The Lamb Co-operative, Inc.

Recipes developed by David Burke

2 (8-rib) frenched Australian
  racks of lamb

1½ teaspoons salt

¾ teaspoon cracked black pepper

1 teaspoon canola oil

1½ teaspoons extra-virgin olive oil

HERB COATING

½ head of garlic, finely chopped

¼ cup chopped fresh parsley

2 teaspoons chopped fresh rosemary

1 tablespoon chopped fresh thyme

1 teaspoon grated lemon zest

Preheat oven to 350°F. Heat a large skillet over medium-high heat. Season racks of lamb with salt and pepper. Add canola oil to the skillet.

Place the lamb racks in the hot pan, fat side down. Sear on both sides for about 4 minutes, or until nicely browned. Remove from the skillet and let rest.

Prepare the herb coating: In a bowl, combine garlic, herbs and lemon zest; stir to blend.

Rub the lamb with olive oil. Spread the herb coating evenly over the lamb. Place on a baking pan or oven-safe dish.

Place the pan in the middle of the oven and cook to desired doneness: approximately 20-25 minutes for medium-rare, or until a meat thermometer inserted into the thickest part reads 130°F. Makes 6-8 servings.

Tips: Cut the racks into double chops. Serve with mint and lemon or yogurt, or with Dijon mustard.

Grilled Australian Lamb Loin Chops

The Lamb Co-operative, Inc.

Salt and pepper

8 Australian lamb loin chops

1½ tablespoons olive oil

2 sticks (8 ounces) butter

½ cup balsamic vinegar

4 tablespoons chopped fresh
  parsley and chives

Turn your barbecue on medium to high heat; be sure the grill is hot.

Salt and pepper both sides of chops (don't be shy; lamb is great with salt and pepper). Drizzle oil on top.

Place the chops on the grill for about 6 minutes on each side, charring both sides well.

On the stove, in a hot sauté pan, add butter and heat until brown (foaming and smells nutty). Remove the pan from the heat. Add vinegar and mix together. Add parsley and chives.

To serve, place the lamb chops on plates and spoon sauce over the top of each chop. Makes 4 servings.

Tip: These are great served with wilted spinach.

Spiced Roasted Australian Boneless Leg of Lamb

The Lamb Co-operative, Inc.

1 cup red wine (suggested Pinot Noir)
¼ cup of your favorite chili sauce
¼ cup water
⅓ cup orange juice
½ cup chopped white onion
½ cup whole garlic cloves
1 tablespoon chili powder

1 teaspoon honey
1 teaspoon brown sugar
1 teaspoon ground cumin
Salt and pepper
2 tablespoons grape seed oil
1 Australian boneless lamb leg

In a large bowl, combine wine, chili sauce, water, orange juice, onion, garlic, chili powder, honey, brown sugar, cumin, salt and pepper to taste.

Rub grape seed oil all over the lamb. In a shallow pan, cover the lamb with the marinade and let sit, refrigerated, overnight.

Preheat oven to 450°F for 30 minutes and then lower the temperature to 350°F.

Place the lamb in the middle of the oven in a nonreactive cooking pan. Roast for approximately 1½ hours (for medium-rare) while frequently basting with the pan juices.

When the lamb reaches the desired temperature (130°F for medium-rare), remove from the oven and carefully transfer to a cutting board, tent with foil, and let rest for 10 minutes. Remove the netting from the leg, then slice and serve. Makes 6-8 servings.

Tip: Serve with creamy polenta, roasted farmers' market vegetables or oven-roasted potatoes.

MIKI DUISTERHOF

Chloe Coscarelli

Chloe Coscarelli won first place in the Food Network's Cupcake Wars, *making her the first vegan to win a Food Network competition. She is a graduate of the Natural Gourmet Institute for Health and Culinary Arts NYC and the University of California, Berkeley, as well as Cornell University's Plant-Based Nutrition Program. She is the author of* Chloe's Kitchen *and* Chloe's Vegan Desserts. *Learn more at chefchloe.com.*

Peach Cobbler recipe on page 114.

Peach Cobbler

Trinity Fruit

Recipes developed by Chloe Coscarelli

DOUGH

1⅓ cups all-purpose flour

2 tablespoons sugar,
  plus extra for sprinkling

1½ teaspoons baking powder

½ teaspoon salt

¼ cup canola oil or
  vegan margarine

½ cup soy, almond or rice milk,
  plus extra for brushing

FRUIT

½ cup sugar

2 tablespoons all-purpose flour

1 teaspoon ground cinnamon

6 fresh Trinity peaches, peeled,
  pitted and sliced (or about
  18 ounces frozen peaches)

Prepare the dough: In a medium bowl, whisk together flour, sugar, baking powder and salt.

In a separate small bowl, whisk oil and nondairy milk, and add it to the flour mixture.

Mix with a wooden spoon until combined and it is sticky and doughy. Do not overmix.

Prepare the fruit: In a medium bowl, whisk together sugar, flour and cinnamon. Add peaches and toss with a large spoon until the fruit is coated with the sugar mixture.

Preheat oven to 375°F.

Pour the peaches into an 8- or 9-inch baking pan or distribute evenly into 6 ramekins. Using a tablespoon, scoop lumps of dough on top of the peaches. Brush the top of the dough with nondairy milk and generously sprinkle with sugar. Bake for 35-40 minutes, or until the dough is thoroughly cooked and lightly browned on top. Be sure to rotate after 20 minutes, so that it bakes evenly. Makes 6 servings.

Peach Cobbler photo on page 113.

Minted Couscous with Arugula, Butternut Squash and Pomegranate

Trinity Fruit

4 tablespoons olive oil, divided

3 cups ½-inch cubes peeled
  butternut squash

Sea salt

Freshly ground black pepper

2 cups Israeli pearl couscous

2½ cups vegetable broth

1 cup arugula

¼ cup Trinity pomegranate arils

½ cup slivered almonds, toasted

2 tablespoons finely chopped
  fresh mint

Preheat oven to 375°F. In a large bowl, toss 2 tablespoons olive oil with squash and season generously with salt and pepper. Transfer to a large rimmed baking sheet and roast for 30-35 minutes, or until the squash is fork tender, turning once or twice with a spatula. Let cool.

In the meantime, combine 1 tablespoon oil, couscous, 1 teaspoon salt and vegetable broth in a medium saucepan. Bring to a boil, then reduce the heat and simmer, covered, for 10 minutes, or until tender. Remove from the heat and let sit, covered, for 5 minutes, or until all the liquid has been absorbed.

Toss the couscous with the remaining 1 tablespoon oil and spread on a large rimmed baking sheet to cool.

In a large bowl, toss the cooled couscous with the cooled butternut squash, arugula, pomegranate, almonds and mint. Adjust the seasoning to taste and serve. Makes 8 servings.

Mandarin Peanut-Crunch Salad with Crispy Wontons
Trinity Fruit

4 ounces mixed greens of choice

1 cup shredded red cabbage

¼ cup shredded carrot

1 scallion, trimmed and thinly sliced

1 cup Trinity mandarin orange segments, membranes and pith removed, if desired

¼ cup chopped roasted peanuts

DRESSING

¼ cup rice vinegar

2 tablespoons canola oil

2 tablespoons brown sugar

1 tablespoon orange marmalade

1¼ teaspoons chili-garlic sauce

CRISPY WONTONS

20 egg-free gyoza or wonton wrappers

Canola oil for frying

Prepare the dressing: In a blender, combine all ingredients and process until smooth. Adjust sweetness to taste.

Prepare the crispy wontons: Using a pizza cutter or sharp knife, cut each wrapper into ¼-inch strips. Fill a small skillet with ½ inch oil and heat over medium heat until a small piece of wrapper sizzles when dropped into the oil. Gently place wonton strips in the heated oil and fry until crisp, about 15-20 seconds, watching very carefully so they don't burn. Drain on paper towels.

In a large bowl, combine greens, cabbage, carrot, scallion, oranges and peanuts. Toss with the desired amount of dressing. Top with a handful of crispy wontons. Makes 6 servings.

Tom Douglas

ED ANDERSON

Tom Douglas creates deliciousness, served with graciousness, at 15 different joints, all in Seattle. With more than 30 years dedicated to the Seattle restaurant scene, he is credited with putting the city on the culinary map. Douglas is the author of four cookbooks, including his latest title, The Dahlia Bakery Cookbook (Morrow, 2012). He was also recently named Outstanding Restaurateur 2012 by the James Beard Foundation.

Jackie's Favorite Strata with Wild Mushrooms and Sausage
Premio

Recipes developed by Tom Douglas

1 pound Premio mild Italian sausages, casings removed, sausages crumbled

2 tablespoons butter, divided

1 medium onion, chopped

2 tablespoons olive oil

¾ pound wild or domestic mushrooms, cleaned and sliced

1 pound chard, washed, stems removed

6 cups loosely packed ¾-inch cubes of bread cut from a rustic loaf

2 teaspoons thinly sliced chives

2 teaspoons chopped fresh thyme

¾ pound white or yellow Cheddar, grated, divided

5 large eggs

2½ cups heavy cream

¾ teaspoon kosher salt

¼ teaspoon black pepper

Cook sausage over medium heat in a skillet (add a little oil if needed), turning with a spatula and breaking up clumps. Drain off fat and set aside.

Melt 1 tablespoon butter in another skillet over medium-high heat. Add onion and cook until starting to brown. Transfer to a large bowl. Add 1 tablespoon butter and olive oil to the skillet. Add mushrooms and cook until tender. Transfer to the bowl.

Bring a pot of salted water to a boil, add chard, and cook until tender, 2 minutes. Drain the chard and then rinse with cold water, drain, and squeeze out all excess water with your hands. Roughly chop the chard and add to the bowl. Add the sausage, bread and herbs to the bowl. Add cheese (reserving ¾ cup) and stir to combine. Transfer the mixture to a buttered 13-by-9-inch baking pan, spreading evenly.

In a bowl, whisk eggs, cream, salt and pepper. Pour into the baking dish, pressing the bread down with a spatula. Sprinkle the remaining cheese over the top. Cover and refrigerate for 2 hours or overnight.

Preheat oven to 350°F.

Bake the strata, uncovered, until golden and the custard is set, about 55-60 minutes. Cool for 10 minutes before serving. Makes 8 servings.

Grilled Italian Sausages with Peperonata
Premio

6 Premio hot Italian sausages

4 garlic cloves, peeled

6 slices rustic bread, ½ inch thick

Olive oil

Kosher salt and black pepper

PEPERONATA

⅓ cup extra-virgin olive oil, more as needed

2 pounds mild to medium peppers, cut into ½-inch pieces

½ yellow onion, roughly chopped

1 tablespoon minced garlic

¼ cup chopped black olives (Kalamata)

¼ cup chopped green olives (picholine)

¼ cup minced flat-leaf parsley

3 tablespoons capers, chopped

2 tablespoons red wine vinegar, more as needed

1½ teaspoons anchovy paste

Kosher salt and black pepper

Prepare the peperonata: Heat oil in a 12-inch skillet over high heat. Sauté peppers and onion, stirring. Lower the heat and cook until soft, about 25 minutes, adding garlic for the last minute. Transfer to a bowl and stir in olives, parsley, capers, vinegar, anchovy and oil to moisten. Season with salt, pepper and vinegar. Cool to room temperature.

Grill sausages over medium heat until cooked through, 15-20 minutes.

Smash garlic cloves. Rub one side of each bread slice with garlic. Brush both sides with oil and season with salt and pepper. Grill until golden, 1-2 minutes per side.

Serve toast and sausage with a big spoonful of peperonata. Makes 6 servings.

SUSAN PARDYS

Mindy Silver

Mindy Silver, corporate chef for Atlantic Capes Fisheries, Inc., trained at the Restaurant School, Philadelphia, Pennsylvania, and La Varenne, Paris. She finds inspiration for recipes from her travel destinations. Her secret to cooking great scallops at home—and impressing your friends—is to not overcook them. Perfect scallops, she says, "are caramelized brown on the outside and translucent and creamy on the inside."

Scallops with Curried Coconut Milk
Atlantic Capes Fisheries

Recipes developed by Mindy Silver

¼ cup plus 1 tablespoon vegetable oil

2 onions, finely chopped

4 garlic cloves, minced

2 tablespoons minced fresh ginger

1½ tablespoons ground coriander

½ teaspoon ground cumin

¼ teaspoon cinnamon

¼ teaspoon turmeric

⅛ teaspoon cayenne

1 cup chopped canned tomatoes, drained

2½ cups canned unsweetened coconut milk

1 tablespoon brown sugar

1¼ teaspoons salt, plus more to taste

1½ pounds Atlantic Capes sea scallops, thawed

Pepper

1 cup snow peas or snap peas

Cilantro or parsley, for garnish

Steamed jasmine or basmati rice, for serving

Lime wedges, for serving

In a large frying pan, heat ¼ cup oil over moderately high heat. Add onions and cook, stirring frequently, until golden. Add garlic and ginger; cook, stirring, for 1-2 minutes.

Add coriander, cumin, cinnamon, turmeric and cayenne; cook for 30-60 seconds, stirring. Add tomatoes and cook, stirring, for 1 minute.

Add coconut milk, brown sugar and salt; bring to a low boil. Reduce the heat to a simmer and cook, stirring frequently, until thickened (about 5-10 minutes).

While the sauce is simmering, heat a large nonstick pan over high heat. Add 1 tablespoon oil to the pan. Season scallops with salt and pepper to taste and place them in the hot pan. Cook until browned on one side (about 2 minutes), turn over and cook until just done (1-2 minutes). Remove the scallops from the pan and place in a large serving bowl.

Add snow peas to the simmering sauce mixture and cook just until the peas are cooked through (1-2 minutes). Pour the sauce over the scallops and garnish with cilantro or parsley. Serve with steamed rice and lime wedges. Makes 4 servings.

Scallop and Asparagus Stir-Fry with Cashews
Atlantic Capes Fisheries

4 tablespoons vegetable oil, divided

1½ pounds Atlantic Capes sea scallops, thawed

Salt and pepper

1 red onion, sliced

2 garlic cloves, chopped

1 pound asparagus, cut in 1-inch diagonal pieces

½ cup canned chicken stock

2 tablespoons Asian fish sauce

1 tablespoon oyster sauce

1 tablespoon fresh lime juice

½ cup roasted cashews

½ cup chopped fresh basil

¼ cup chopped green onions

White rice, preferably jasmine or basmati, for serving

Heat 2 tablespoons oil in a sauté pan over medium-high heat. Season scallops to taste with salt and pepper. Cook the scallops in the hot pan, searing on each side until golden brown (about 2 minutes per side). Remove to a plate and cover with foil.

In a wok or large skillet over medium-high heat, heat 2 tablespoons oil. Sauté onion until translucent. Add garlic and asparagus; cook for about 2 minutes. Add chicken stock, fish sauce, oyster sauce and lime juice; simmer for 2 minutes.

Remove the pan from the heat and stir in cashews and basil. Season to taste with salt and pepper. Toss in the seared scallops and garnish with chopped green onions. Serve with rice. Makes 4 servings.

Aida Mollenkamp

Chef, television personality and food writer Aida Mollenkamp followed her passion for cooking, first at Cornell University's School of Hotel Administration and then at Le Cordon Bleu Paris. She became food editor at Chow magazine before hosting the Food Network television show Ask Aida in 2008. Mollenkamp's second show, FoodCrafters, debuted in 2010. Her first cookbook is Keys to the Kitchen (Chronicle, 2012).

Herb Chicken Paillard Salad with Creamy Mango Dressing

Foster Farms

Recipes developed by Aida Mollenkamp

SALAD

½ head red or green leaf lettuce, torn into bite-size pieces

3 ounces baby arugula

1 cup packed watercress leaves

¼ cup snipped fresh basil

⅓ cup thinly sliced red onion

2 Japanese cucumbers, thinly sliced

1 medium avocado, cut in ½-inch slices

¼ cup chopped toasted peanuts

DRESSING

1 large ripe mango, peeled and chopped

4 teaspoons plain yogurt

3 tablespoons rice wine vinegar

1 teaspoon Dijon mustard

¼ teaspoon kosher salt

⅛ teaspoon freshly ground black pepper

CHICKEN

4 Foster Farms fresh boneless, skinless chicken breasts

2 tablespoons olive oil, plus more for drizzling

¾ teaspoon roughly chopped fresh thyme

2 tablespoons finely chopped fresh flat-leaf parsley

Grated zest and juice of 1 lemon

1 teaspoon kosher salt

½ teaspoon freshly ground black pepper

In a salad bowl, combine lettuce, arugula, watercress and basil; toss gently.

In a blender, combine dressing ingredients and blend until smooth. Stir in a spoonful of water.

Place each chicken breast in a medium-size resealable plastic bag, sprinkle with water, push out air and seal. Using a meat mallet, gently pound each piece until about ½ inch thick.

Heat oil over medium-high heat in a large nonstick skillet. Lightly coat chicken with oil. Stir together chopped herbs, lemon zest and juice, salt and pepper. Rub onto the chicken. Cook chicken in the skillet about 4-5 minutes on each side (165°F). Cut into ½-inch slices.

Place greens on 4 plates; top with onion, cucumbers and avocado. Drizzle with dressing. Top with chicken and peanuts. Makes 4 servings.

Sonoma Turkey Burgers with Rosemary Aïoli

Foster Farms

1½ pounds Foster Farms fresh ground turkey

¼ cup chopped fresh basil leaves, tightly packed

¼ cup minced California ripe olives

2 tablespoons water

1¼ teaspoons kosher salt

½ teaspoon freshly ground black pepper

2 tablespoons olive oil

6 slices California Jalapeño Jack cheese

6 potato buns or good-quality hamburger buns, toasted

¾ cup wild or baby arugula

1 avocado, thinly sliced

ROSEMARY AÏOLI

¾ cup mayonnaise

2 teaspoons Dijon mustard

1 tablespoon lemon juice

1 large garlic clove, minced

2 teaspoons finely chopped fresh rosemary leaves

Prepare the aïoli: Combine all ingredients and stir until well blended. Set aside.

In a large bowl, combine turkey, basil, olives, water, salt and pepper. Handle the meat as little as possible to avoid compacting, but mix well. Divide the mixture into 6 equal portions and form into patties.

In a large skillet, heat olive oil over medium-high heat. Add the patties and cook for 4 minutes. Then turn, cover and cook for 2 minutes. Uncover, top with cheese, re-cover and cook until the internal patty temperature is 165°F, approximately 2-4 minutes.

To assemble the burgers, spread a generous amount of Rosemary Aïoli on the cut sides of the buns. On each bun bottom, add some arugula, top with a patty, and add a few slices of avocado. Add bun tops. Makes 6 servings.

Tip: For added indulgence, sprinkle crumbled cooked bacon on each bun before adding the patty.

Pancetta Chicken and Brussels Sprouts

Foster Farms

1 pound fresh Brussels sprouts

2 tablespoons olive oil

3 ounces paper-thin slices pancetta

2 garlic cloves, minced

1 pound Foster Farms fully cooked chicken breast strips, cut into 1-inch pieces

¾ cup dried cranberries

¼ cup Sauvignon Blanc

1 teaspoon fresh thyme leaves

½ cup almond slivers, lightly toasted

½ teaspoon salt

½ teaspoon freshly ground pepper

Wash Brussels sprouts thoroughly; pat dry. Trim stems, remove yellow leaves and coarsely chop, preferably by hand. Steam in a covered microwave-safe bowl or on the stovetop for 5-6 minutes.

Immediately add to an ice-water bath and let cool for 5 minutes.

Meanwhile, warm olive oil in a large skillet over medium-high heat. Add pancetta pieces individually and sauté until crispy, about 3 minutes. Add garlic and chicken; continue to sauté for about 4 minutes, or until the chicken is warmed through. Add dried cranberries, Sauvignon Blanc and thyme. Stir to combine.

Drain the Brussels sprouts, transfer to a salad spinner, and spin until dry. Place the Brussels sprouts in a large bowl. Add the chicken mixture, toasted almond slivers, salt and pepper. Gently toss together and serve immediately. Makes 4 servings.

Fabio Viviani

Chef Fabio Viviani has possessed a passion for food since his childhood in Florence, Italy. Viviani is perhaps best known for his appearance on season 5 of Bravo's Top Chef. His cookbook of family recipes is Fabio's Italian Kitchen (Hyperion, 2013). Viviani regularly shares recipes with his fans through his newsletter, "Fabio's Kitchen Academy." For more information, visit his website, http://fabioviviani.com.

Rigatoni delle Nonna recipe on page 124.

Rigatoni delle Nonna (Grandma's Rigatoni)
Tarantino

Recipes developed by Fabio Viviani

1 pound rigatoni

1 tablespoon olive oil

2 small red onions, diced

1 red bell pepper, cut in small dice

1½ pounds Tarantino Italian sausages, removed from casings

3 small heads of radicchio di Treviso, leaves separated

1 cup heavy cream

½ cup grated Parmigiano cheese

Cook rigatoni in salted boiling water until al dente. Drain the pasta, reserving ¼ cup of cooking liquid.

In a large skillet, heat olive oil over medium-high heat. Add onions and pepper; cook until tender and beginning to brown. Add sausage, crumbling with your hands. Continue to cook over high heat, breaking the pieces apart with your spatula, until browned.

Turn the heat down to medium and add radicchio to the pan. Sauté gently until the leaves are very wilted and reduced in size by half.

Add cream and cook for a few minutes until incorporated. Add cheese and toss to combine. Add the drained pasta to the pot and continue to cook for a minute or so. If the sauce is too thick, add a bit of the cooking water. Makes 4 servings.

Rigatoni delle Nonna photo on page 123.

Broiled Stuffed Tomatoes
Tarantino

4 green tomatoes

1 cup ricotta cheese

1 cup grated Parmesan cheese

¼ pound mortadella, chopped

¼ pound Tarantino Italian sausage, casings removed, crumbled, cooked

½ cup pitted black olives, chopped

4 tablespoons olive oil

Extra-virgin olive oil, for serving

Preheat the oven broiler to the highest setting.

Cut the tops off the tomatoes. Scoop out the flesh with a spoon and discard.

In a bowl, combine cheeses, meats and olives; mix well. Fill the hollowed-out tomatoes with the mixture, mounding the top. Drizzle 1 tablespoon of olive oil over each tomato and place in an oven-safe pan.

Broil the tomatoes for 10-12 minutes, or until golden brown and crusty.

Remove from the oven and drizzle with extra-virgin olive oil. Makes 4 servings.

Adapted from Fabio's Italian Kitchen, by Fabio Viviani (Hyperion, 2013).

Sausage Strata
Tarantino

16 ounces Tarantino breakfast link
  sausage, sliced into small rounds

⅓ cup butter, softened, or as needed

12 English muffins, split

12 ounces shredded sharp Cheddar
  cheese, divided

8 ounces shredded provolone
  cheese, divided

8 large eggs

1½ cups sour cream

1 cup chopped green bell pepper

Heat a large skillet over medium-high heat. Add sausage and cook, stirring, until each piece is browned on both sides, about 10 minutes. Lightly grease a 13-by-9-inch baking dish. Spread butter on the inside of each English muffin half. Arrange 6 of the English muffin halves buttered side down in the prepared baking dish. Top with half the sausage, half the Cheddar and half the provolone.

In a large bowl, whisk eggs, sour cream and bell pepper together; pour evenly over the sausage and cheese layer. Top with the remaining muffin halves, sausage, Cheddar and provolone. Cover and refrigerate overnight. Preheat oven to 375°F. Bake the strata until lightly browned and set in the middle, about 45 minutes, covering the pan if necessary to prevent overbrowning. Makes 6 servings.

INSPIRED BY FLAVOR™

Mollie Katzen

LISA KEATING

Mollie Katzen changed the way a generation cooked with the publication of the Moosewood Cookbook. Hailed by The New York Times as "one of the best-selling cookbook authors of all time," Katzen is an award-winning illustrator and designer and has been inducted into the James Beard Cookbook Hall of Fame. Her new cookbook is The Heart of the Plate: Vegetarian Recipes for a New Generation (Houghton Mifflin, 2013).

Fattoush
SUNSET

Recipes developed by Mollie Katzen

2-3 SUNSET cucumbers (peeled if desired), diced (about ½ pound)

1 medium SUNSET bell pepper (any color), diced

1 pint SUNSET Zima grape tomatoes, halved if large (about 2 cups)

4 scallions, minced (whites and light greens)

2 large handfuls fresh flat-leaf parsley (1 packed cup), coarsely chopped (larger stems discarded)

2 large handfuls fresh mint leaves (1 packed cup), whole or coarsely chopped

Vinaigrette (your favorite brand)

Black pepper

1 medium head purslane (about ½ pound), sturdier stems removed, leaves and smaller stems coarsely chopped, *or* romaine hearts, cored and torn or chopped

2 whole-wheat pita breads (ideally thin-walled ones), lightly toasted and broken into large bite-size pieces

Salt

Combine cucumbers, bell pepper, tomatoes, scallions and herbs in a shallow dish and toss with about 6 tablespoons of vinaigrette and black pepper to taste. Add the purslane (hold off if using the romaine) and toss to coat. Cover and let it sit for at least 30 minutes and up to 2 hours (refrigerate if the room is hot).

About 30 minutes before serving, toss in the pita (and romaine, if using) and mix until thoroughly coated.

Taste and adjust the amount of vinaigrette if necessary. Add a light sprinkling of salt and pepper, if desired. Serve cold or at cool room temperature. Makes 3-4 modest main-course servings.

Roasted One Sweet Pepper Saladita
SUNSET

Olive oil

About 2 pounds SUNSET One Sweet Peppers

1 teaspoon minced or crushed garlic

½ teaspoon salt, or more to taste

½ teaspoon ground cumin, or more to taste

2 teaspoons cider vinegar, or more to taste

1 tablespoon fresh lemon or lime juice, or more to taste

½ teaspoon agave nectar or sugar (optional)

Cayenne or crushed red pepper

Preheat the broiler. Lightly brush a foil-lined baking sheet with olive oil.

Place the whole peppers on the baking sheet. Broil until they are blistered all over and covered with black patches, using tongs to carefully turn the peppers a few times while they are cooking. This will take up to 15 minutes, depending on your broiler.

Transfer the peppers to a bowl, cover with a plate, and let cool for at least 45 minutes. They will give off a good amount of delicious juice while they cool—save all of it.

Peel the peppers and remove and discard the seeds and stems. Mince the flesh, and return the minced peppers to the bowl. Stir in garlic, starting with ½ teaspoon and possibly going up from there, then salt, cumin, vinegar and lemon or lime juice. Add as much of the saved juice from the peppers as you wish. Stir to combine, adjust the seasonings to taste, adding some sweetener if you like, and heating things up a touch with cayenne or crushed red pepper.

Serve cold or at cool room temperature. If you are going to store the saladita in the refrigerator, coat the top with a slick of olive oil. Makes 6-8 servings.

Note: This can be served with crackers or toast.

STUDIO YOU PHOTOGRAPHY

Tony Seta

Master Chef Anthony (Tony) Seta is a culinary professional with more than 25 years of experience in successfully developing creative and signature items for restaurant chains and food manufacturers. As Butterball's director of culinary services, Chef Seta applies his expert knowledge of ethnic cuisines and current culinary trends to recipe and formula development with a primary focus on flavor.

Bahama Breeze Burgers
Butterball

Recipes developed by Tony Seta

Cooking spray

1 pound Butterball fresh
 ground turkey

4 slices Cheddar cheese

4 pineapple slices

4 hamburger buns, horizontally
 cut in half, toasted

1 cup shredded lettuce

8 thinly sliced red onion rings

SWEET CHILI MAYO

¼ cup chili sauce

¼ cup mayonnaise

Prepare the Sweet Chili Mayo: In a small bowl, combine ingredients and stir to blend. Set aside.

Spray the cooking grates of an outdoor grill. Preheat the grill to medium direct heat.

Form ground turkey into 4 patties, each 4-5 inches in diameter. Grill for 8-10 minutes, turning over after 5 minutes. Continue cooking until the internal temperature is 165°F. Place 1 slice of cheese on each burger. Grill until the cheese is melted. Remove the burgers from the grill and keep warm.

Grill pineapple slices 1-2 minutes per side, or until there are grill marks. Remove from the grill.

Spread Sweet Chili Mayo evenly over the cut surfaces of each bun. Layer the bottom halves of the buns with lettuce, cooked burger, onions and pineapple. Cover with the bun tops and serve. Makes 4 servings.

Nutritional information: Each serving has 485 calories, 33 g protein, 38 g carbohydrates, 23 g fat (8 g saturated), 107 mg cholesterol, 2 g fiber, 743 mg sodium, 376 mg potassium, 11 g sugar.

Easy Turkey Chili
Quick & Easy

Butterball

2 tablespoons vegetable oil

1 pound Butterball fresh
 ground turkey

1 1.6-ounce packet chili seasoning

1 14.5-ounce can diced
 fire-roasted tomatoes

1 4-ounce can diced mild
 green chiles, drained

Heat oil in a medium saucepan on medium-high heat. Add turkey and cook until no longer pink, stirring frequently.

Stir seasoning into the turkey. Add remaining ingredients. Bring to a boil, stirring frequently. Reduce the heat to medium-low and simmer, uncovered, for 15 minutes. Makes 4 servings.

Nutritional information: Each serving has 293 calories, 25 g protein, 13 g carbohydrates, 17 g fat (3 g saturated), 78 mg cholesterol, 2 g fiber, 1056 mg sodium, 486 mg potassium, 3 g sugar.

MICHAEL HARLAN TURKEL

Alexandra Raij

Alexandra Raij is the co-owner, co-Chef, with her husband, Eder Montero, of Txikito, El Quinto Pino and La Vara, three Spanish restaurants in New York City. This year Raij was named Best Chef New York by Eater.com. Raij and Montero have set a new standard for tapas and Spanish food stateside and developed a singular style of cooking that is both traditional and authentic but also personal and innovative.

Catalan-Style Braised Veal Leg Cutlets with Mushrooms and Almond Sauce

Plume De Veau

Recipes developed by Alexandra Raij

6 Plume De Veau veal leg cutlets
Salt
White pepper
Flour
Olive oil
2 large onions, minced
2 sprigs of thyme
1 pinch of saffron
3 plum tomatoes, grated on a box grater to obtain pulp, skins discarded
1 cup Cognac, brandy or white wine

4 cups veal stock
1 cup diced exotic mushrooms of choice, preferably chanterelles or porcini (or substitute small button mushrooms)
Chopped flat-leaf parsley, for serving

ALMOND PICADA
½ cup toasted blanched almonds
⅓ cup panko bread crumbs
1 cup olive oil
3 garlic cloves, finely grated

Prepare the Almond Picada: In a food processor or coffee grinder, combine almonds and bread crumbs. Pulse until a fine paste forms. Place in a sauté pan over medium heat with olive oil. Cook, stirring constantly, until it takes on a light golden color. Add garlic and cook, stirring, until just golden. Remove to a plate to cool.

Heat a large, deep sauté pan over medium heat.

Working in batches, season the meat with salt and white pepper to taste and dust with flour, shaking off excess. Add olive oil to coat the pan and sear the meat on both sides in batches, moving the cutlets to a plate once seared.

To the same pan, add onions and salt to taste; sweat until translucent and tender. Add thyme and saffron; cook 3 minutes more. Raise the heat and add the tomato pulp. Cook until dry and darkened.

Add Cognac and stir, bringing to a simmer; cook for 2 minutes. Stir in stock and return to a simmer.

Nestle the cutlets back in the pan, making sure they are covered with sauce. Cook at a very low simmer, uncovered, for 35 minutes.

Add mushrooms and simmer until the meat is tender, another 15-20 minutes. Stir in the picada and adjust the seasoning.

Sprinkle with parsley and serve. Makes 6 servings.

Recipes printed with permission of Alexandra Raij, Txikito, La Vara, El Quinto Pino. All rights reserved.

Spicy Veal Loin Chops with Pineapple Salsa

Plume De Veau

1 tablespoon ground cumin
1 teaspoon dried marjoram
3 chipotle peppers from a can of chipotles in adobo sauce
1 garlic clove
2 tablespoons salt
¼ cup canola oil, plus more for searing
4 Plume De Veau veal loin chops

PINEAPPLE SALSA
2 cups small-diced pineapple
Salt
1 cup roughly chopped cilantro
1 jalapeño or serrano pepper, minced
Juice of 2 limes
1 small red onion, minced
1 cup olive oil

In a blender, combine cumin, marjoram, chipotles, garlic, salt and oil. Process until a paste forms.

Massage the paste into the chops. Marinate for 3 hours in the refrigerator.

Prepare the salsa: Combine all ingredients and stir to blend.

Bring the chops to room temperature.

Preheat oven to 450°F.

Heat a cast-iron sauté pan over high heat and add a little canola oil. Reduce the heat to medium and sear the meat on both sides, then transfer to the oven and roast until medium (140-145°F), about 8 minutes. Let rest for a few minutes, then serve with the salsa. Makes 4 servings.

Veal Rib Chops with Lemon Caper Gremolata

Plume De Veau

4 Plume De Veau veal rib chops

Salt and pepper

1 tablespoon Spanish paprika

½ cup olive oil, or as needed

LEMON CAPER GREMOLATA

¼ cup capers, rinsed and minced

1 bunch flat-leaf parsley, chopped

½ cup grated Parmesan cheese

1 garlic clove, minced

1 anchovy, minced

Grated zest of 2 lemons

½ cup olive oil

Juice of 1 lemon

2 tablespoons butter,
   at room temperature

Preheat oven to 450°F. Heat a cast-iron sauté pan large enough to accommodate all 4 chops, over medium heat. Season the chops with salt and pepper to taste and paprika. Brush with olive oil. Sear the chops until golden, about 3 minutes per side. Move to the oven and cook to medium, about 7 minutes. Remove to a plate to rest for 5 minutes. Meanwhile, prepare the gremolata: In a small bowl, mix together capers, parsley, Parmesan, garlic, anchovy and lemon zest. Stir in olive oil and lemon juice. Stir in butter. Reheat the chops for 1 minute and serve with a large spoonful of gremolata on top. Makes 4 servings.

MORGAN TRINKER

Heather Baird

Heather Baird's passion is creating eye-popping, mouthwatering desserts. She writes about her adventures in the world of creative dessert-making in her award-winning blog at www. sprinklebakes.com. She is the author of SprinkleBakes: Dessert Recipes to Inspire Your Inner Artist *(Sterling Epicure, 2012), and lives in Knoxville, Tennessee, with her husband, Mark, and two mischievous pugs named Biscuit and Churro.*

Pumpkin Croissant Breakfast Bake recipe on page 134.

Pumpkin Croissant Breakfast Bake
Puratos

Recipes developed by Heather Baird

6 croissants, cubed
2 cups heavy cream
1 15-ounce can pumpkin
1 cup whole milk
1¼ cups sugar
4 large eggs
1 large egg yolk
1 teaspoon ground cinnamon
¼ teaspoon ground allspice
Pure maple syrup, for serving

STREUSEL TOPPING
¾ cup sugar
¾ cup flour
1 tablespoon water
1 teaspoon ground cinnamon
¼ cup butter, softened
¼ teaspoon salt
⅓ cup chopped pecans

Prepare the streusel topping: Place all ingredients in a medium bowl and mash together with a fork until crumbly. Store the mixture in the refrigerator while the custard is being prepared.

Spray a 13-by-9-inch casserole dish with cooking spray. Place cubed croissants in the dish and set aside.

In a bowl, whisk together cream, pumpkin, milk, sugar, eggs, egg yolk, cinnamon and allspice. Pour over the croissant cubes. Press the croissant pieces down into the custard so they are thoroughly coated with the mixture. Cover and refrigerate for 1 hour.

Preheat oven to 350°F.

Bake for 35 minutes, and then sprinkle on the streusel topping. Bake for an additional 20-25 minutes, or until the custard is just set. Serve warm with pure maple syrup. Makes 12 servings.

Pumpkin Croissant Breakfast Bake photo on page 133.

Caramel Apple Strudels with Candied Walnuts
Puratos

CANDIED WALNUTS
Cooking spray
1 egg white
½ cup walnut pieces
Pinch of salt
2 tablespoons granulated sugar
¼ teaspoon ground cinnamon

CARAMEL STRUDELS
1 cup sugar
8 tablespoons unsalted butter, cut into cubes
½ cup heavy cream
¼ teaspoon salt
8 braided apple strudels

Prepare the walnuts: Preheat oven to 350°F. Grease a baking sheet with cooking spray. Whisk egg white in a small cup until frothy. Place walnuts in a bowl and pour in just enough egg white to coat the nuts. Add remaining ingredients and toss to coat. Spread the walnuts on the baking sheet. Bake for 15-20 minutes, or until they begin to dry and turn golden. Cool on a wire rack.

Prepare the strudels: Place sugar in a medium saucepan over medium-high heat. Cook, stirring occasionally, until the sugar is liquefied. When the mixture turns a deep amber, add cubed butter and whisk until incorporated. Remove from the heat and whisk in cream a little at a time. The mixture will bubble and foam. Whisk in salt. Transfer to a medium bowl and let cool.

Place strudels in a 13-by-9-inch baking dish. Pour warm caramel over the strudels and sprinkle with candied walnuts. Makes 8 servings.

Red Wine Poached Pears with Danish Pastry
Puratos

3 firm medium-size Bosc pears
1 bottle dry red wine
1 cup sugar
2 tablespoons lemon juice

3 cinnamon sticks
¼ teaspoon aniseed (optional)
6 pull-apart Danish pastries

Peel pears and core them from the bottom, leaving the stem intact at the top. In a saucepan large enough to hold the pears in a single layer, combine wine, sugar and lemon juice; stir well. Add cinnamon sticks and aniseed. Bring to a simmer over medium-high heat. Add the pears and simmer until fork-tender, about 20 minutes, depending on the firmness of the pears.

Transfer the poached pears to a plate using a slotted spoon. Let cool completely. Carefully slice the pears in half lengthwise, beginning at the stem. Place the pears cut side down on a cutting board. Cut into ½-inch slices beginning ½ inch below the stem so the slices are still attached at the top.

To serve, place a cut pear half on top of each Danish. Separate the pear slices and fan them out from the uncut top portion. Makes 6 servings.

Daphne Oz

ELLEN SILVERMAN

Daphne Oz is co-host of ABC's The Chew and author of the New York Times best-seller Relish (William Morrow, 2013) and the national best-seller The Dorm Room Diet. She received her chef's degree from the Natural Gourmet Institute and is a graduate of the Institute for Integrative Nutrition. She lives with her husband, John, in New York City.

Fruit Yogurt Pops
Alpine Fresh

Recipes developed by Daphne Oz

2 cups mixed Alpine Fresh blueberries, blackberries and fresh-cut mango (see note)

1½ cups plain yogurt

1 banana

2-3 tablespoons honey

Juice of 2 limes

Special equipment: ice pop molds and sticks

Place all ingredients in a blender with 1 cup water. Blend on high until smooth.

Pour into the ice pop molds or cups and cover with aluminum foil. Insert the ice pop sticks and freeze for 4 hours or overnight. Makes 6-12 ice pops.

Note: If preferred, the pops can be made with just one kind of fruit—blueberries, blackberries or mango.

Sweet Corn Succotash
Alpine Fresh

3 ears sweet corn, shucked

Salt

½ pound Alpine Fresh green beans, trimmed

2 large shallots, peeled and minced

¼ cup olive oil

¼ cup white wine vinegar or champagne vinegar

1 tablespoon Dijon mustard

1 teaspoon raw honey

½ teaspoon sea salt

Fresh-cracked black pepper

¾ cup chopped flat-leaf parsley, divided

1 medium tomato, seeded and chopped

¼ cup raw or smoked almonds, chopped

½ jalapeño, minced

1 large ripe avocado, pitted, peeled and diced in ½-inch cubes

Cut the corn kernels from the cobs and reserve them in a large bowl.

Bring 3 cups water and a large pinch of salt to a boil. Blanch green beans by boiling them for 1-2 minutes, uncovered, until tender but still crisp. Drain the beans and plunge them into an ice bath. Drain the beans, then chop them into bite-size pieces. Reserve them with the corn.

In a blender, combine shallots, olive oil, vinegar, mustard, honey, salt, pepper to taste and ¼ cup of the parsley. Blend until smooth and creamy.

To the corn and beans, add tomato, almonds, jalapeño and the vinaigrette. Toss well.

Serve the salad garnished with avocado and the remaining parsley. Makes 4 servings.

Mark Bittman

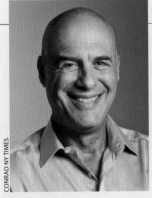

CONRAD NY TIMES

Mark Bittman is one of the country's most respected food writers. His How to Cook Everything *books are a mainstay of the modern kitchen. Bittman writes for* The New York Times *on food policy and cooking and is a columnist for* The New York Times Magazine. *His cooking show,* The Minimalist, *airs on the Cooking Channel. He is also the author of* VB6: Eat Vegan Before 6:00, Food Matters, The Food Matters Cookbook *and* Fish.

Blueberry-Banana Parfaits
Rainier Fruit Company

Recipes developed by Mark Bittman

2 ripe medium bananas
2 tablespoons fresh lemon juice
½ cup low-sugar, high-fiber cereal

3 cups Rainier Fruit blueberries, or 1½ cups blueberries and 1½ cups other chopped fresh fruit
Lemon zest (optional)

Put bananas in a medium bowl and squeeze lemon juice over all. Mash and stir the mixture with a fork or potato masher until it's as smooth or lumpy as you like.

Assemble parfaits in short, wide glasses in alternating layers of mashed banana, cereal and blueberries until you use everything up. Top with lemon zest, if desired. Serve immediately. Makes 4 servings.

Tip: Mashed bananas give you all the creamy richness and sweetness you expect in a parfait without a bit of dairy. For an even creamier version, add a layer of silken tofu.

Spiced Apple Jam
Rainier Fruit Company

1½ pounds Rainier Fruit Organic Fuji apples, cored, peeled if you like, and roughly chopped ●Organic
1-2 tablespoons sugar (optional)
2 tablespoons minced fresh ginger, or 2 teaspoons ground ginger

¼ teaspoon ground cinnamon
½ teaspoon salt
2 tablespoons fresh lemon juice
Whole-grain toast, for serving (optional)

In a medium saucepan, combine apples, sugar, ginger, cinnamon, salt and lemon juice. Bring to a boil over medium heat, stirring occasionally.

Reduce the heat to a gentle bubble and cook, stirring occasionally and adding a bit of water if the mixture gets too dry, until it darkens and thickens, about 1½ hours.

Once the apples are quite soft, you can mash them a bit with a fork or potato masher, if you like. Taste, and adjust the seasoning. Cool and refrigerate until you're ready to use. (It will keep for at least a week.) Makes about 8 servings.

Tip: This jam is great on toast or hot cereal, or eaten like applesauce.

Six Sisters

LARRY ADAMSON

Elyse Ellis, Camille Beckstrand, Stephanie Loaiza, Kristen Hills, Lauren Adamson and Kendra Adamson are six sisters who share their easy, affordable recipes and crafts on their blog, SixSistersStuff.com. Their blog is filled with family recipes using common ingredients, with easy-to-follow instructions and photographs of each dish. Believing that time spent eating together around the dinner table is priceless, they are out to build families one meal at a time!

Red Velvet Cake Truffles

CSM Bakery Products

Recipes developed by Six Sisters

¼ of a Kirkland Signature 10-inch red velvet cake with cream cheese frosting

6 ounces Baker's Premium White Chocolate

Remove the custard filling from the middle of the cake.

Take the remaining cake and frosting and place it in a bowl. Mix the cake and frosting with a fork until it is blended and a wet mixture forms.

With your hands, form the mixture into small balls about 1 inch by 1 inch. Place the balls on a small cooking sheet and put in the freezer for 30 minutes.

Once the balls are cold, melt white chocolate in a small microwavable bowl on high for 2 minutes, stirring every 30 seconds. Stir until the chocolate is completely melted.

Dip the cold cake balls into the chocolate. Let the excess chocolate drip off. Place on waxed paper and let stand until the chocolate is firm. Makes 20 truffles.

Granola Snack Mix Cookies

CSM Bakery Products

1 cup butter, softened
1 cup packed light brown sugar
¼ cup granulated sugar
2 large eggs
1 teaspoon vanilla extract
¼ teaspoon salt

1 cup sweetened coconut flakes
3 cups all-purpose flour
1 cup semisweet chocolate chips
2 cups Kirkland Signature granola snack mix, crushed

Preheat oven to 375°F. Line a baking sheet with parchment paper.

In a large bowl, cream together butter, brown sugar and granulated sugar. Beat in eggs one at a time. Mix in vanilla and salt. Add coconut and flour; mix until combined. Fold in chocolate chips and crushed granola snack mix.

Drop by rounded tablespoonfuls onto the baking sheet 2 inches apart. Gently flatten the dough with your fingertips. Bake for 10-12 minutes, or until golden brown. Makes 4 dozen cookies.

Entrées

Marinated Beef Tri-Tip Roast with Parsley Cherry-Tomato Sauce

National Beef

1 garlic clove, chopped
1 tablespoon brown sugar
½ teaspoon black pepper
½ teaspoon ground ginger
1 tablespoon cooking oil
2 tablespoons water
¼ cup soy sauce
1 beef tri-tip roast (2 pounds)

PARSLEY CHERRY-TOMATO SAUCE

1½ pounds cherry tomatoes (5 cups)
½ teaspoon salt
¼ teaspoon red pepper flakes
¼ cup plus 2 tablespoons extra-virgin olive oil, divided
1 cup firmly packed fresh flat-leaf parsley leaves
1 garlic clove, sliced
1 tablespoon red wine vinegar

In a small bowl, combine garlic, brown sugar, pepper, ginger, oil, water and soy sauce.

Place beef roast and the marinade in a plastic ziplock bag, turning the roast to coat. Marinate in the refrigerator for 1 hour.

Preheat oven to 425°F.

Place the roast in a shallow roasting pan. Do not add water or cover. Roast for 30-40 minutes for medium rare (135°F), 40-45 minutes for medium (150°F). Transfer the roast to a carving board and let stand for 15 minutes.

Prepare the sauce while the meat cooks: In a 13-by-9-inch glass baking dish, toss together tomatoes, salt, red pepper flakes and ¼ cup olive oil. Roast on the lower oven rack until the tomatoes burst and release their juices, about 30 minutes.

Meanwhile, in a food processor combine parsley, garlic, vinegar and remaining 2 tablespoons olive oil; pulse until chopped. Transfer to a bowl.

Stir the tomatoes with their juices into the parsley mixture. Serve with the sliced beef. Makes 4-6 servings.

National Beef.
Leading the Way in Quality Beef.

Tri-Tip Street Tacos

Cargill Meat Solutions

1 Morton's of Omaha Steakhouse Classic Tri-Tip
24 4-inch corn or flour tortillas
½ red onion, thinly sliced
1 pound coleslaw cabbage mix
¼ cup jalapeño jelly
3 tablespoons cider vinegar
½ cup chopped fresh cilantro
12 lime wedges
Rice and guacamole, for serving

Prepare tri-tip according to package directions.

Wrap tortillas in a slightly damp towel and microwave on high for 1 minute. Wrap in aluminum foil and let steam for 20 minutes.

In a bowl, combine onion, coleslaw mix, jelly, vinegar and cilantro.

Serve sliced tri-tip on tortillas and top with jalapeño coleslaw. Garnish with lime wedges. Serve with your favorite rice and guacamole. Makes 8 servings.

Sustainable Gourmet Beef Wellington
Katama Foods

1 Sustainable Gourmet beef tenderloin ●Organic

3 tablespoons grape seed oil

1 sheet frozen puff pastry, thawed

Egg wash – 1 egg, 2 tablespoons water, whisked together

Duxelles (see recipe below)

Let tenderloin sit at room temperature for about 30 minutes. Line a baking sheet with parchment paper.

Preheat oven to 425°F.

Heat a sauté pan or skillet over medium-high heat until very hot and pour in oil. Sear the tenderloin until the meat is brown and crispy, about 1 minute per side, then sear the edges. Remove from the pan.

Roll out puff pastry to 1-2 inches greater than its original size. Brush with egg wash. Place about 9 tablespoons of duxelles in the center of the puff pastry and spread evenly. Place the seared tenderloin in the center and fold in the sides of the pastry, sealing the edges. Brush the pastry with egg wash and place seam side down on the prepared baking sheet.

Bake for 15-20 minutes, or until the pastry is golden brown and the meat is cooked to taste. Remove from the baking sheet and let rest for 2 minutes. Makes 4 servings.

Duxelles
Katama Foods

1 tablespoon unsalted butter

1 medium shallot, finely chopped

½ pound mushrooms, cleaned and finely chopped

½ cup ruby or tawny port

Sea salt

Freshly ground black pepper

Heat a sauté pan over medium heat. Add butter and let it melt.

Add shallot and sauté until translucent, about 2 minutes.

Add mushrooms and sauté until juicy and aromatic, about 5 minutes.

Add port and season with salt and pepper to taste. Simmer until the juices have reduced and the mushrooms are almost dry. Remove from the heat and let cool before using in the Wellington. Makes 4 servings.

Beef Wellington with Cherry Port Demi-Glace

Chelan Fresh

2 6-ounce beef tenderloin steaks

Salt and pepper

2 tablespoons plus 1 teaspoon
olive oil, divided

1 portobello mushroom

2 garlic cloves, chopped

1 shallot, chopped

Pinch of thyme

Pinch of rosemary

8-9 ounces puff pastry dough

1 teaspoon butter

1 egg, lightly beaten

CHERRY PORT DEMI-GLACE

1 cup Trout Brand cherries, halved and pitted

1 teaspoon butter

¼ shallot, chopped

¼ cup ruby port

1 quart beef demi-glace,
made from powdered demi-glace
(or 50/50 chicken/beef broth)

Preheat oven to 450°F. Season tenderloins with salt and pepper. Heat 1 teaspoon olive oil in a hot pan; add tenderloins and sear.

Prepare the demi-glace: Sauté cherries with butter and shallot over medium-high heat until tender. Add port and cook until the alcohol has evaporated. Add demi-glace and simmer to desired consistency. Add salt and pepper to taste.

Scrape gills from mushroom. Peel off skin. Cut into ¼-inch squares. Heat 2 tablespoons olive oil in a sauté pan over medium-high heat. Sauté mushroom until tender. Lower heat to medium; stir in garlic, shallot, thyme and rosemary.

Cut pastry dough into 2 pieces; roll out. Place a tenderloin in the center of each pastry; top with mushrooms and butter. Fold in sides of pastry and seal. Vent tops with a few slits; brush with egg. Place on a baking sheet. Bake for 7-10 minutes, or until internal temperature is 130°F. Reduce heat to 425°F when pastry starts to become golden brown. Let rest for 10 minutes.

Serve with Cherry Port Demi-Glace. Makes 2 servings.

Recipe created by Executive Chef Joseph Nagy of Rivers Restaurant.

Filet Mignon in Red Wine and Grape Sauce
Divine Flavor

10 8- to 10-ounce
  filet mignons

1 tablespoon salt

Freshly ground
  black pepper

1 tablespoon minced garlic

1 cup thinly sliced onions

3 tablespoons olive oil

1 pound Divine Flavor red
  seedless grapes, divided

1 quart beef stock

1 cup red wine (Zinfandel)

Place the steaks in a nonreactive container and season with salt, pepper to taste, garlic, onions and olive oil. Marinate in the refrigerator for at least 2 hours and up to 24 hours.

Preheat the grill to medium-high.

Puree half of the grapes in a blender. Cut the remaining grapes in half.

In a small, heavy saucepan, combine the pureed grapes, beef stock and wine. Bring to a boil, then simmer for 10-15 minutes. Stir in the halved grapes.

Place the filets on the grill and cook to taste.

To serve, top the filets with the sauce. Makes 10 servings.

A TASTE THAT CAN ONLY BE DESCRIBED AS **DIVINE FLAVOR**

Montreal Roasted NY Strip with Caramelized Mushrooms and Shallots
Cargill Meat Solutions

1 New York strip loin
  (4-6 pounds)

2 tablespoons olive oil

¼ cup Montreal
  steak seasoning

2 cups whole shallots
  (10 ounces), peeled

4 cups quartered button
  mushrooms

¼ cup sherry vinegar

2 tablespoons honey

Preheat oven to 350°F.

Rub strip loin with olive oil and then rub Montreal seasoning on all surfaces. Place on a roasting rack in a roasting pan. Add remaining ingredients to the bottom of the roasting pan.

Roast for 30 minutes. Remove from the oven and raise the heat to 450°F. When the oven is ready, return the roast to the oven for 15 minutes, or until the internal temperature is 130°F, for medium-rare. Remove and let rest for 15 minutes.

Slice the roast into ⅓-inch slices and serve with mushrooms and shallots from the pan. Makes 4-6 servings.

The Best Meat Loaf You Ever Made
Kirkland Signature/Orleans International

1½ pounds Kirkland Signature ground beef

1 onion, chopped

2 large eggs, beaten

½ cup barbecue sauce (such as Open Pit)

¾ cup crushed crackers (such as Ritz)

1 cup crushed potato chips

¾ teaspoon liquid smoke flavoring

¾ teaspoon ground black pepper

1 teaspoon kosher salt

¾ teaspoon garlic powder

1 major pinch cayenne pepper

6 slices thick-cut bacon

Preheat oven to 375°F.

In a large bowl, combine ground beef, onion, eggs, barbecue sauce, cracker crumbs, potato chips, liquid smoke, black pepper, salt, garlic powder and cayenne pepper. Mix well.

On a lightly greased cookie sheet, shape the mixture into a loaf. Lay bacon slices across the width of the loaf so the entire surface is covered. Cover loosely with foil.

Bake for 90 minutes, or until the internal temperature is 160°F. Makes 6 servings.

Sweet Mini Pepper and Meat Lasagna
Royal Flavor

1 pound Royal Flavor sweet mini peppers, halved and seeded

2 tablespoons olive oil, divided

1 pound ground beef

8 ounces tomato sauce

8 ounces mozzarella cheese, shredded

4 ounces Parmigiano-Reggiano cheese, grated

Preheat oven to 375°F. Grease a 6-by-6-inch pan.

Place peppers on a sheet pan and drizzle with 1 tablespoon olive oil. Roast for about 10 minutes, or until very tender. Remove from the oven and let cool.

Heat 1 tablespoon olive oil in a sauté pan over medium heat. Add ground beef and cook, crumbling until browned, about 5 minutes. Add tomato sauce to the pan and cook for another 5 minutes. Remove from the heat and let cool.

Place a third of the peppers evenly in the prepared pan. In even layers, add half the meat sauce, then half the mozzarella and another third of the peppers. Repeat the layers. Spread Parmigiano-Reggiano evenly over the top.

Bake for 15 minutes, or until the cheese is melted and the top is browned. Serve immediately. Makes 4-6 servings.

Slow-Cooked Chuck Roast with Chili-Apricot Sauce
Cargill Meat Solutions

½ cup vegetable oil

1 choice boneless chuck roast (3-4 pounds)

2 envelopes dry onion soup mix

1 quart beef broth

1¼ cups chili sauce

12 ounces apricot preserves

1 cup cola

1 teaspoon ground black pepper

Preheat oven to 250°F.

Heat oil in a large sauté pan over medium-high heat. Add chuck roast and cook until browned well on all sides.

Place the meat in a deep sauce pot. Cover with remaining ingredients.

Cook, covered, for 5 hours, or until fork-tender. Makes 3-4 servings.

Tip: Serve with braised greens and grits.

Beef and Potato Pie
Reser's Fine Foods

1 40-ounce Reser's Main St. Bistro Baked Scalloped Potatoes

1 15-ounce package prepared beef roast au jus

1 bunch green onions, sliced, including some of the green

1 14.1-ounce package pie-crust dough (for a 2-crust 9-inch pie)

1 egg

1 tablespoon milk

Preheat oven to 375°F.

In a large mixing bowl, with clean hands break scalloped potatoes into small chunks. Then break beef roast into small chunks; reserve the au jus in the container. Add sliced green onions. Mix gently with hands until combined.

Place bottom pie crust in a 9-inch pie plate. Add the potato/meat mixture to the crust. Drizzle the reserved au jus over the top. Add the top pie crust and seal the edges.

In a small bowl, beat together egg and milk. Brush on the pie crust. Pierce the top of the crust with a knife in several places for venting.

Bake for 45-55 minutes, or until golden brown and bubbling. Makes 6-8 servings.

Tip: Add a drizzle of ketchup for an added kick.

Beef and Broccoli Stir-Fry
Mr. Yoshida's

1 pound lean sirloin steak

1 cup Mr. Yoshida's Original Gourmet Sauce, divided

1 tablespoon cornstarch

2 tablespoons water

1 tablespoon vegetable oil

1 12-ounce bag frozen cut broccoli, thawed

Rice, for serving

Cut meat into thin slices. Place in a resealable plastic bag and add ½ cup Mr. Yoshida's sauce. Refrigerate for 30 minutes.

In a small bowl, combine cornstarch and water, stirring until the cornstarch is dissolved. Stir in the remaining ½ cup Mr. Yoshida's sauce. Set aside.

Heat oil in a large skillet over high heat. Add the steak to the skillet and cook until browned, about 3-4 minutes. Add broccoli and cook for an additional 2 minutes, stirring.

Stir in the sauce mixture and cook until it thickens and boils. Serve over rice. Makes 5 servings.

Chicken and Broccoli Ramen Supreme
Nissin Top Ramen

1 tablespoon olive oil

½ cup chopped white onion

8 ounces fresh mushrooms, sliced

6 ounces chicken breast, diced

2 3-ounce packages Nissin Chicken Flavor Top Ramen

4 ounces broccoli florets

1 8-ounce container light sour cream

In a frying pan, heat oil over medium heat. Add onion and sauté until translucent. Add mushrooms and cook until golden brown.

Add chicken to the pan and cook until lightly browned.

In a separate pot, boil 4 cups of water. Add noodles and cook for 3 minutes, stirring occasionally. Drain.

While the noodles cook, put broccoli in a microwave-safe bowl, add 2 tablespoons of water, and cover. Microwave for 2 minutes in a 1,000-watt microwave.

Mix sour cream and the 2 seasoning packets. Toss noodles with the mixture, then add the rest of the ingredients. Cover and let the ingredients blend for a few minutes. Makes 2 servings.

Japanese Kushiyaki Combo

Kirkland Signature/Tyson

2 pounds baby cucumbers, cut in large dice

2 Kirkland Signature boneless, skinless chicken breasts, cut into thin 5-inch-long strips

2 pounds Kirkland Signature beef tenderloin, cut into thin 5-inch-long strips

32-34 wooden skewers, soaked in water for 30 minutes

2 cups baby arugula

1 cup mâche

MISO VINAIGRETTE

2 tablespoons white miso

1½ tablespoons rice wine vinegar

1 teaspoon mirin

1 tablespoon honey

2 teaspoons Dijon mustard

¼ cup canola oil

SPICY CHARRED SOY SAUCE

⅓ cup soy sauce

¼ cup orange marmalade

1 teaspoon finely chopped fresh garlic

1 teaspoon finely chopped fresh ginger

1½ teaspoons Sriracha sauce

2 tablespoons thinly sliced green onion

⅛ teaspoon toasted sesame oil

TOGARASHI RUB

1 tablespoon grated grapefruit zest

1 teaspoon ground red pepper

½ teaspoon ground ginger

½ teaspoon dry mustard

CRUNCHY GARLIC CONDIMENT

2 tablespoons fried garlic (see note)

1 tablespoon thinly sliced toasted nori

2 tablespoons toasted sesame seeds

Prepare the vinaigrette: Combine all ingredients. Add cucumbers and marinate for 1 hour.

Prepare the spicy sauce: In a skillet, combine all ingredients. Set over high heat until it comes to a slow boil. Set aside.

Prepare the rub and condiment: Combine all rub ingredients; in a separate bowl combine all condiment ingredients. Preheat grill to medium-high. Thread chicken and beef onto separate skewers. Season with rub. Grill chicken for 7-10 minutes. Grill beef for 4-5 minutes, basting with the sauce. Encrust the grilled chicken with the condiment.

Drain cucumbers, saving vinaigrette. Top with arugula and mâche. Drizzle with vinaigrette. Serve with the skewers. Makes 8-10 servings or 16-17 appetizer servings.

Note: Packaged fried garlic is available at Asian stores.

Wine-Glazed Chicken
Sunkist Growers

3 cups red wine, preferably Pinot Noir
½ cup sugar
1 medium shallot, finely chopped
2 garlic cloves, peeled and smashed
2 teaspoons chopped fresh rosemary
2 teaspoons chopped fresh thyme
Kosher salt and freshly ground black pepper
4 chicken drumsticks with thighs attached

SAUCE
1 tablespoon olive oil
4 slices bacon, chopped
½ cup diced onion
½ carrot, diced
½ celery stalk, diced
½ cup halved Sunkist black seedless grapes
½ cup halved Sunkist red seedless grapes

In a medium saucepan, combine wine, sugar, shallot, garlic, rosemary, thyme, 1½ teaspoons kosher salt and ½ teaspoon pepper. Bring to a boil, then simmer over medium-low heat until thickened and reduced to 1 cup (about 20 minutes). Let cool completely.

Pour the wine mixture into a medium bowl. Add chicken, cover, and marinate, refrigerated, for 1 hour.

Preheat oven to 400°F. Cover a baking sheet with foil. Place the chicken on the sheet skin side up, reserving the marinade. Roast the chicken until cooked through, about 30-40 minutes.

Prepare the sauce: In a medium skillet, heat olive oil over medium heat. Add bacon, onion, carrot and celery; cook until tender and slightly caramelized, about 8-10 minutes. Season well with salt and pepper. Add the reserved marinade and bring to a simmer. Add grapes and cook until tender, about 5 minutes. Add the chicken and gently toss to coat.

Serve the chicken with the sauce spooned over the top. Makes 4 servings.

Sunkist

Meyer Lemon Greek Grilled Chicken
Duda Farm Fresh Foods

4 boneless, skinless chicken breasts
¼ cup olive oil
Grated zest and juice of 2 Dandy
  Meyer lemons

1 tablespoon dried oregano
2 garlic cloves, minced
1 teaspoon salt
½ teaspoon red pepper flakes

Place chicken breasts in a glass dish.

In a small bowl, whisk together olive oil, lemon zest and juice, oregano, garlic, salt and red pepper flakes. Pour the mixture over the chicken breasts and marinate for 30 minutes or overnight in the refrigerator.

When you're ready to prepare the chicken, preheat the grill to high. If the chicken has been in the refrigerator, let it stand at room temperature for 15 minutes before placing on the hot grill to ensure even cooking.

Grill the chicken for 5 minutes per side, or until the internal temperature is 160°F. Let rest for 5 minutes before slicing to allow the juices to evenly distribute. Makes 4 servings.

Duda
farm fresh foods

Empanadas with Hand-Pulled Rotisserie Chicken
GoodHeart Brand Specialty Foods

2 tablespoons butter

2 tablespoons extra-virgin olive oil

¼ cup diced yellow onion

¼ cup roasted corn kernels

¼ cup diced roasted red and
yellow bell peppers

¼ cup diced roasted,
peeled poblano peppers

5 cups Kirkland Signature
hand-pulled rotisserie chicken

¼ cup sliced (¼ inch) green onions

½ cup GoodHeart's authentic
Red Mole (optional)

Salt, pepper and red pepper flakes

10 prepared empanada dough discs

Vegetable oil, for deep-frying

Heat butter and olive oil in a sauté pan over medium-high heat. Add onion, corn and peppers; sauté until tender. Transfer the mixture to a bowl and add chicken, green onions, red mole, and salt, pepper and red peppter flakes to taste. Toss to combine. Put a generous amount of filling on each empanada disc. Fold in half and seal the edges. Heat vegetable oil to 375°F. Add the empanadas and fry until golden brown, 5-8 minutes. Makes 10 servings.

Hearty Chicken Pot Pie
General Mills

1 16-ounce package frozen mixed vegetables, thawed

1 cup cut-up cooked chicken

1 10¾-ounce can condensed cream of chicken soup

1 cup Original Bisquick mix

½ cup milk

1 large egg

Preheat oven to 400°F.

In an ungreased 2-quart casserole, mix vegetables, chicken and soup.

In a small bowl, stir remaining ingredients with a fork until blended. Pour over the ingredients in the casserole. Bake for 30 minutes, or until golden brown. Makes 6 servings.

Variations: Stir in ½ teaspoon dried thyme leaves, dried sage leaves or pepper. Use condensed cream of mushroom soup or condensed cheese soup instead of the chicken soup to give this dish a whole new taste.

For Hearty Beef Pot Pie, use 1 cup cut-up cooked leftover or deli roast beef instead of the chicken and condensed cream of mushroom soup instead of cream of chicken.

Nutritional information: Each serving has 225 calories (80 calories from fat), 13 g protein, 27 g carbohydrates, 9 g fat (3 g saturated), 60 mg cholesterol, 4 g fiber, 710 mg sodium.

Bisquick

Seared Pork Medallions with Vegetable Ratatouille
Oppenheimer Group

4 center-cut pork loin steaks

Salt and pepper

4 tablespoons extra-virgin olive oil, plus more for searing pork

1 onion, diced

1 zucchini, sliced

1 red greenhouse bell pepper, diced

1 yellow greenhouse bell pepper, diced

1 orange greenhouse bell pepper, diced

4 tomatoes, diced

2 garlic cloves, minced

1 tablespoon capers

¼ cup raisins

¼ cup kalamata olives, pitted

1 tablespoon *each* chopped fresh rosemary, sage, basil and thyme

½ cup dry white wine

1 cup tomato sauce

Season pork to taste with salt and pepper. Heat a frying pan with oil to coat over medium-high heat. Sear pork for 5-7 minutes per side, or until cooked to taste. Let rest for 3 minutes before cutting in 1-inch-thick slices.

Meanwhile, preheat a large pot over medium heat. Add 4 tablespoons olive oil, onion, zucchini, peppers, and salt and pepper to taste. Cook for 5 minutes, stirring regularly. Add tomatoes, garlic, capers, raisins, olives and herbs. Cook for 5 minutes. Add wine and tomato sauce; cook 5 minutes more, stirring often. Adjust seasoning.

Spoon ratatouille onto each plate and arrange sliced pork on top. Makes 4 servings.

Recipe courtesy of SunSelect and Chef Jeff Massey of Restaurant 62.

Roast Pork with Pears
California Pear Advisory Board

Cooking oil

3 cups fresh root vegetables (potatoes, carrots, onions) cut into large chunks

4-pound boneless pork loin roast

Salt and pepper

¼ cup plus 2 tablespoons olive oil, divided

3 tablespoons mustard

3 tablespoons finely chopped fresh herbs (thyme, sage, marjoram)

3-4 fresh California pears

Preheat oven to 350°F. Coat the bottom of a roasting pan with cooking oil.

Place vegetables in the center of the pan.

Rinse pork and dry with paper towels. Season with salt and pepper. In a large skillet, heat 2 tablespoons olive oil over medium-high heat. Brown the roast on all sides. Place on top of the vegetables.

Mix ¼ cup olive oil, mustard and herbs; brush on top and sides of roast. Roast for 1 hour.

Cut pears in half lengthwise. Remove core and seeds. Place cut side down in the pan.

Return to the oven for 15 minutes, or until the internal temperature of the roast is 155°F. Remove from the oven and let stand for 10 minutes, until the internal temperature is 160°F.

Place the roast on a platter. Arrange vegetables and pears around it. Makes 8 servings.

CALIFORNIA
PEARS

Grilled Coffee-and-Garlic-Rubbed Pork Chops
J.M. Smucker Co.

2 teaspoons Folgers Black Silk Coffee, ground

2 teaspoons garlic powder

1 teaspoon dry mustard

1 teaspoon paprika

1 teaspoon firmly packed brown sugar

¾ teaspoon salt

½ teaspoon ground black pepper

4 bone-in center-cut pork chops (¾ to 1 inch thick)

¼ cup Crisco Pure Olive Oil

Preheat the grill.

In a small bowl, combine coffee, garlic powder, mustard, paprika, brown sugar, salt and pepper.

Coat pork chops with the spice mixture. Let rest for 5 minutes.

Brush the pork chops with olive oil. Grill over high heat for 3-4 minutes on each side, or until the internal temperature is 145°F. Remove from the grill. Cover and let rest for 5 minutes. Makes 4 servings.

Easy Slow-Cooker Pulled Pork
Kirkland Signature/Farmland Foods

1 large onion, thinly sliced
1 Farmland boneless pork butt
8 slices Kirkland Signature hickory-smoked bacon, finely chopped

2 cups barbecue sauce
1 teaspoon minced garlic
1 teaspoon ground black pepper

In a 3½- to 4-quart slow cooker, layer onions and pork butt. In a bowl, combine bacon, barbecue sauce, garlic and pepper. Pour over the top of the pork butt.

Cook on low for 8-10 hours (on high: 4-5 hours). Remove the pork from the cooker. Using 2 forks, pull the meat apart and place back in the cooker. Stir to combine with the onions, bacon and sauce. Makes 8-10 servings.

Sweet and Hot Dried Plum Chipotle Ribs

Kirkland Signature/Sunsweet

1 large slab pork ribs (about 4 pounds)

1 cup Kirkland Signature/Sunsweet dried plums

1 cup chicken or vegetable stock

1 cup chopped onion

3 tablespoons honey

2 tablespoons lime juice

1 8-ounce can tomato sauce

2-3 canned chipotle chile peppers in adobo sauce, plus 2 teaspoons adobo sauce from the same can

Chopped fresh cilantro (optional)

Preheat oven to 400°F. Place ribs in a large shallow baking pan. Add 1 inch of water to the pan and cover tightly with foil. Bake for 1 hour.

Meanwhile, combine dried plums, stock, onion, honey, lime juice, tomato sauce, chipotles and adobo sauce in a medium saucepan. Bring to a boil, then reduce the heat and simmer, uncovered, for 15 minutes. Let cool slightly, then puree in a blender or food processor. Return to the saucepan and cook until fairly thick.

Remove the foil from the ribs and drain off the water. Bake, uncovered, for 30 minutes, basting liberally with the sauce several times. Serve the ribs with extra sauce, and sprinkle with cilantro. Makes 4-6 servings.

Grilled Australian Lamb Loin Chops with Mango and Lime Salad

JBS

½ cup olive oil

2 garlic cloves, crushed

2 tablespoons fresh thyme, roughly chopped

8 Australian loin lamb chops

Salt and freshly ground black pepper

MANGO AND LIME SALAD

2 firm mangoes

2 limes

1 English cucumber, thinly sliced

1 teaspoon grated fresh ginger

1 teaspoon brown sugar

1 teaspoon fish sauce

4 ounces Greek-style feta cheese, drained

½ cup cilantro leaves

1 mild red chile, seeded and finely chopped

In a large, shallow baking dish, whisk together olive oil, garlic and thyme. Add lamb chops and turn to coat. Season to taste with salt and pepper. Heat outdoor grill to high and grill the chops 5-6 minutes per side for medium doneness.

Remove and let rest in a warm place for 5 minutes.

Prepare the salad: Peel and slice mangoes into thin matchstick strips. Remove skin and white pith from limes and divide into segments, catching any of the juices. Place the prepared mango and lime in a bowl. Add cucumber and ginger, and gently toss together.

Mix the reserved lime juice, brown sugar and fish sauce together; drizzle over the salad. Place the salad on a serving platter and crumble feta over the top. Scatter cilantro leaves and red chile over the salad. Serve with the grilled chops. Makes 4 servings.

JBS

Grilled Australian Lamb Loin Chops with Garlic Pepper

Kirkland Signature/Thomas Foods International

2 teaspoons cracked black pepper
Pinch of cayenne pepper
2 tablespoons crushed garlic
1 tablespoon chopped fresh rosemary

2 tablespoons chopped fresh parsley
1 teaspoon salt
8-12 Australian loin lamb chops
3 tablespoons olive oil

Preheat the grill to medium-high. Heat olive oil in a skillet over medium-high heat. Add the chops and quickly sear on both sides until light brown. Transfer the chops to the grill and cook to taste. Makes 4-6 servings.

In a shallow bowl, combine black pepper, cayenne pepper, garlic, rosemary, parsley and salt. With a paper towel, pat lamb chops dry. Roll in the seasoning blend. Press the mixture firmly into the meat. Refrigerate for 30 minutes. Remove the lamb chops from the refrigerator and let warm to room temperature.

Honey-Roasted Rack of Australian Lamb

Kirkland Signature/Thomas Foods International

3 tablespoons honey
3 tablespoons lemon juice
3 tablespoons soy sauce

2 teaspoons crushed garlic
1 medium 8-rib rack of Australian lamb

Preheat oven to 475°F. In a small bowl, combine honey, lemon juice, soy sauce and garlic. Preheat a heavy skillet over high heat. Add rack of lamb and sear for 3 minutes per side. Season with the honey mixture.

Place the rack, fat side up, in a roasting pan and roast in the middle of the oven for 14-16 minutes for medium-rare. Transfer the rack to a warm plate and let rest for 10 minutes before slicing. Makes 4 servings.

Tip: The firmer the feel of the meat, the more well-done it is. Just press the lamb—when it has a springy but firm texture and is moderately juicy, the meat is done.

Butterflied Australian Leg of Lamb with Chimichurri
JBS

1 medium onion, quartered

4 garlic cloves, peeled

1 bunch green onions, both white and green parts, trimmed

1 bunch fresh cilantro

1 teaspoon dried oregano

3 bay leaves

1 teaspoon salt

1 teaspoon freshly ground black pepper

1 cup dry white wine

½ cup olive oil

1 Australian boneless leg of lamb

CHIMICHURRI

¾ cup olive oil

3 tablespoons red wine vinegar

1 tablespoon lemon juice

½ cup parsley leaves

2 garlic cloves

1 bunch green onions, both white and green parts, trimmed

1 tablespoon dried chile

Salt and freshly ground black pepper, to taste

In a blender, combine onion, garlic, green onions, cilantro leaves, oregano, bay leaves, salt, pepper, wine and olive oil; process until slightly coarse. Turn the lamb so the bottom faces you. Remove the netting, cut halfway through the meat, and lay the leg flat. Place the lamb in a large tray and pour the marinade over, rubbing into the meat. Cover with plastic wrap and refrigerate overnight. Remove the lamb from the refrigerator 30 minutes before cooking.

Prepare the chimichurri: Place all ingredients in a food processor and blend together; do not mix too much. Let stand for 1 hour.

While the chimichurri is resting, preheat outdoor grill to medium-high. Cook the lamb for 30 minutes, turning once, or until the internal temperature is 140°F (medium). Rest the lamb for 20 minutes. Makes 4-6 servings.

Captain Jack's Blackened Salmon
Multiexport Foods

2 tablespoons paprika

1 tablespoon sea salt

1½ tablespoons black pepper

1½ tablespoons garlic powder

2 teaspoons cayenne pepper

1 teaspoon dried oregano

1 teaspoon dried thyme

1 teaspoon ground cumin

½ cup unsalted butter, melted, divided

4 6-ounce salmon fillets (boneless, skinless)

Preheat the grill. Combine all the seasonings in a bowl, mixing well. With ¼ cup melted butter, brush both sides of salmon fillets. Sprinkle evenly with the seasoning mix. With half of the remaining butter, drizzle one side of each fillet. On a hot grill, cook the salmon, butter side down, until blackened, 2-5 minutes. Drizzle with the remaining butter and turn the fillets. Continue cooking until blackened. The salmon should be opaque in color and flake easily through the thickest part. Makes 4 servings.

Multiexport Foods
Nourishing the future

Miso-Marinated Fish Fillets

Lusamerica Fish

¼ cup mirin (sweet Japanese rice wine) or sake

2 tablespoons rice wine vinegar

Juice of ½ Meyer lemon (or 1 lime)

2 tablespoons soy sauce

1 teaspoon toasted sesame oil

4 tablespoons miso paste (white for sweeter, red for saltier)

2 tablespoons sugar

4 6-ounce salmon, black cod or California halibut portions

Green onions, sliced diagonally, for serving

In a medium saucepan, combine mirin, vinegar, lemon juice, soy sauce and sesame oil; bring to a boil over high heat. Stir in miso paste slowly until dissolved.

Reduce the heat to low. Add sugar and stir until dissolved. Simmer for 5 minutes. Set aside and let cool to room temperature.

Preheat the oven broiler.

Baste fish fillets with miso marinade. Broil until cooked to taste.

To serve, garnish with green onions. Makes 4 servings.

Orange Ginger Salmon

Marine Harvest

¼ cup hoisin sauce

3 tablespoons frozen orange juice concentrate

1½ tablespoons minced ginger

1 tablespoon honey

2 teaspoons mirin

1 teaspoon soy sauce

½ teaspoon toasted sesame oil

4 6-ounce salmon fillets

Nonstick cooking spray

In a square baking dish, combine hoisin, orange juice concentrate, ginger, honey, mirin, soy sauce and sesame oil. Add salmon fillets and turn to coat. Cover with plastic wrap and refrigerate for 1-4 hours, turning the fillets every 30 minutes.

Preheat the oven broiler. Place a stainless steel rack in a rimmed baking sheet and coat with cooking spray.

Place the salmon fillets on the rack and spoon the marinade on top. Place the salmon on the second oven rack from the top. Broil until the marinade bubbles and caramelizes, 7-10 minutes. Turn the salmon over, spoon marinade on top, and broil for 5-7 minutes, or until the marinade bubbles and the edges of the salmon start to brown. Turn off the broiler and let the salmon sit in the residual heat for 5 minutes. Serve immediately. Makes 4 servings.

Grilled Salmon on Portabella Mushrooms with Ginger Vinaigrette

C&M Mushrooms/Giorgio Fresh Co./Monterey Mushrooms

4 7-ounce salmon fillets
Salt and pepper, to taste
4 portabella caps, sliced in ½-inch strips
1 teaspoon garlic seasoning
¼ cup vegetable or olive oil
¼ cup chopped fresh mint leaves

VINAIGRETTE
¼ cup rice vinegar
1 teaspoon grated fresh ginger
1 teaspoon sugar
¼ teaspoon salt
½ cup vegetable or olive oil

Prepare the vinaigrette: In a bowl, whisk together vinegar, ginger, sugar and salt. Whisk in oil and set aside. Preheat the grill to medium-high. Season salmon with salt and pepper. Grill until cooked to taste, about 4 minutes per side.

Meanwhile, sprinkle portabella strips with garlic seasoning. Heat oil in a sauté pan over medium-high heat. Add the mushrooms and sauté until just browned.

Make a bed of portabella slices in the center of each dinner plate and top with a salmon fillet. Drizzle each fillet with 3 tablespoons of vinaigrette. Sprinkle with chopped mint. Makes 4 servings.

Southeast Grilled Salmon
Alaska Glacier Seafoods

1 salmon fillet, 1½-2 pounds

¼ cup (approximately) butter, softened, or olive oil

Salt

Pepper

Garlic powder

Red chile powder (optional)

Fresh or dried dill (optional)

1 onion

1 lemon

Preheat the grill to 300°F.

Rinse fresh (or thawed) salmon fillet. Pat dry with paper towels (both sides). Cut into pieces that you can manage with your spatula.

Coat the salmon liberally with softened butter or olive oil. Season to taste with salt, pepper, garlic powder, chile powder and dill.

Slice onion horizontally and separate into rings. Slice the lemon. Place the onion rings and lemon slices on the salmon.

Lightly oil the grill and cook the salmon skin side down until you can see the white fat of the salmon developing on the surface and edges of the fillet and the fish flakes easily, about 12 minutes. When the fish is done, the meat should separate easily from the skin with a metal spatula. Makes 4-8 servings.

Sockeye Salmon Wellington
Orca Bay Seafoods

4 Orca Bay frozen wild sockeye salmon fillets

16 sheets frozen phyllo pastry dough, thawed

Nonstick cooking spray

½ cup prepared chili and cheese dip (or other favorite)

Thaw fillets according to package directions and pat dry with paper towels.

Preheat oven to 375°F.

On a cutting board, layer 4 sheets of phyllo dough, first spraying each sheet lightly with cooking spray. Place a fillet across the sheets ⅓ of the way up from the bottom. Spread 2 tablespoons of dip over the fillet.

Fold the bottom of the stacked sheets up over the fillet, then roll the fillet and dough once. Fold the sides in to the center, and roll the complete pouch once more to finish. If any dough extends beyond the completed roll, tuck it into the Wellington. Spray the surface of the pouch lightly with cooking spray. Transfer to a baking sheet.

Repeat with the remaining phyllo sheets, fillets and dip.

Bake for 25-30 minutes, or until golden brown. Makes 4 servings.

Atlantic Salmon with Creole Mustard Sauce

Camanchaca

4 tablespoons unsalted butter
  (½ stick), melted

3 tablespoons light brown sugar

3 tablespoons soy sauce

2 tablespoons fresh lemon juice

2 tablespoons white wine

1 Kirkland Signature fresh Atlantic
  salmon fillet (about 3 pounds),
  cut into 4-6 portions

CREOLE MUSTARD SAUCE

1 cup whipping cream (or half-and-half)

¾ cup stone-ground or
  whole-grain mustard

1 teaspoon Dijon mustard

4 teaspoons Lea & Perrins
  Worcestershire sauce

½ teaspoon dried basil

¾ teaspoon ground black pepper

⅛ teaspoon white pepper

⅛ teaspoon cayenne pepper

1 cup sour cream

In a small bowl, combine butter, brown sugar, soy sauce, lemon juice and wine. Place salmon in a ziplock bag and pour in the marinade. Refrigerate for 1-6 hours. Preheat oven to 400°F. Place the salmon with the marinade in a baking dish and bake for 20 minutes. Then broil for an additional 2 minutes.

Prepare the sauce: In a heavy saucepan, combine cream, mustards, Worcestershire, basil and peppers. Cook, stirring, over medium heat until thick, about 5 minutes. Add sour cream and stir well.

Spoon the sauce over each salmon portion. Makes 4-6 servings.

Summer Rolls with Seasoned Grill Salmon
Morey's

4 fillets Morey's Seasoned Grill Salmon

4 ounces rice vermicelli

6-8 rice paper sheets

Fresh cilantro leaves, to taste

6 green onions, chopped

1 avocado, sliced

1 cucumber, cut julienne style

2 carrots, cut julienne style

Dipping sauce, optional (fish sauce or other sauce of choice)

Cook salmon and vermicelli according to package directions. Flake the salmon.

Once the salmon and vermicelli are ready, dip each rice paper sheet in hot water for 5 seconds. When the wrapper begins to soften, place on a plate or glass cutting board; the wrapper will continue to soften as it sits.

On each wrapper, 1 inch from the bottom, layer salmon, vermicelli, cilantro, green onions, avocado, cucumber and carrots. Leave 1-2 inches of wrapper uncovered on both sides. Pull the bottom of the wrapper up to cover the filling and fold in both sides to cover the edges. Roll the wrap until sealed. Refrigerate until chilled.

Serve with dipping sauce. Makes 3-4 servings or 6-8 appetizer servings.

Tip: Customize this recipe by using your own favorite veggies and dipping sauce.

Salmon in Red and Yellow Bell Pepper Sauce
Divine Flavor

10 8- to 10-ounce salmon fillets

1 tablespoon salt, plus more to taste

Freshly ground black pepper

1 tablespoon minced garlic

½ onion, chopped

3 tablespoons olive oil

3 Divine Flavor red bell peppers

3 Divine Flavor yellow bell peppers

2 onion slices, divided

2 teaspoons dried oregano, divided

1-2 cups cream cheese

Season salmon fillets with 1 tablespoon salt, pepper to taste, garlic, chopped onion and olive oil. Marinate, refrigerated, for at least 2 hours and up to 24 hours.

Preheat the grill to medium-high.

Clean bell peppers and cut into pieces. Place in 2 saucepans, one for each color. To each saucepan add 1 quart water, a slice of onion, salt to taste and 1 teaspoon oregano. Bring to a boil. Drain the peppers, reserving a little of the water.

In a blender, puree the peppers in separate batches, adding a little water.

Transfer to 2 saucepans and bring to a boil. Stir in cream cheese, salt and pepper to taste; heat gently.

Grill the salmon until cooked to taste.

To serve, drizzle the salmon with sauces. Makes 10 servings.

Captain Jack's Zorba Salmon

Multiexport Foods

1 lemon, halved

4 6-ounce Multiexport Foods fresh
  farmed salmon fillets (skinless)

Prepared Greek vinaigrette
  salad dressing

¾ cup pitted black olives

¾ cup canned artichoke hearts,
  cut into pieces

1 large cucumber, peeled and cut in
  ¼-inch cubes

¾ cup cherry tomatoes, cut into quarters

¾ cup crumbled feta cheese

Squeeze ½ lemon over salmon fillets and then cover with Greek vinaigrette.
Marinate in the refrigerator for about 1 hour.

In a bowl, combine olives, artichoke hearts, cucumbers and tomatoes. Squeeze
on some fresh lemon juice and add vinaigrette to taste.

To bake: Preheat oven to 375°F. Place the salmon in a greased baking dish
and top with mixed vegetables. Sprinkle with feta. Bake on the center rack
for about 15 minutes, or until the salmon flakes easily with a fork.

To grill: Preheat grill to medium-high. Place the salmon on greased foil. Top
the salmon with vegetables and sprinkle with feta. Grill for about 20 minutes
on medium heat. The salmon does not have to be turned while it is grilling.
Makes 4 servings.

Multiexport Foods
Nourishing the future

Salmon Burger Loaf
Trident Seafoods

Cooking spray

3 Trident Seafoods frozen salmon burgers, cooked according to package directions

¾ cup panko bread crumbs

¼ cup chopped green onions or chives

2 eggs

¼ cup low-fat milk

1 tablespoon olive oil

1 teaspoon grated lemon zest

½ teaspoon ground black pepper

Tartar sauce or other sauce of your choice

Preheat oven to 375°F. Coat a 5¾-by-3-by-2-inch loaf pan with nonstick cooking spray. Flake salmon burgers and place in a medium bowl. Add bread crumbs, green onions, eggs, milk, olive oil, lemon zest and pepper. Mix well. Press the mixture into the prepared pan. Bake, uncovered, for 20-25 minutes, or until lightly browned and set. Slice and serve with sauce. Makes 2-3 servings.

Pan-Seared Steelhead with Lemongrass-Ginger Coconut Milk

AquaGold Seafood

2-inch piece fresh ginger, peeled

4-inch piece lemongrass, halved

1 13.5-ounce can whole coconut milk

Juice of ½ lime

4 4-ounce steelhead portions (skin on)

Sea salt and pepper

1 tablespoon coconut oil

2 ice cubes

Grated zest of 1 lime

Cut ginger into 3 pieces. Hit with a kitchen mallet a few times to release oils. Lightly crush lemongrass with the mallet.

In a small saucepan, combine ginger, lemongrass and coconut milk. Bring to a slow boil over medium heat and cook until reduced by ⅔ and it coats the back of a spoon, about 45 minutes. Remove lemongrass and ginger. Add lime juice and cook until reduced by ⅓, about 10 minutes.

Season fish with salt and pepper.

Heat coconut oil in a frying pan over medium heat. Add the fish skin side down and cook for 3 minutes. Turn the fish over, peel off the skin and discard. Cook for 5 minutes, then add ice cubes and cover to finish cooking.

To serve, spoon coconut milk over the fish and sprinkle with lime zest. Makes 4 servings.

Hickory Grilled Steelhead Trout with Spinach and Honey Mustard Glaze

F.W. Bryce

½ teaspoon hickory liquid smoke

1 tablespoon kosher salt

1 tablespoon sugar

4 6-ounce portions fresh steelhead trout

1 teaspoon cracked black pepper

2 tablespoons vegetable oil

4 tablespoons butter

½ cup diced onion

½ tablespoon minced garlic

2 tablespoons diced cooked bacon

8 ounces baby spinach

½ cup heavy cream

HONEY MUSTARD GLAZE

1 cup mayonnaise

½ cup honey

½ cup yellow mustard

1 teaspoon fresh tarragon leaves

In a small dish, combine liquid smoke, salt and sugar. Rub gently into the fish. Sprinkle with cracked pepper.

Preheat grill to medium-high. Lubricate grill with vegetable oil and place the fish directly on the bottom grate. Cook for 2 minutes. Gently flip the fish and move to the upper grate. Cook until the internal temperature is 145°F.

In a large sauté pan, melt butter over medium heat. Add onion, garlic and bacon; cook until the onion is translucent. Add spinach and cook until wilted. Add cream and simmer for 3 minutes.

Combine all the glaze ingredients and mix until blended. Drizzle over the cooked steelhead. Serve with the spinach. Makes 4 servings.

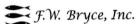 *F.W. Bryce, Inc.*

Pan-Seared Columbia River Steelhead with Tarragon Cream

Pacific Seafood Group

4 6-ounce portions Columbia River steelhead

Grated zest and juice of 1 lemon, divided

Salt and pepper

2 green onions, chopped, divided

1 tablespoon chopped fresh tarragon, divided

1 shallot, chopped

1 cup white wine (dry or semi-dry)

1 pint heavy whipping cream

Hearty rice blend, for serving

Heat a nonstick sauté pan over medium heat. Season steelhead fillets with lemon zest and salt and pepper to taste. Sprinkle with half the green onions and 1 teaspoon of the tarragon. Place the fillets skin side up in the preheated pan and cook until golden brown, about 4 minutes. Turn the fillets over and continue cooking until golden brown and cooked through, about 3 more minutes. Remove the fillets to a serving platter and keep warm. Add shallot and the remaining tarragon to the pan and deglaze with wine, reducing until nearly evaporated. Add cream and cook until reduced by half. Add the remaining green onions and season to taste with salt, pepper and lemon juice. Pour over the fillets. Serve with hearty rice blend. Makes 4 servings.

PacificSeafood™

Tataki Ahi Tuna
Western United Fish Company

2 fresh Western United ahi
  tuna steaks
  (1½-2 pounds)
Salt and pepper
Sesame seeds, to taste
Black sesame seeds, to taste
2 tablespoons vegetable oil
1 tablespoon toasted
  sesame oil
Ponzu sauce

WASABI MAYONNAISE

2 tablespoons
  wasabi powder
1½ tablespoons water
½ cup mayonnaise

Sprinkle ahi steaks on both sides with salt, pepper and sesame seeds to taste. (If the steaks are too large, cut in half.)

Prepare the mayonnaise: In a small bowl, stir together wasabi powder and water. Add mayonnaise and stir to blend.

Heat a heavy sauté pan over medium-high heat. Add vegetable oil and sesame oil to the pan. Add the ahi and sear for about 1 minute on each side.

Remove the ahi from the pan and slice thinly, no more than ¼ inch thick.

Arrange the ahi slices on a plate and drizzle lightly with ponzu sauce. Serve with the mayonnaise as a dipping sauce. Makes 4 servings.

Tip: Serve with a side of mixed greens and sliced avocados.

Your Direct Source·

Blackened Tuna with Banana Pineapple Chutney
Dole

¾ cup packed brown sugar
½ cup cider vinegar
½ cup water
2 teaspoons curry powder
½ teaspoon
  ground cinnamon
½ teaspoon minced garlic
⅛ teaspoon ground
  red pepper
4 medium Dole Bananas,
  sliced, divided
2 cups diced Dole Tropical
  Gold Pineapple
¼ cup raisins
6 ahi tuna steaks
6 Dole Portobello
  Mushrooms, cleaned,
  stems removed
1 tablespoon vegetable oil
1-2 teaspoons blackening
  seasoning

In a saucepan, combine first 7 ingredients. Heat to a simmer, then cook for 1 minute. Stir in 3 bananas and pineapple; simmer for 10 minutes, or until thickened. Stir in remaining banana and raisins, then remove from the heat, cover, and let stand for 30 minutes.

Preheat oven to 375°F. Line a sheet pan with foil.

Heat a large nonstick skillet over high heat. Brush tuna and mushrooms with oil; sprinkle with seasoning. Sear the tuna until browned. Sear the mushrooms until soft. Place the tuna and mushrooms on the sheet pan. Bake for 10 minutes, or until cooked to taste.

Place mushrooms on plates, arrange sliced tuna on top; spoon chutney over. Makes 6 servings.

Halibut Ceviche
S.M. Products (BC) Ltd.

4 6-ounce frozen halibut fillets, thawed and diced into small cubes

Sea salt

Freshly ground pepper

2 tablespoons rice vinegar

Juice of 4 limes

¼ cup diced red onion

3 Roma tomatoes, quartered, seeded and diced

1 mango, diced

1 green chile, seeded and finely diced

1 large avocado, diced

¼ cup chopped fresh cilantro

1 tablespoon extra-virgin olive oil

Tortilla chips, for serving

Place halibut cubes in a glass or nonreactive bowl and season to taste with salt and pepper. Stir in vinegar and lime juice. Marinate, refrigerated, for 3-4 hours, or until the lime juice has cooked the halibut through.

Strain off all the liquid and discard.

In a bowl, combine onion, tomatoes, mango, chile, avocado, cilantro and olive oil. Add the halibut cubes and gently toss. Season to taste with salt and pepper.

Serve with tortilla chips. Makes 4 servings.

Petrale Sole Summer-Style
Regatta Tropicals

3 tablespoons olive oil

2 pounds petrale sole fillets

Salt and pepper

½ cup white flour

Egg wash – 3 eggs, 3 ounces water

1 tablespoon grated fresh ginger

1 garlic clove, thinly sliced

½ cup Riesling

Juice of 1 Meyer lemon

2 tablespoons butter

4 green onions, chopped

1 cup halved and seeded Chilean red grapes

Quinoa, couscous or risotto, for serving

Heat a large nonstick frying pan over medium heat. Add olive oil to the pan.

Season fish with salt and pepper to taste. Dredge the fish in flour, then dip into the egg wash to coat. Once the oil is heated, add the fish and brown on both sides. Remove from the pan and keep warm.

Add ginger, garlic and wine to the pan; cook, stirring, until thickened. Add lemon juice and butter, stirring to blend. Stir in green onions and grapes.

Serve the sole over quinoa, couscous or risotto. Top with sauce, reserving some for the table. Makes 4 servings.

Recipe courtesy of Giuseppe DiFronzo, owner of Giuseppe's Cucina Italiana in Pismo Beach and Palazzo Giuseppe in San Luis Obispo, California.

Fish Tacos with Creamy Lime Drizzle

Trident Seafoods

16 Trident Seafoods Ultimate Fish Sticks
8 6-inch round flour tortillas
1 medium lime, cut into 10 pieces
½ cup sour cream

2 cups finely shredded red and green cabbage
16 cilantro sprigs
Prepared pico de gallo or other salsa

Cook fish sticks according to package directions. Meanwhile, wrap tortillas in foil and warm in a 425°F oven for 8 minutes. In a bowl, squeeze 2 lime pieces into sour cream and mix well.

Place 2 fish sticks in each tortilla. Divide cabbage evenly among the tortillas and top each with 2 cilantro sprigs. Drizzle each taco with sour cream sauce. Serve with a lime squeeze and pico de gallo on the side. Makes 4 servings.

Tip: Trident Panko Tilapia can be used instead of Trident Ultimate Fish Sticks, substituting 1 piece of tilapia for every 2 fish sticks.

Coconut-Lime Tilapia
Market Source

Grated zest of 3 Market Source limes

4 garlic cloves, minced

¼ teaspoon salt

¼ teaspoon pepper

2 tablespoons plus 1 teaspoon coconut oil, melted, divided

4 5-ounce tilapia fillets

8 cups fresh spinach

¼ cup plus 1 tablespoon freshly squeezed lime juice from Market Source limes

Heat a large frying pan over medium-high heat.

In a small bowl, combine lime zest, garlic, salt, pepper and 4 teaspoons coconut oil.

Coat tilapia with the oil mixture on both sides. Place fillets, 2 at a time, in the pan and cook for 3-4 minutes on each side, or until golden brown and crisp.

In a large bowl, toss spinach with the remaining tablespoon of coconut oil and 1 tablespoon of lime juice. Divide among 4 plates.

To serve, top each plate with a fillet and drizzle with lime juice. Makes 4 servings.

Nutritional information: Each serving has 230 calories, 30 g protein, 4 g carbohydrates, 11 g fat (8 g saturated), 1 g fiber, 250 mg sodium.

Spiced Tilapia with Creamed Spinach
Rain Forest Aquaculture

2 teaspoons turmeric

2 teaspoons salt

¼ teaspoon ground cardamom

¼ teaspoon ground cinnamon

⅛ teaspoon cayenne pepper

⅛ teaspoon ground ginger

1½ pounds Rain Forest Aquaculture tilapia, cut into 12 long thin strips

1 tablespoon butter

2 tablespoons chopped shallot

1 tablespoon chopped fresh ginger

2 teaspoons minced garlic

12 ounces baby spinach

⅓ cup unsweetened coconut milk

¼ cup heavy cream

Freshly ground pepper

Preheat oven to 350°F. Butter a 12-cup muffin pan.

Combine the first 6 ingredients. Sprinkle over the fish. Arrange 1 piece of fish in each muffin cup, leaving the center open for stuffing. Bake the fish for 6-8 minutes, or until the fillets are firm.

Melt butter in a sauté pan over medium heat. Add shallots and cook for 3 minutes. Add ginger and garlic; cook for 1 minute. Add spinach and toss. When the spinach wilts, add coconut milk and cream.

Turn the fish out of the molds and place 3 fillets on each plate. Fill the centers with spinach and drizzle with hot coconut milk. Season with pepper. Makes 4 servings.

Rain Forest
AQUACULTURE

Tilapia Marsala with Mushrooms

Slade Gorton

5 tablespoons unsalted butter, divided

2 tablespoons finely chopped shallot

10 ounces mushrooms (combination of button and shiitake), sliced

¼ teaspoon salt

⅛ teaspoon black pepper

2 tablespoons extra-virgin olive oil, divided

4 portions fresh toasted crumb tilapia

½ cup plus 2 tablespoons dry Marsala wine, divided

1 cup chicken broth

⅔ cup heavy cream

1 teaspoon fresh lemon juice

Wild rice pilaf, for serving

Position rack in the center of the oven. Preheat oven to 200°F. Melt 3 tablespoons butter in a heavy skillet over medium heat. Add shallot and cook, stirring, until it begins to turn golden, about 1 minute. Add mushrooms, salt and pepper; cook until the mushrooms begin to brown, 6-8 minutes. Set aside. Heat 1 tablespoon *each* of oil and butter in a nonstick skillet over medium heat. Add 2 tilapia portions and sauté, turning over once, until golden and cooked through, about 4 minutes. Transfer the cooked fish to a large heatproof platter, arranging in one layer. Put the platter in the oven to keep warm. Repeat with the remaining oil, butter and fish. Add ½ cup wine to the skillet and boil over high heat, stirring and scraping up brown bits, for about 30 seconds. Add broth, cream and the mushrooms; simmer, stirring occasionally, until the sauce is slightly thickened, 6-8 minutes. Add lemon juice and remaining wine. Pour the sauce over the warm tilapia and serve with your favorite wild rice pilaf. Makes 4 servings.

Tilapia with Chimichurri Sauce

Regal Springs

¼ cup olive oil

⅔ cup sherry vinegar

¾ cup chopped fresh parsley

3 tablespoons chopped fresh oregano

3 tablespoons fresh lemon juice

6 large garlic cloves, chopped

Salt and pepper

6 6-ounce Regal Springs frozen tilapia loins, thawed

Preheat oven to 375°F.

In a bowl, combine olive oil, vinegar, parsley, oregano, lemon juice and garlic; stir to blend. Season to taste with salt and pepper. Set aside.

Place tilapia on a baking sheet lined with parchment paper. Bake for 10 minutes, or until the flesh is opaque and flakes with a fork. To serve, spoon the chimichurri sauce onto the fish. Makes 6 servings.

Tip: Serve with salad, rice or roasted root vegetables.

Grilled Tilapia with Mango Salsa

Regal Springs

⅓ cup extra-virgin olive oil

1 tablespoon lemon juice

1 tablespoon minced fresh parsley

1 garlic clove, minced

1 teaspoon dried basil

1 teaspoon ground black pepper

½ teaspoon salt

2 6-ounce Regal Springs fresh
 tilapia fillets

MANGO SALSA

1 large ripe mango, peeled, pitted and diced

½ red bell pepper, diced

2 tablespoons minced red onion

1 tablespoon chopped fresh cilantro

1 jalapeño, seeded and minced

2 tablespoons lime juice

1 tablespoon lemon juice

Salt and pepper

In a bowl, whisk together olive oil, lemon juice, parsley, garlic, basil, pepper and salt. Pour into a resealable plastic bag. Add tilapia, coat with the marinade, squeeze out excess air, and seal the bag. Marinate in the refrigerator for 1 hour.

Prepare the salsa: In a bowl, combine mango, bell pepper, onion, cilantro and jalapeño. Add lime juice and lemon juice; toss well. Season to taste with salt and pepper. Refrigerate until ready to serve.

Preheat an outdoor grill to medium-high. Lightly oil the grate. Remove the tilapia from the marinade and shake off excess. Discard the remaining marinade. Grill the fillets until the fish is no longer translucent in the center and flakes easily with a fork, 3-4 minutes per side, depending on the thickness of the fillets. Serve the tilapia topped with mango salsa. Makes 2 servings.

Sweet and Savory Tilapia Tacos
Naturipe Farms

1 cup thinly sliced red onion
¼ cup lime juice, divided
Salt
1 cup diced (¼ inch) avocado
1 cup diced (¼ inch) fresh strawberries

6 tilapia fillets
1 tablespoon vegetable oil
6 6-inch flour tortillas
6 tablespoons crema mexicana
 (or sour cream, thinned)
3 tablespoons minced jalapeño

In a bowl, combine red onion with 2 tablespoons lime juice and ½ teaspoon salt; stir to blend. Refrigerate for at least 1 hour. In another bowl, combine diced avocado and strawberries; toss in the remaining lime juice.

Season fish with salt to taste. Heat oil in a large sauté pan over medium-high heat until nearly smoking. Add the fish and sear on both sides until golden brown and cooked through (about 2-3 minutes per side, depending on the thickness of the fish).

Lay the tortillas flat and top each with 1 tablespoon crema, 1 tilapia fillet, ½ tablespoon jalapeño and 1 tablespoon of the pickled red onion. Top with the strawberry/avocado mixture. Serve immediately. Makes 6 servings.

naturipe

Trota alla Milanese (Trout Milanese Style)
Clear Springs

4 eggs
1 cup milk
1 cup flour
6 cups panko bread crumbs
6 6-ounce Clear·Cuts Rainbow Trout Natural Fillets
Sea salt and freshly ground pepper
1 cup olive oil

⅓ cup balsamic vinegar
1 cup extra-virgin olive oil
1 pound fresh arugula, washed, tough stems removed
½ small red onion, thinly sliced into rings
24 cherry tomatoes, halved
12 shavings of Parmigiano-Reggiano cheese
1 lemon, cut into wedges

In a medium bowl, beat eggs, then whisk in milk. Place flour and bread crumbs in 2 separate bowls. Season trout with salt and pepper. Dust each fillet with flour, then dip into the egg mixture, allowing any excess to drain. Coat the fish with bread crumbs. Refrigerate, covered, until ready to use.

Preheat oven to 350°F. Heat oil in a large ovenproof sauté pan over medium heat. Add the trout, skin side up, and cook until browned, about 5 minutes. Flip the fish over and transfer to the oven to finish cooking, 5-7 minutes. Remove the fish from the oven and place on paper towels to drain.

Make the vinaigrette: Pour vinegar into a bowl. Add a generous pinch of salt and pepper. Whisk in extra-virgin olive oil in a slow stream until well combined.

In a large bowl, toss arugula, onion and tomatoes with vinaigrette. Adjust for seasoning. To serve, place a fillet on each of 6 warmed plates. Top with salad and garnish with Parmigiano shavings and lemon wedges. Serve immediately. Makes 6 servings.

CLEAR SPRINGS FOODS®

Hawaiian Opakapaka en Papillote
Norpac Fisheries Export

Kirkland Signature Parchment Paper
¼ cup olive oil
1 large onion, julienned
1 tablespoon grated ginger
1 tablespoon chopped garlic
1 dried spicy Chinese sausage, diced
¼ cup orange juice
4 8-ounce opakapaka fillets
¼ cup white wine
Salt and pepper
¼ cup peanut oil
1 bunch cilantro, chopped
1 tablespoon soy sauce

Preheat oven to 350°F. Cut four 15-inch sheets of parchment paper. Fold the sheets in half, crease and unfold.

Heat olive oil in a sauté pan over medium heat. Add onion, ginger, garlic and sausage; sauté for 2-3 minutes. Add orange juice.

For each serving, place ¼ of the onion mixture on a parchment sheet near the crease. Place a fillet on top, skin side up. Drizzle with wine.

Season with salt and pepper. Fold the parchment to enclose. Starting at the top corner, make overlapping folds around the packet. Twist the last fold for a tight seal. Bake for 20 minutes.

Heat peanut oil over medium heat. Cut an X on the top of each packet. Top each fillet with cilantro, hot peanut oil and soy sauce. Makes 4 servings.

Miso-Glazed Haddock
North Coast Seafoods

⅓ cup sake
⅓ cup mirin (sweet Japanese rice wine)
⅓ cup miso paste (light or dark)
3 tablespoons brown sugar
2 tablespoons soy sauce
1 teaspoon black pepper
2 teaspoons ground ginger
4 8-ounce skinless fresh haddock portions

In a bowl, combine all ingredients except the haddock. Stir until the sugar is dissolved.

Place haddock in a ziplock bag and pour in the marinade. Marinate in the refrigerator for 3-6 hours.

Preheat the oven broiler.

Remove the fish from the marinade, draining off excess marinade. Broil until golden brown and cooked through, about 7-10 minutes, depending on the thickness of the fish. If the fish is golden brown before it is cooked through, switch off the broiler and bake (350°F) until done.

Serve with rice and green vegetables. Makes 4 servings.

Mediterranean Catfish
Consolidated Catfish Producers

2 tablespoons olive oil, divided
1 cup diced zucchini
½ cup sliced red onion
2 garlic cloves, minced
½ cup halved mixed
    Mediterranean olives
½ cup halved grape tomatoes

2 tablespoons chopped fresh basil
1 tablespoon capers
4 fresh U.S. farm-raised catfish fillets
½ teaspoon salt
¼ teaspoon ground black pepper
½ cup crumbled feta cheese

Preheat oven to 450°F. Heat 1 tablespoon olive oil in a sauté pan over medium heat. Add zucchini, onion and garlic. Cook for about 4 minutes, or until the onions are translucent. Remove from the heat and stir in olives, tomatoes, basil and capers.

Brush catfish fillets with 1 tablespoon olive oil. Season with salt and pepper. Place on a lightly oiled baking dish. Spoon an equal amount of the vegetable mixture on top of each fillet. Bake for 15 minutes, or until the fish flakes easily with a fork.

Top with crumbled feta cheese and serve immediately. Makes 4 servings.

Mussels Fra Diavolo

North Coast Seafoods

4 tablespoons olive oil

1 tablespoon chopped garlic

½ cup chopped onion

1 teaspoon crushed red pepper
(add more if you like it hotter)

1 tablespoon chopped fresh oregano

½ cup dry white wine

3 cups chopped canned, peeled
    tomatoes, with juice

2 pounds PEI mussels

Salt and pepper

1 tablespoon chopped fresh parsley

Garlic bread or pasta, for serving

In a large pot (with a lid), heat olive oil over medium heat. Add garlic and sauté just until it starts to brown. Add onion and continue cooking until they are soft. Add crushed red pepper and oregano; cook for 2 minutes. Add wine and cook for 2-3 minutes. Add tomatoes and simmer for 30 minutes. Bring the sauce to a boil and add mussels. Cover the pot and steam the mussels in the sauce until they have opened and are cooked, about 4-5 minutes.

Season to taste with salt and pepper. Sprinkle with parsley. Serve with garlic bread or over your favorite pasta. Makes 2 servings.

Tip: This serves 4 as an appetizer.

Mussels Rockefeller
Penn Cove Shellfish

1-2 tablespoons butter

2 tablespoons thinly sliced shallots

2 tablespoons chopped garlic

½ cup dry white wine

Dash of salt and pepper

1 ounce cooked smoked bacon, chopped

2-3 ounces heavy cream

1 tablespoon Pernod (or other anise-flavored liqueur)

1 pound Penn Cove mussels

2 ounces spinach leaves

French bread, for serving

In a sauté pan, melt butter over medium heat. Add shallots, garlic, wine, salt and pepper; sauté for 2-3 minutes.

Add bacon, cream, Pernod and mussels to the pan. Cover and continue cooking until the mussels have opened and are not translucent, about 5 minutes. Discard any mussels that do not open.

Dish the mussels into serving bowls, add the spinach leaves and then pour the cream sauce over the top.

Serve with French bread. Makes 1 serving or 4 appetizer servings.

Tip: This can also be served over linguine (2 entrées).

Recipe courtesy of Front Street Grill, Coupeville, Washington.

Steamed Manila Clams
Pacific American Fish Company

5 pounds Manila clams

1 cup diced onions

1 cup diced celery

Italian seasoning

12 tablespoons unsalted butter, divided

¼ cup dry white wine

3 tablespoons fresh lemon juice

2 garlic cloves, crushed

Rinse clams well in cold water and drain. Discard any clams with broken shells.

Use a large soup pot that remains half empty once the clams are added. Layer ⅓ of the clams, ⅓ onions, ⅓ celery and several shakes of Italian seasoning. Repeat 2 more times.

Cut 4 tablespoons butter into small pieces and dot the top of the clams. Add wine. Cover with a tight-fitting lid. Cook over medium-high heat until the clams steam, then lower the heat and cook until all the shells are open, about 10 minutes. The clams on top will open first, so it is OK to stir the pot once. Do not overcook, or the meat will become rubbery.

Melt 8 tablespoons butter and stir in lemon juice and garlic.

Serve the clams in bowls with a drizzle of the melted butter. Makes 4 servings (or 6 appetizer servings).

Florida Clam Scampi

Cedar Key Aquaculture Farms

4 tablespoons butter

2 tablespoons olive oil

4 garlic cloves, minced

2 dozen hard clams, rinsed well

1 cup chopped fresh parsley

2 tablespoons lemon juice

Salt and pepper

½ cup dry white wine

¼ cup chopped sun-dried tomatoes

1 pint grape tomatoes, halved

8 ounces spinach fettuccine, cooked

Melt butter with olive oil in a medium skillet over medium heat. Add garlic and cook, stirring, for 1 minute.

Add clams and cook, stirring, for 5 minutes.

Add parsley, lemon juice, salt and pepper to taste, and wine. Continue steaming, stirring occasionally, until the clams open.

Stir in tomatoes and serve over fettuccine. Makes 2 servings.

Recipe courtesy of Chef Justin Timineri. © 2013 "Fresh From Florida" Recipes. All rights reserved.

Pistachio-Encrusted Scallops with Asparagus Risotto

Kirkland Signature

12 sea scallops

1 cup milk

⅓ cup shelled, chopped Kirkland Signature pistachio kernels

1 tablespoon cornmeal

¼ teaspoon black pepper

¼ cup olive oil

ASPARAGUS RISOTTO

12 asparagus spears, cut into 1-inch pieces

6 cups chicken broth, simmering

4 tablespoons butter, divided

2 shallots, chopped

1½ cups Arborio rice

1½ cups dry white wine

½ cup grated Parmesan cheese

½ teaspoon salt

½ teaspoon black pepper

Prepare the risotto: Blanch asparagus in broth for 2 minutes. Remove asparagus and keep the broth simmering. In another saucepan, melt 1 teaspoon butter over medium heat. Add shallots and cook 3 minutes. Stir in rice; cook 3 minutes. Add wine; simmer 3 minutes. Add ½ cup broth and stir 2 minutes. Continue cooking, adding broth ½ cup at a time, 20 minutes total. Stir in asparagus, butter, Parmesan, salt and pepper.

Place scallops in a dish and cover with milk. Mix pistachios and cornmeal.

Remove scallops from milk and season with salt and pepper. Coat with pistachio mixture. Sauté scallops in oil over medium heat, turning once, about 8 minutes. Serve with risotto. Makes 4 servings.

Medjool Date and Kiwifruit Salsa with Sea Scallops
Bard Valley Medjool Dates/AJ Trucco

1 cup pitted, chopped Medjool dates

4 kiwifruit, peeled and chopped

¼ cup finely chopped red onion

¼ cup finely chopped red bell pepper

2 tablespoons chopped fresh cilantro

1 jalapeño, seeded and finely chopped

1 tablespoon lemon juice

½ teaspoon salt, divided

¼ teaspoon pepper, divided

1 tablespoon olive oil

1½ pounds sea scallops (about 18 large scallops)

Lemon curls and cilantro leaves, for garnish (optional)

In a bowl, combine dates, kiwifruit, onion, bell pepper, cilantro, jalapeño, lemon juice, ¼ teaspoon salt and ⅛ teaspoon pepper.

Heat olive oil in a skillet over medium-high heat. Rinse scallops and pat dry with a paper towel. Sprinkle with the remaining salt and pepper. Sauté the scallops for 2-3 minutes on each side, or until they are opaque and lightly browned.

Serve immediately with the salsa. Garnish with lemon curls and cilantro leaves. Makes 4-6 servings.

Cranberry Curry Scallops
American Pride Seafoods

2 tablespoons peanut oil

2 tablespoons red curry paste

2 tablespoons tomato paste

2 teaspoons ground cumin

2 teaspoons ground coriander

2 teaspoons curry powder

9 American Pride Seafoods sea scallops

1 cup sliced mushrooms

1 shallot, minced

2 garlic cloves, minced

½ cup cranberries

2 tablespoons minced fresh ginger

2 tablespoons fish sauce

¾ cup coconut milk

2 tablespoons brown sugar

Rice, for serving

Preheat a sauté pan over medium-high heat and add peanut oil.

In a bowl, combine curry paste, tomato paste, cumin, coriander and curry powder. Set aside.

When the pan and peanut oil are hot, add scallops and sear until they develop a golden brown crust, about 2-3 minutes on each side. Remove from the pan.

Add mushrooms, shallot, garlic, cranberries and ginger to the pan and sauté for 2-3 minutes.

Add the curry/tomato paste mixture, fish sauce, coconut milk and brown sugar. Bring to a boil, then reduce to a simmer. Add the scallops and cook for 8-10 minutes, stirring occasionally.

Serve over rice. Makes 1-2 servings.

Dungeness Crab and Sweet Pea Pot Pies
Pacific Seafood Group

¼ cup butter

¼ cup flour

½ onion, chopped

1 carrot, chopped

¼ cup white wine
(your favorite)

2 cups whole milk

1 cup fresh sweet peas

1 tablespoon plus
1 teaspoon chopped
fresh parsley, divided

1 pound fresh Dungeness
crab meat

Salt and pepper

Pastry dough for single-
crust 9-inch pie

1 egg

Melt butter in a medium saucepan over medium heat. Add flour and cook for 3 minutes, stirring occasionally. Add onion and carrot; cook for another 2 minutes. Add wine and stir to blend.

Slowly add milk and heat until the sauce thickens. Add peas, 1 tablespoon parsley and crab. Season to taste with salt and pepper. This can be prepared a day ahead and kept in the refrigerator.

Preheat oven to 350°F.

Place the crab filling in 4 individual 8- to 12-ounce round ramekins.

Roll out the pie crust and cut into 4 round circles slightly larger than the ramekins. Place the crust on top of the ramekins. It should drape over the sides a little.

Beat egg with 1 tablespoon water. Brush the top of each pie crust with egg wash. Sprinkle with the remaining parsley.

Bake for about 45 minutes, or until the tops are golden brown and the filling is hot. Makes 4 servings.

Pacific Seafood™

King Crab Legs and Grits
International Seafood Ventures

3 cups chicken broth

1 cup grits

3 tablespoons butter

4 bacon slices, diced

¼ cup dry white wine

1 sweet onion, diced

1 tablespoon minced garlic

1 pinch of cayenne pepper

1 red bell pepper, diced

1 tomato, seeded and diced

¼ cup sliced green
onions, divided

2 pounds cooked king
crab leg meat

Salt and pepper

In a medium saucepan, bring chicken broth to a boil. Gradually stir in grits. Reduce the heat and simmer, stirring occasionally, until creamy, about 20 minutes. Fold in butter.

Meanwhile, cook bacon in a sauté pan over medium-high heat, stirring frequently, until crisp. Deglaze with wine, then add onion, garlic, cayenne and red bell pepper to the pan. Cook, stirring, until the onion is translucent.

Add tomato and 2 tablespoons green onions; sauté for 3-4 minutes. Lower the heat and gently fold in crab meat, stirring until heated through. Season to taste with salt and pepper.

Spoon the grits into a serving bowl, top with the crab mixture, and garnish with the remaining green onions. Makes 4-6 servings.

Nectarine-Glazed Shrimp with Grilled Nectarines

I.M. Ripe

GLAZE

2 tablespoons butter

5 I.M. Ripe nectarines, quartered and pitted

Grated zest of 1 lime

Grated zest and juice of 1 lemon

4 serrano chiles, 3 thinly sliced, 1 minced

½ cup tequila

½ cup blue agave syrup or honey

2 tablespoons chopped fresh cilantro

GRILLED NECTARINES

6 I.M. Ripe nectarines, halved and pitted

3 tablespoons olive oil

GRILLED SHRIMP

2 pounds raw shrimp, peeled and deveined

2 tablespoons olive oil

Juice of 1 lime

Kosher salt

Prepare the glaze: Melt butter in a skillet over medium heat. Add nectarines, lime zest, lemon zest, lemon juice and 3 thinly sliced serrano chiles. Sauté for 10 minutes, or until the nectarines are soft. Add tequila and agave; simmer, uncovered, for 15 minutes. Puree the mixture in a blender. Pour the puree into a bowl and add minced serrano chile and cilantro.

Prepare the nectarines: Prepare a hot fire in the grill. Brush the flesh of each nectarine with olive oil and grill flesh side down for 3-5 minutes, or until black grill marks appear. Set aside.

Prepare the shrimp: Thread shrimp onto metal or wooden skewers. Lightly brush with olive oil. Place the skewers on the hot grill and generously brush with the nectarine glaze. Grill for 2-4 minutes per side or until done, with good grill marks, basting again after turning.

Remove the skewers from the grill and place the shrimp on a serving platter. Squeeze lime juice over the shrimp and add salt to taste. Serve with the grilled nectarines. Makes 6 servings.

Sugar Snaps with Fettuccine and Smoked Salmon

Southern Selects

½ stick unsalted butter

1 medium red onion, diced

Salt and freshly ground pepper

8 ounces Southern Selects sugar snap peas

12 ounces fettuccine

4 ounces smoked salmon, cut in ½-inch pieces

½ cup ricotta cheese

½ cup grated Parmesan cheese

Bring a large pot of salted water to a boil.

Melt butter in a large skillet over medium-high heat. Add onion and a pinch of salt; cook until the onion is soft and translucent, about 6 minutes. Turn off the heat and season generously with pepper.

Add sugar snap peas to the boiling water and cook until bright green and crisp, about 2 minutes. Scoop the peas from the water and transfer to a plate.

Cook fettuccine in the boiling water according to package directions. Transfer fettuccine to the skillet, reserving the cooking water.

Add salmon and peas to the skillet, stirring gently to combine over low heat. Add a small amount of cooking water, alternating with a small amount of ricotta. Continue adding ricotta, water and Parmesan until the pasta is coated and the sauce is creamy. Makes 4 servings.

Spaghetti with Shrimp and Garlic-Chili Oil
Kirkland Signature/Olde Thompson

2 tablespoons plus
  1 teaspoon Kirkland
  Signature Mediterranean
  sea salt, divided, plus
  more to taste
1 pound spaghetti
1 tablespoon olive oil
1 pound large raw shrimp,
  peeled and deveined
8 ounces baby spinach,
  cleaned
¼ cup coarsely chopped
  fresh parsley

GARLIC-CHILI OIL
½ cup olive oil
2 teaspoons Kirkland
  Signature crushed
  red pepper
1 tablespoon Kirkland
  Signature chopped
  dehydrated onion
⅜ teaspoon Kirkland
  Signature granulated
  California garlic

Prepare the garlic-chili oil: In a small saucepan, combine olive oil and crushed red pepper; cook over low to medium-low heat for 3 minutes. Add chopped onion and cook for another 2 minutes. Reduce the heat to low and add granulated garlic. Cook for an additional minute, being sure not to burn the garlic. Strain the oil through a fine-mesh sieve and set aside.

Bring a large pot of water to a boil. Season with 2 tablespoons sea salt and cook spaghetti according to package directions, about 9-10 minutes. Drain the pasta, reserving ¼ cup of the cooking liquid, and set aside.

Meanwhile, heat olive oil in a large nonstick skillet over medium-high heat. Season shrimp with 1 teaspoon sea salt and sauté until cooked through, about 4-5 minutes. Remove the shrimp from the pan and set aside.

Turn the heat to low and add the cooked spaghetti, spinach and reserved pasta water to the pan. Toss until the spinach just begins to wilt. Add ⅓ cup of the garlic-chili oil and toss to combine. Season to taste with additional garlic-chili oil and sea salt. Return the shrimp to the pan, sprinkle with parsley, and serve. Makes 4-6 servings.

KIRKLAND *Signature*

Thai Shrimp Curry
Seattle Shrimp & Seafood

3 tablespoons cooking oil
2 tablespoons Thai red curry
  paste (Mae Ploy brand)
4 teaspoons palm or
  brown sugar
2 teaspoons fish sauce
½ teaspoon red
  pepper flakes
1 13.5-ounce can coconut
  milk (Chaokoh brand)
1 19-ounce can sliced
  bamboo shoots, drained
1 red bell pepper, seeded
  and cut into strips
1 pound 13/15 raw
  easy-peel shrimp
20 fresh Thai basil leaves
Cooked rice, for serving

Heat a skillet over medium-high heat. Add oil and red curry paste. Whisk for about 30 seconds.

Stir in sugar, fish sauce and red pepper flakes. Pour in coconut milk, then continue whisking and bring to a boil.

Add bamboo shoots and bell pepper; continue cooking for 3 minutes.

Add shrimp to the curry and cook for another 4 minutes, or until the shrimp are cooked.

Stir in basil and serve over rice. Makes 4 servings.

Wild-Caught Langostino Lobster Tails over Angel Hair Pasta
Camanchaca

4 tablespoons plus 1 teaspoon olive oil, divided

1 tablespoon plus ½ teaspoon kosher salt, divided

¾ pound angel hair pasta

4 tablespoons butter

4 garlic cloves, minced

½ cup dry white wine (Chardonnay)

Juice of 1 large lemon

1 pound frozen fully cooked Langostino Lobster Tails, thawed

¼ teaspoon ground pepper

⅓ cup chopped fresh parsley leaves

⅛ teaspoon red pepper flakes

Grated Parmesan cheese, for serving

Bring a large pot of water to a boil. Drizzle with 1 teaspoon olive oil and add 1 tablespoon salt. Add pasta and cook according to package directions.

In a large skillet, melt butter and 4 tablespoons olive oil over low heat. Add garlic and sauté for 1 minute. Add wine and lemon juice; heat for 1 minute.

Squeeze the thawed lobster tails gently to remove any excess water. Add to the skillet, plus ½ teaspoon salt and ¼ teaspoon pepper. Sauté for 2 minutes. Remove from the heat and add parsley and red pepper flakes.

Drain the pasta well, add to the sauce in the skillet, and toss. Serve with grated Parmesan. Makes 4 servings.

Camanchaca
Gourmet Seafood

Spinach Pesto Sauce with Pasta
River Ranch Fresh Foods

4 cups washed and dried, torn spinach
leaves, stems removed, well packed
(about 6-8 ounces)

3 garlic cloves, peeled and halved

3 tablespoons pine nuts (toasted or not)

1½-2 tablespoons chopped fresh basil

¼ cup extra-virgin olive oil

⅓ cup grated fresh Parmesan cheese

⅛ teaspoon salt

1 pound spaghetti or other pasta
of choice

Shaved or grated fresh Parmesan
cheese, for serving

In a blender or food processor, combine a few spinach leaves, garlic, pine nuts, basil and a little olive oil. Cover and puree until the leaves begin to look crushed. Continue adding spinach leaves a few at a time with small amounts of oil, using a rubber spatula to help combine the pureed mixture. Add Parmesan and salt. Cover and process until smooth. Meanwhile, cook pasta according to package directions and drain in a colander. To serve, add the spinach pesto sauce to the pasta a little at a time and toss until you have the desired amount on your pasta. Top with shaved or grated Parmesan cheese. Makes 4-6 servings.

Tip: Pesto can be frozen in ice cube trays for future use.

Broccoli Mac 'n' Cheese
Eat Smart

2 cups elbow macaroni

1 pound Eat Smart broccoli florets

2 10-ounce containers refrigerated light Alfredo sauce

1½ cups chicken broth

½ cup minced shallots

2 teaspoons dry mustard

⅛ teaspoon grated nutmeg

3 cups shredded sharp Cheddar cheese

¼ cup real bacon bits or pieces

Cook macaroni according to package directions; drain.

Cut broccoli into small florets. Cook in boiling water for 5 minutes, or until crisp-tender; drain well.

In a medium saucepan, combine Alfredo sauce, chicken broth, shallots, mustard and nutmeg. Bring to a boil, then reduce the heat and simmer for 10 minutes. Add cheese a little at a time, stirring until it is melted.

Stir in macaroni, broccoli and bacon. Serve immediately. Makes 6-8 servings.

Tips: Bacon bits are actually not too bad on the health scale—and with their great smoky flavor, a little goes a long way. To up the nutrition in this dish, try using a whole-grain pasta; elbows or penne both work well. Serve alongside a rotisserie chicken for a great quick meal.

Baked Eggplant Parmesan
Classico

3 eggplants, peeled and thinly sliced

2 eggs, beaten

4 cups Italian-seasoned bread crumbs

6 cups Classico Tomato & Basil Pasta Sauce, divided

1 pound mozzarella cheese, shredded, divided

½ cup grated Parmesan cheese, divided

½ teaspoon dried basil

Preheat oven to 350°F.

Dip eggplant slices in egg, then in bread crumbs. Place in a single layer on a baking sheet. Bake for 5 minutes on each side.

In a 13-by-9-inch baking dish, spread some pasta sauce in an even layer. Place a layer of eggplant slices in the sauce. Sprinkle with mozzarella and Parmesan. Repeat with the remaining ingredients, ending with the cheeses. Sprinkle basil on top.

Bake for 35 minutes, or until golden brown. Makes 10 servings.

Orzo Pasta
New York Style Sausage

1 pound New York Style Italian
   sausage links, casings removed

3-4 teaspoons olive oil, divided

1 onion, chopped small

1 red bell pepper, finely chopped

2 garlic cloves, minced

½ pound mushrooms,
   coarsely chopped

½ teaspoon cayenne pepper

Salt and pepper

¼ cup chicken stock

1 7- to 8-ounce bag baby spinach

½ cup grated Romano or
   Parmesan cheese

½ pound orzo pasta, cooked

Fry sausage in 1 teaspoon olive oil in a large sauté pan over medium heat for 10-12 minutes, or until cooked through, breaking up into pieces. Remove from the pan and set aside.

Use 1 teaspoon of the pan drippings and 1 teaspoon olive oil to sauté onion and bell pepper over medium heat for 4-5 minutes, stirring occasionally, until soft. Add garlic, mushrooms, cayenne, and salt and pepper to taste; cook for about 2 minutes. Add chicken stock and cook for 1 minute.

Add spinach, the sausage, cheese and the hot cooked orzo to the pan. Toss to blend.

Drizzle with 1-2 teaspoons olive oil just before serving. Makes 4-6 servings.

California Chicken Club Pizza
Kirkland Signature

5 bacon slices, cooked and cut in half

1 Kirkland Signature frozen cheese pizza

12 ounces boneless, skinless chicken breast, cooked and seasoned

1 large tomato, thinly sliced

2 ounces romaine lettuce, shredded

3 tablespoons mayonnaise

1 large avocado, halved and sliced

Lay bacon evenly over the pizza. Cut chicken into bite-size pieces and arrange on the pizza. Bake the pizza according to package directions. Cut the pizza into 8 portions. Arrange sliced tomatoes on the pizza. Toss shredded lettuce with mayonnaise. Evenly distribute over the pizza. Top with avocado slices. Makes 8 servings.

KIRKLAND *Signature*

Stuffed Burgers for Cheese Lovers
Kirkland Signature/Orleans International

4 slices American cheese, mild Cheddar or pepper jack (about 4 ounces)

1½ pounds Kirkland Signature ground beef (15-20% fat)

1¼ teaspoons kosher salt

½ teaspoon garlic powder

1 teaspoon Worcestershire sauce

¼ teaspoon ground black pepper

Vegetable oil, for grilling

4 soft premium hamburger buns

Sliced pickles

Cut each piece of cheese into 4 squares; set aside.

In a large bowl, combine ground beef, salt, garlic powder, Worcestershire and pepper. Mix by hand just until evenly combined.

Divide the meat into 8 equal portions and shape into ¼-inch-thick burger patties. For each serving, arrange 4 cheese squares on a patty, then top with another patty and press the edges together.

Transfer to a plate. Refrigerate while you prepare the grill.

Heat a grill pan or outdoor grill to medium-high. Using tongs and paper towels, coat grill with vegetable oil.

Place the burgers on the grill, close the grill, and cook *undisturbed* (do not press down on the burgers) for 3-4 minutes, or until you see grill marks. Flip the burgers and cook for 3-5 minutes on the second side, or until cooked through. Remove the burgers from the grill and let rest for 3-5 minutes.

Place the burgers on buns and top with pickles. Makes 4 servings.

Sloppy Janes
Lea & Perrins

Nonstick cooking spray

1 large onion, chopped

2 pounds lean ground beef

¼ cup Lea & Perrins Worcestershire sauce

1 cup Heinz ketchup

¼ cup Heinz white vinegar

¼ cup lemon juice

2 tablespoons brown sugar

Buns, for serving

In a large saucepan sprayed with cooking spray, sauté onion over medium-high heat for 8-10 minutes, stirring occasionally. Remove the onion from the pan.

In the same pan, brown beef for 8-10 minutes, stirring occasionally. Drain off the fat and return the onion to the pan. Stir in Worcestershire sauce, ketchup, vinegar, lemon juice and sugar. Add ½ cup hot water and bring to a boil. Reduce the heat and simmer, covered, for 50-60 minutes, stirring occasionally.

Serve hot with your favorite buns. Makes 8 servings.

Tip: To prepare in a slow cooker, sauté onion as above. Transfer to a 3- to 4-quart slow cooker. Brown beef as above and place in the slow cooker. Add remaining ingredients and stir. Cook for 4 hours on low heat.

Korean BBQ Burgers with Sriracha Slaw and Potato Salad

Sandridge Food Corporation/Rikki Rikki

KOREAN BBQ BURGERS

2 pounds ground beef

2 eggs, beaten

½ cup panko bread crumbs

1 cup Rikki Rikki Korean BBQ Sauce

1½ sesame seed baguettes

Sandridge Foods Ultimate Potato Salad, for serving

SRIRACHA SLAW

1 large carrot, julienned

6 green onions, sliced

2 cups chopped cabbage

½ cup julienned cucumber

1 teaspoon salt

1 cup Rikki Rikki Sriracha Mayonnaise

Place ground beef in a bowl. Add eggs, bread crumbs and BBQ sauce; knead into the meat to mix thoroughly. Optional: Marinate in the refrigerator overnight. Divide into 6 portions and shape into patties.

Preheat the grill to high.

Prepare the slaw: In a bowl, mix carrot, onions, cabbage, cucumber and salt. Add mayonnaise and stir to blend.

Grill the burgers.

Cut the baguettes into burger-size portions. Toast lightly.

Place the grilled burgers on the bread and top with slaw. Serve with potato salad. Makes 6 servings.

Cherry Burgers

Delta Packing Company

¼ cup (½ stick) butter

4 large yellow onions, sliced thin

Kosher salt

Black pepper

1 teaspoon sugar

1 pound ground beef

1 cup Delta Fresh cherries, pitted and chopped

2 tablespoons soy sauce

¼ teaspoon granulated garlic

1 tablespoon dried savory

½ cup toasted walnuts, chopped

3 cups arugula

1 tablespoon balsamic vinegar

⅔ cup mayonnaise

2 tablespoons cherry preserves

2 tablespoons Pickapeppa sauce

6 slices smoked Gouda cheese (optional)

6 brioche buns, sliced and toasted

12 bacon slices, fried crisp

Melt butter in a large sauté pan over medium heat. Add onions, a pinch of salt and pepper, and sugar. Cook until golden.

In a bowl, combine beef, cherries, ¾ teaspoon pepper, soy sauce, garlic, savory and nuts. Form into 6 patties.

In a bowl, toss arugula and vinegar. In another bowl, blend mayonnaise, cherry preserves and Pickapeppa sauce.

Grill burgers over medium-high heat for 3 minutes, then flip and grill for 2 minutes. Add cheese, if desired, and cook for 1 minute.

Spread half of each bun with the mayo mixture; add burger, 2 bacon slices, onions and arugula. Top with other half of bun. Makes 6 servings.

Bacon Cheese SPAMburgers

Hormel Foods/Kirkland Signature

1 12-ounce can SPAM Less Sodium,
cut into 6 slices

3 tablespoons mayonnaise
or salad dressing

6 hamburger buns, split

6 lettuce leaves

2 tomatoes, sliced

6 slices American cheese

12 slices Hormel/Kirkland Signature
fully cooked bacon

In a large skillet, cook SPAM over medium heat, turning once, for 3-5 minutes,
or until lightly browned.

Spread mayonnaise on cut sides of buns. Layer lettuce, tomatoes, SPAM,
cheese and bacon on the bottom halves of the buns. Cover with the top
halves of the buns. Makes 6 servings.

Savory Mediterranean Burgers
Quick'N Eat

1 large eggplant
Salt and pepper
Olive oil
4 Quick'N Eat Beef Patties
20 bocconcini
   mozzarella balls
12 basil leaves
1 red onion, thinly sliced
1 roasted red bell pepper,
   cut in 4 equal pieces

BLACK OLIVE SPREAD

1 cup pitted Kalamata
   olives, soaked in cold
   water for an hour
   and drained
2 garlic cloves,
   finely chopped
1 pinch of crushed
   red pepper
½ cup extra-virgin olive oil
Pepper, to taste

Cut eight ½-inch-thick horizontal slices from the eggplant. Lightly salt the slices and stack on top of each other for at least an hour to remove bitterness.

Prepare the spread: Combine all ingredients in a food processor. Pulse until the mixture becomes spreadable.

Brush eggplant slices with olive oil and season with pepper. Grill the eggplant and Quick'N Eat Beef Patties according to package directions.

Spread the olive spread on the eggplant slices. Place 5 mozzarella balls on each of 4 eggplant slices, then beef patties, basil, onion and bell pepper. Place the remaining eggplant slices on top, spread side down. Makes 4 servings.
Recipe created by Chef Kurt Fleischfresser.

Cheesy Bacon Chicken Burgers with Cilantro Aïoli
Better Than Bouillon

2 teaspoons Better Than
   Bouillon All-Natural
   Reduced Sodium
   Chicken Base
2 tablespoons milk
8 ounces bacon, cooked
4 ounces sharp Cheddar
   cheese, cut into
   ¼-inch pieces
1 pound ground chicken
½ cup plain dry bread crumbs
1 tablespoon stone-
   ground mustard
½ teaspoon garlic powder
¼ teaspoon salt
⅛ teaspoon cayenne pepper
1½ tablespoons olive oil
Lettuce leaves, optional
6 whole-grain buns, toasted

CILANTRO AÏOLI

½ cup mayonnaise
½ cup sour cream
2 tablespoons chopped
   cilantro leaves
1 tablespoon freshly
   squeezed lemon juice
¼ teaspoon
   cayenne pepper
¼ teaspoon garlic powder

Prepare the aïoli: Place all ingredients in a medium bowl and stir to combine. Cover and refrigerate until ready to use.

In a large bowl, whisk chicken base with milk until dissolved. Chop the bacon. Add it and the next 7 ingredients to the bowl; mix to combine. Divide the mixture into 6 equal portions and shape into patties.

Heat olive oil in a large nonstick skillet over medium heat. Add the patties and cook until done, about 10-12 minutes, turning once.

Place the lettuce leaves and burgers on buns and serve with Cilantro Aioli. Serve with vegetable chips. Makes 6 servings.

SOUTHEASTERN

Hearty Meatball Sandwiches

Panné Provincio

Quick & Easy

2 loaves Panné Provincio roasted garlic bread

5 Del Destino Sweet Piquillo Peppers, halved

1 3-pound package large beef meatballs, thawed

1 cup Cello shredded Four Cheese Italian Blend

¾ cup Alpino Brand Hot Pepper Mix "Giardiniera"

Preheat oven to 425°F. Slice bread loaves in half lengthwise. Top the bottom half of each loaf evenly with peppers, 3-4 meatballs, shredded cheese and giardiniera. Add the top bread half and wrap tightly in aluminum foil. Bake for 15-20 minutes, or until the meatballs are heated through and the cheese is melted. Remove from the foil and cut each loaf into 3-4 even portions. Serve immediately. Makes 6-8 servings.

Blackened Salmon Sandwiches with Tartar Sauce

La Brea Bakery

1 tomato, cut into eight
⅛-inch-thick slices

Salt and pepper

4 La Brea Bakery Torta Sandwich Rolls

4 5-ounce salmon fillets

2 tablespoons canola oil

¼ cup unsalted butter, melted

TARTAR SAUCE

¼ cup chopped dill pickles

¼ cup peeled, finely julienned
celery root

¼ cup sour cream

⅓ cup mayonnaise

1¼ teaspoons Worcestershire sauce

2 tablespoons Dijon mustard

2 tablespoons chopped shallots

¾ teaspoon Tabasco sauce

2 teaspoons chopped fresh parsley

SPICE MIX

2¼ teaspoons paprika

⅜ teaspoon cayenne pepper

1½ teaspoons sugar

¾ teaspoon salt

¼ teaspoon *each* garlic powder, onion
powder and ground black pepper

½ teaspoon *each* dried oregano
and dried thyme

Prepare the tartar sauce: In a bowl, combine all ingredients and mix until blended. Refrigerate.

Prepare the spice mix: In a spice grinder, combine all ingredients and grind for 1 minute.

Preheat oven to 375°F. Season tomato slices with salt and pepper to taste. Split rolls and toast lightly (cut side up) in the oven, about 8 minutes.

Preheat an iron skillet over high heat. Gently rub the spice mix onto the large sides of each salmon fillet. Remove excess. Add canola oil to the skillet, let smoke slightly, and then dip each fillet in melted butter. Lay the fillets in the pan with space between them. Cook for 2-3 minutes on each side, or until a dark crust forms. Using a slotted spatula, place the fillets on the roll bottoms. Top with tomato slices, tartar sauce and roll tops. Makes 4 servings.

LA BREA BAKERY

Lobster Rolls
Vie de France

Butter, softened

2 large Vie de France butter croissants, sliced in half lengthwise

FILLING

12 ounces cooked lobster meat, cut in bite-size pieces

2 tablespoons mayonnaise

1 teaspoon fresh lemon juice

2 tablespoons finely diced celery

Salt and pepper to taste

Prepare the filling: In a bowl, combine all ingredients and stir to blend. Cover and chill for an hour.

Heat a grill or sauté pan over medium heat.

Spread softened butter on the croissant halves. Place the croissants butter side down in the pan and cook until golden brown, 1-2 minutes.

Fill the croissants with the lobster mixture and serve. Makes 2 servings.

Avocado Tuna Sandwiches
Chicken of the Sea

2 ripe avocados, peeled, pitted and coarsely mashed

2 tablespoons fresh squeezed lime juice or lemon juice

¼ cup roasted red pepper strips, fresh or jarred

2 tablespoons chopped fresh parsley

½ teaspoon garlic salt

¼ teaspoon black pepper

2 7-ounce cans Chicken of the Sea chunk light tuna in water, drained

8 slices bread

8 slices tomato

8 slices red onion

In a medium bowl, combine avocado, lime juice, red pepper strips, parsley, garlic salt and pepper. Gently flake and fold in Chicken of the Sea tuna.

Layer each sandwich with ¼ avocado-tuna filling, 2 tomato slices and 2 red onion slices. Serve immediately. Makes 4 sandwiches.

Bagel Tortas
Einstein Brothers Bagels

1 rotisserie chicken breast
¼ teaspoon ground black pepper
¼ teaspoon garlic powder
¼ teaspoon ground cumin
½ teaspoon chili powder
1 lime, halved, divided
4 Kirkland Signature plain bagels

3 ounces cream cheese
½ cup shredded cheese
  (mozzarella or blend)
¾ cup seasoned refried beans
1 onion, thinly sliced
2 tomatoes, thinly sliced
1 ripe avocado, thinly sliced

Preheat oven to 375°F. Pull the chicken into thin strips. In a bowl, combine the chicken with the dry spices and juice of ½ lime, stirring to blend. Cut bagels in half and scoop out the insides. Spread cream cheese evenly on the 4 bagel tops. Top with shredded cheese. Spread refried beans on the bagel bottoms. Top with the seasoned pulled chicken. Place on a baking tray and bake for 8-10 minutes, or until the cheese has started to bubble. Remove from the oven and place onions, tomatoes and avocado on the bagel bottoms. Squeeze the remaining ½ lime over the toppings. Close the sandwiches and let sit for a minute before cutting in half or quarters to eat or share. Makes 4 servings.

  NOAH'S BAGELS

Baked Monte Cristo
New York Style Sausage

1 pound New York Style Italian
   sausage links (4-5 links)
1 teaspoon olive oil
8 slices deli ham
9 slices Swiss cheese
5-6 slices buttermilk or potato bread
4 large eggs

1 cup milk
1 tablespoon Dijon mustard
Salt and pepper
Chopped cooked turkey bacon,
   for topping (optional)
Tomato slices, sour cream and chopped
   chives, for garnish (optional)

Fry sausage links in olive oil over medium heat for 10-12 minutes, turning occasionally, until just cooked through. Cool and then carefully slice lengthwise into thirds. Set aside. Butter a baking dish (approximately 12 by 6 by 2 inches). Lay 4 slices of ham in the pan, then layer with 3 slices of cheese, half the sausage slices and 2½-3 bread slices. Repeat the layers (ham, cheese, sausage, bread), then top with the remaining 3 cheese slices.

In a bowl, whisk together eggs, milk, mustard, and salt and pepper to taste. Pour over the casserole. Cover with plastic wrap and refrigerate for 2-24 hours (so the egg mixture soaks into the bread).

Preheat oven to 350°F. Remove the plastic wrap and cover the casserole with foil. Bake for 20 minutes. Remove the foil and bake another 25 minutes, or until the cheese is melted and the bread doesn't look soggy. Finish off under the broiler to brown the top.

If desired, sprinkle with bacon and garnish with tomato slices, sour cream and chives. Makes 4-6 servings.

Asparagus, Poached Egg, Prosciutto and Fontina Sandwiches

La Brea Bakery

16-20 asparagus spears, tough ends broken off

Extra-virgin olive oil

½ teaspoon kosher salt

20 sprigs fresh thyme, divided

4 slices La Brea Bakery Whole Grain Loaf Bread

1 garlic clove, peeled

4 eggs, poached

3 ounces Fontina or Gruyère cheese, sliced into four ⅛-inch-thick slices

2 ounces prosciutto di Parma, cut into 8 thin slices

Cracked black pepper, to taste

Adjust the oven rack to the middle position. Preheat oven to 450°F. Place asparagus in a bowl, drizzle with 1 tablespoon olive oil, and sprinkle with salt, tossing to coat. Scatter 16 thyme sprigs onto a baking sheet and cover with the asparagus. Roast for about 10 minutes, until tender to the touch yet firm in the center.

Brush bread with olive oil and lightly brown each side over medium heat in a heavy-bottomed pan. Rub each bread slice with the garlic clove, then place on a baking sheet, garlic side up. Arrange the asparagus on the bread slices. Adjust the oven rack to the upper position. Preheat the broiler.

Place eggs in the center of the asparagus. Drape a cheese slice over each egg. Broil the sandwiches just until the cheese melts. Remove from the oven, and rumple a slice of prosciutto over each end of the asparagus. Top each sandwich with a drizzle of olive oil, pepper and a thyme sprig. Makes 4 servings.

LA BREA BAKERY

Egg Salad with a Kick

Cal-Maine Foods/Hickman's Family Farms/Hillandale Farms/ Moark/NuCal Foods/Oakdell Egg Farms/Wilcox Farms

½ medium red onion, chopped

12 extra-large eggs

1 celery stalk (with leaves), chopped

¼ cup mayonnaise

¼ cup sour cream

2 tablespoons chopped fresh dill

2 tablespoons yellow mustard

1 tablespoon plus 1 teaspoon freshly squeezed lemon juice

2 teaspoons kosher salt

1 teaspoon cayenne pepper

Freshly ground black pepper

8 slices sourdough bread, toasted

Mayonnaise, for serving (optional)

Watercress sprigs

Salad greens

2 tomatoes, sliced

2 avocados, sliced

Soak onion in cold water for 15 minutes. Drain.

Place eggs in a large saucepan with a tight-fitting lid and cover with cold water by 1 inch. Bring to a boil and cook for 1 minute. Cover the pan, remove from the heat, and set aside for 8 minutes. Drain the water from the pan and cool the eggs in the pan under cold running water. Peel the eggs and cut into sixths.

In a large bowl, mix together the onion, celery, mayonnaise, sour cream, dill, mustard, lemon juice, salt and cayenne pepper.

Add the eggs to the mayonnaise/sour cream mixture and gently mix. Season with pepper to taste.

Spread 4 slices of toast with mayonnaise, if you like. Spread each with ¼ of the egg salad and arrange watercress sprigs on top. Garnish with salad greens, tomato and avocado. Top each sandwich with another slice of toast and serve. Makes 4 servings.

Gluten-Free Watermelon Mozzarella Sandwiches

Big Chuy & Sons/George Perry & Sons/Growers Select Produce/Leger & Son/Timco Worldwide

2 cups homemade (see note) or homemade-style bread-and-butter pickles

8 slices seedless watermelon, 4 by 6 by ½ inch thick

2 cups chopped fresh basil

16 ¼-inch-thick slices fresh mozzarella cheese

8 decorative picks

Corn chips or salad greens, for serving

Divide pickles in an even layer over 4 watermelon slices. Sprinkle basil over the pickles.

On each sandwich, place 4 slices of cheese in an even layer over the basil. Place another slice of watermelon on top.

Secure each sandwich with 2 decorative picks and cut diagonally into 2 pieces.

Serve the sandwiches with corn chips or over greens as "fork sandwiches." Makes 4 servings.

Note: These are available at a lot of farmers' markets as well as gourmet supermarkets.

National Watermelon Promotion Board

Brie and Apple Turkey Pinwheels
West Liberty Foods

- 4 12-inch spinach wraps
- 1 mini Brie wheel, cut lengthwise into 20 thin slices
- 1 medium Granny Smith apple, cored and sliced into 32 thin wedges
- 12 slices oven-roasted turkey breast from a Kirkland Signature deli meat and cheese platter
- 1 head green leaf lettuce, cleaned, with leaves removed

HONEY MUSTARD DRESSING

- 5 tablespoons honey
- 2 tablespoons rice wine vinegar
- 3½ tablespoons Dijon mustard

Prepare the dressing: Mix all ingredients in a bowl.

Lay each wrap on a work surface and spread with 2 tablespoons of dressing, leaving a 1-inch border.

Place 5 cheese slices across the width of the wrap. Lay 8 apple slices across the wrap.

Place 3 turkey slices on top. Add a large lettuce leaf.

Roll the wraps up snugly from the bottom and slice each wrap into 3 pinwheels.

Serve on a platter. Makes 4 servings of 3 pinwheels each.

WLF | West Liberty Foods.

Chicken Caesar Salad Wraps
Foxy Vegetables

- ¼ cup mayonnaise
- ¼ cup grated Parmesan cheese
- 2 tablespoons lemon juice
- 1 tablespoon Worcestershire sauce
- 1 tablespoon Dijon mustard
- 1 garlic clove, minced
- ¼ cup olive oil
- 1 2½-pound rotisserie chicken, skin and bones discarded, meat shredded into bite-size pieces (3 cups)
- 1 Foxy romaine lettuce heart (6 ounces), torn into bite-size pieces
- 4 10-inch flour tortillas

In a bowl, whisk together mayonnaise, Parmesan, lemon juice, Worcestershire, mustard and garlic. Gradually whisk in olive oil until thoroughly incorporated.

In a bowl, toss chicken with half of the dressing.

In another bowl, toss romaine with the remaining dressing.

Lay tortillas on a flat surface. Divide the chicken equally among the tortillas. Top each with 1 cup of the dressed lettuce mixture. Roll into wraps. Makes 4 servings.

Desserts

Spiced D'Anjou Pear Sundaes with Cinnamon-Caramel Sauce
Domex Superfresh Growers

4 cups water

1 cup granulated sugar

1 teaspoon pure vanilla extract

4 star anise

1 cinnamon stick

10 whole black peppercorns

2 ripe but firm D'Anjou pears

Vanilla ice cream, for serving

CINNAMON-CARAMEL SAUCE

2 tablespoons unsalted butter

½ cup packed light brown sugar

½ teaspoon ground cinnamon

Pinch of salt

½ cup heavy cream

In a medium saucepan, combine water, granulated sugar, vanilla and spices. Set over medium-high heat and bring just to a boil, stirring to help the sugar dissolve. When the syrup boils, reduce the heat to medium-low and simmer for 10 minutes.

Meanwhile, halve, core and peel the pears.

Gently add the pear halves to the syrup and simmer until just tender when pierced with the tip of a knife, about 20 minutes, turning every 5 minutes to poach evenly. The syrup should bubble gently but not boil; reduce the heat to low if needed. Set the pan aside until the pears are cooled to room temperature.

While the pears are cooling, make the sauce: Melt butter in a small saucepan over medium heat. Add brown sugar and cook, stirring often, until melted and bubbly, about 4 minutes. Stir in cinnamon and salt, then add cream and cook, stirring, until smooth (the sugar may solidify a bit when the cream is added), 2-3 minutes longer. Set aside.

Lift the pear halves from the syrup with a slotted spoon and set aside on paper towels to drain. Use a paring knife to cut ½-inch slices lengthwise in the pears, leaving the slices attached at the top (stem) end.

To serve, press gently on each pear half to spread the slices a bit and set in a shallow bowl. Add 1-2 scoops of ice cream. Drizzle with sauce. Garnish with chocolate curls, if desired. Makes 4 servings.

Coconut Chocolate Frozen Mousse
Michael Foods

1¾ cups coconut cream (see note)

⅓ cup AllWhites liquid egg whites

⅓ cup unsweetened cocoa

½ teaspoon vanilla extract

¼ teaspoon almond extract

1 cup chocolate ice cream syrup

1 large ripe mango, chopped

Shaved sweetened coconut

In a large mixing bowl, combine coconut cream and AllWhites. Beat with a mixer for 3 minutes, or until slightly thickened. Add cocoa and vanilla; beat about 2 minutes longer, or until thickened.

Cover the bowl and place in the freezer for at least 2 hours or up to overnight.

To serve, mix almond extract into chocolate syrup. Scoop the mousse into dessert glasses. Drizzle the syrup over the desserts. Garnish with mango and shaved coconut. Makes 8 servings.

Note: Look for coconut cream in the beverage aisle, with the ingredients for making cocktails.

Tip: To make parfaits, layer small scoops of mousse with whipped cream, mango, coconut and crumbled amaretti cookies.

Mocha Malted Hot Fudge Sauce
Starbucks Coffee

¼ cup cocoa powder
½ cup sugar
⅛ teaspoon salt
½ cup whole milk
1 cup heavy cream
1 cup light corn syrup
⅛ teaspoon cider vinegar
3 ounces semisweet chocolate, finely chopped, divided
2 tablespoons unsalted butter
6 tablespoons malted milk powder
1 teaspoon vanilla extract
3 sticks Starbucks VIA Italian Roast

In a heavy saucepan, whisk together cocoa, sugar, salt and milk until the mixture forms a smooth paste.

Place over medium heat and stir in cream, corn syrup, vinegar and ⅔ of the chocolate.

Bring the mixture to a boil, whisking or stirring frequently. Boil, whisking frequently, until the sauce reaches 220 to 225°F on a candy thermometer, about 8 minutes.

Remove from the heat. Whisk in butter, malted milk powder, vanilla, Starbucks VIA sticks and the remaining chocolate until the sauce is smooth.

Strain and set aside for a few minutes before serving. Goes great with ice cream, brownies or your favorite dessert. Makes 2 cups.

Tips: If not using the sauce right away, chill in an airtight container. Rewarm before serving. This keeps well, chilled, for 3 weeks.

Fresh Strawberry-Agave Granita
West Lake Fresh

16 ounces fresh strawberries
8 ounces Kirkland Signature drinking water
2 tablespoons fresh Meyer lemon juice
4 ounces agave nectar, or 6 ounces honey
Grated lemon zest

Thoroughly rinse strawberries under cold running water. Next, using a paring knife, carve out and discard the leafy green calyx and stem core from the top of each berry.

Put berries, water and lemon juice in a blender and puree. If desired, the puree can be strained through a fine sieve to remove the strawberry seeds.

Add agave nectar or honey to the puree and briefly reblend in a clean blender jar to incorporate. Pour the mixture into ice cube trays and freeze.

To serve, working in batches, place just enough frozen cubes in a food processor to make a single layer. Pulse the cubes to a "snow-cone" texture (about 11 pulses). Spoon the mixture into serving glasses and grate lemon zest on top for eye appeal. Serve immediately. Makes 6 servings.

My Four Boys Blueberry Cheesecake

Townsend Farms

2 8-ounce packages cream
  cheese, softened

1 cup low-fat sour cream

¾ cup sugar

1 teaspoon vanilla extract

2 tablespoons all-purpose flour

4 large eggs

2 cups Townsend Farms blueberries,
  fresh or frozen (thawed)

⅓ cup blueberry jelly

CRUST

1 cup graham cracker crumbs

2 tablespoons sugar

¼ cup melted butter

In a bowl, beat cream cheese until soft and creamy. Gradually add sour cream, sugar, vanilla and flour. Beat in eggs one at a time. Pour the mixture over the crust.

Bake for about 1 hour, or until a toothpick inserted in the cake comes out clean. Let cool to room temperature, then remove from the pan, loosening the edges with a knife.

Place blueberries on top. Melt jelly and spoon over the blueberries to glaze. Chill until ready to eat. Makes 6-8 servings.

Townsend
since 1906   Farms

Preheat oven to 325°F.

Prepare the crust: In a bowl, combine all ingredients and stir until well blended. Pat the mixture into the bottom of a 9-inch springform pan.

Blueberry Shortcake
Vie de France

**1 3.4-ounce box instant
  vanilla pudding**
2 cups fresh blueberries
¼ cup confectioners' sugar

½ teaspoon vanilla or almond extract
8 ounces cream cheese, softened
6 large Vie de France butter croissants
Whipped cream, for garnish

Prepare pudding according to package directions. Let set for up to an hour.

In a medium bowl, mix blueberries, sugar and extract. Add cream cheese and stir until blended. Put the mixture in the refrigerator to chill.

Slice croissants lengthwise. Spread the pudding on the croissants. Top with the chilled berry mixture.

Garnish with whipped cream and serve immediately or refrigerate for up to 60 minutes before serving. Makes 6 servings.

Caramel Apple Cheesecake Bars

Borton & Sons

3 8-ounce packages cream cheese, softened

¾ cup plus 2 tablespoons sugar, divided

3 large eggs

1½ teaspoons vanilla extract

3 Borton & Sons Granny Smith apples, peeled, cored and finely chopped

½ teaspoon ground cinnamon

¼ teaspoon ground nutmeg

CRUST

2 cups all-purpose flour

½ cup firmly packed light brown sugar

1 cup (2 sticks) butter, softened

TOPPING

1 cup packed light brown sugar

1 cup all-purpose flour

½ cup quick-cooking oats

½ cup (1 stick) butter, softened

½ cup prepared caramel topping, for drizzling

Preheat oven to 350°F. Line a 13-by-9-inch baking pan with heavy-duty aluminum foil.

Prepare the crust: In a medium bowl, combine flour and brown sugar. Cut in butter with a pastry blender (or 2 forks) until the mixture is crumbly. Press evenly into the pan. Bake for 15 minutes, or until lightly browned.

In a large bowl, beat cream cheese with ¾ cup sugar with an electric mixer at medium speed until smooth. Beat in eggs one at a time, then vanilla. Pour over the warm crust.

In a small bowl, stir together chopped apples, 2 tablespoons sugar, cinnamon and nutmeg. Spoon evenly over the cream cheese mixture.

Prepare the topping: In a small bowl, combine brown sugar, flour, oats and butter. Sprinkle over the apples.

Bake for 40-60 minutes, or until the filling is set. Drizzle with caramel topping and let cool. Serve chilled. Makes 16-24 servings.

Crustless New York-Style Cheesecake with Cherry Sauce

Oneonta Starr Ranch Growers

2 pounds cream cheese

1½ cups granulated sugar

½ cup sour cream

¼ cup whipping cream

2 tablespoons cornstarch

1 teaspoon vanilla extract

2 large eggs

1 large egg yolk

CHERRY SAUCE

8 cups pitted fresh Starr Ranch Growers sweet dark cherries

1¼ cups granulated sugar

⅓ cup water

⅓ cup apple jelly

1 tablespoon cornstarch

2 tablespoons kirsch (cherry brandy)

Preheat oven to 325°F. Grease a 9-inch springform pan; line the bottom with parchment paper. Using a stand mixer, beat cream cheese and sugar until very smooth. Add sour cream, whipping cream, cornstarch and vanilla; beat on high for 5 minutes. On low speed, beat in eggs and yolk one at a time until well blended. Scrape into the prepared pan. Bake until lightly set in the center, about 45-50 minutes. Run a wet knife around the cake's edge and let cool. Remove the sides of the pan. Refrigerate, covered, until firm, at least 4 hours.

Prepare the cherry sauce: In a saucepan, combine cherries, sugar and water. Bring to a boil, then reduce the heat, cover, and simmer gently for 8-10 minutes, or until the cherries are almost tender.

Stir in jelly; increase the heat to medium-high and boil for 5 minutes.

Mix cornstarch with 1 tablespoon water; stir into the cherries. Return to a boil and cook, stirring, until thickened, about 1 minute. Let cool for 15 minutes. Stir in kirsch. Let cool to room temperature. Slice cheesecake with a wet knife and serve with the sauce. Makes 6-8 servings.

ONEONTA
STARR RANCH *growers*

Red Grapefruit Mini-Cheesecakes

Corona-College Heights/Premier Citrus Marketing/
Florida Classic Growers

36 paper muffin liners

3 12-cup muffin pans

36 vanilla wafers

2 8-ounce packages cream cheese, softened

¾ cup sugar

2 large eggs

4 tablespoons red grapefruit juice

3 cups red grapefruit sections

2 cups prepared strawberry glaze

Whipped cream, for serving (optional)

Preheat oven to 350°F. Place paper liners in the muffin cups.

Put 1 vanilla wafer in the bottom of each muffin cup.

In a bowl, combine cream cheese, sugar, eggs and grapefruit juice. Beat with an electric mixer until smooth and creamy.

Fill each muffin cup half full of the cream cheese mixture. Bake for 15-20 minutes, or until the centers are almost set. Let cool thoroughly.

Gently fold grapefruit sections and strawberry glaze together. Top each cheesecake with the mixture and chill.

Serve with whipped cream. Makes 36 servings.

Peach and Nectarine Cupcakes

Pride Packing Co./HMC Farms

1¼ cups all-purpose flour

½ teaspoon baking powder

¼ teaspoon salt

⅓ cup whole milk

1 teaspoon vanilla extract

6 tablespoons unsalted butter, softened

¾ cup sugar

2 large eggs

1 medium HMC Farms nectarine, peeled and finely chopped

1 medium Mary's Pride peach, peeled and finely chopped

1 small nectarine and 1 small peach, thinly sliced, for garnish

TOPPING

1 cup cold heavy cream

½ cup sour cream

3 tablespoons sugar

Preheat oven to 350°F. Place 12 baking cups in a standard muffin tin.

Sift together flour, baking powder and salt. In a small bowl, blend milk and vanilla.

Beat butter and sugar on medium speed until pale and fluffy. Beat in eggs one at a time. Alternately add flour and milk mixtures in 3 batches.

To each muffin cup add 1 tablespoon batter, 1-1½ tablespoons *each* chopped nectarines and peaches, then 2 tablespoons batter. Bake until the edges turn golden, about 25 minutes. Let cool.

Prepare the topping: Combine all ingredients and whisk to medium peaks. Top each cupcake with topping and peach and nectarine slices. Makes 12 cupcakes.

Apple Cherry Upside-Down Cake
Columbia Marketing International

¼ cup packed light brown sugar

2 CMI Granny Smith or Golden Delicious apples, cored and peeled

⅓ cup dried dark cherries

½ cup (1 stick) unsalted butter, room temperature

1 cup sugar

2 large eggs

1 teaspoon pure vanilla extract

1 teaspoon dark rum (optional)

½ cup whole milk

1½ cups all-purpose flour

1½ teaspoons baking powder

½ teaspoon kosher salt

Preheat oven to 350°F. Butter an 8-by-8-inch square cake pan and sprinkle the bottom with brown sugar.

Slice the apples into ½-inch-thick circles. Pick the wider circles, and place in a single layer in the baking pan on top of the brown sugar. Sprinkle cherries on top.

With an electric mixer, beat the butter and sugar on high until light.

In another bowl, whisk together eggs, vanilla, rum and milk. In a separate bowl, sift together flour, baking powder and salt.

Beat ⅓ of the flour mixture into the butter mixture, then ½ of the milk mixture, scraping down the sides of the bowl. Repeat with ⅓ of the flour mixture, the remaining milk mixture and then the remaining flour. Pour the batter over the apples and smooth the top.

Bake for about 1 hour, or until golden brown on top and a toothpick inserted in the center comes out clean. Cool on a rack for about 30 minutes.

To serve, cover the cake pan with a plate and carefully flip. Give the bottom of the pan a gentle tap to release the cake. Serve warm or cooled. Store, covered, for up to 2 days. Makes about 9 servings.

Recipe courtesy of Lara Ferroni, food writer and epicurean from the Pacific Northwest.

Date and Orange Cake
AMC Direct

1 cup butter, softened

¾ cup superfine sugar

2 large eggs

2 cups flour

Pinch of salt

1 teaspoon baking soda

¾ cup milk

2 tablespoons grated orange zest

½ pound chopped dates

½ cup finely chopped walnuts

1 cup chopped candied cherries

1 cup raisins

SYRUP

1 cup sugar

¾ cup freshly squeezed orange juice

2 teaspoons grated orange zest

Prepare the syrup: Combine all ingredients in a saucepan and bring to a boil. Remove from the heat and let cool to room temperature. Refrigerate.

Preheat oven to 370°F. Butter and flour an 8.5-inch springform pan.

In a bowl, cream butter and sugar. Beat in eggs one by one. Fold in sifted flour and salt.

Mix baking soda and milk together. Fold into the batter.

Fold in remaining ingredients until combined.

Pour into the pan and bake for 45 minutes, or until a cake tester comes out clean. Remove from the oven, pour the syrup over the cake, and bake for another 10 minutes.

Let cool before removing the cake from the pan. Makes 8-10 servings.

Apple Pear Spice Cake
Kingsburg Orchards

2 Kingsburg Orchards Apple Pears, peeled, cored and diced
1¼ cups flour
¾ cup sugar
1½ teaspoons baking powder
½ teaspoon salt

⅛ teaspoon ground cloves
¼ teaspoon pumpkin pie spice
½ teaspoon ground cinnamon
½ cup unsalted butter
1 tablespoon vanilla extract

Preheat oven to 350°F. Place Apple Pears in a greased 9-by-9-inch baking dish and spread in an even layer. Mix together flour, sugar, baking powder, salt and spices. Spread evenly over the Apple Pears. Melt butter and stir in vanilla. Pour evenly over the flour mixture. Bake for 30-35 minutes, or until lightly browned around the edges. Makes 9 servings.

Tuxedo Mousse Baked Alaska

France Délices/Ticklebelly Desserts

2 cups superfine sugar

1 cup egg whites

½ teaspoon cream of tartar

½ teaspoon salt

1 Kirkland Signature Tuxedo Chocolate Mousse Cake, frozen

Special equipment: piping bag with a star tip

In a stainless steel or glass bowl, whisk together sugar, egg whites, cream of tartar and salt. Set the bowl over a saucepan of simmering water, being sure that it does not touch the water. Heat, whisking every few minutes, until the mixture is 170°F. When it is ready, the mixture will be in a very liquid state and the sugar will be melted.

Remove the bowl from the heat and beat with a mixer at high speed until stiff and glossy. Use immediately.

Place the frozen cake on an oven-safe platter (or parchment-lined baking sheet). Put the meringue in the piping bag and pipe the meringue onto the cake, covering the surface. Place the cake back in the freezer.

When ready to serve, preheat oven to 475°F. Bake the cake for 3-5 minutes, or until the meringue is golden brown. Makes 12 servings.

Note: You can also use a propane torch to toast the meringue.

Super-Moist Chocolate Mayo Cake

Unilever

1 16.5-ounce package chocolate cake mix

1 cup Hellmann's or Best Foods Real Mayonnaise

1 cup water

3 large eggs

1 teaspoon ground cinnamon (optional)

Confectioners' sugar or frosting

Preheat oven to 350°F. Grease and lightly flour two 9-inch round cake pans (see note).

In a large bowl, combine cake mix, mayonnaise, water, eggs and cinnamon. Beat with an electric mixer on low speed for 30 seconds. Beat on medium speed, scraping the sides of the bowl occasionally, for 2 minutes. Pour the batter into the prepared pans.

Bake for 30 minutes, or until a toothpick inserted in the center comes out clean. Cool on a wire rack for 10 minutes. Remove the cakes from the pans and cool completely.

Sprinkle, if desired, with confectioners' sugar or fill and frost. Makes 12 servings.

Note: The cake can also be baked in a 13-by-9-inch baking pan for 40 minutes.

Strawberry Coconut Crunch Pie

Kashi

2 cups Kashi GOLEAN Crunch cereal
⅓ cup whole-wheat flour
¾ cup shredded coconut
½ cup apple juice concentrate

3½ cups halved strawberries, divided
2 tablespoons arrowroot or cornstarch
½ cup cold water

Preheat oven to 375°F. Crush cereal with a rolling pin, or process in a food processor or blender until it is semi-fine in texture. Place the crushed cereal in a bowl and add flour, coconut and apple juice concentrate. Stir until well blended.

Pour into an oil-sprayed 9-inch glass pie pan and press into place with a spoon or rubber spatula. Bake for 8 minutes, or until golden brown. Cool completely on a rack before filling. Arrange all but 1 cup strawberries in the cooled baked shell.

Puree the 1 cup strawberries in a blender or food processor. Add arrowroot or cornstarch to the cold water and stir until well blended. Combine with the pureed berries in a microwave-safe bowl (or double boiler). Heat and gently stir until slightly thickened. Pour over the berries in the pie shell. Refrigerate until chilled. Serve cold. Makes 8 servings.

Tip: Sprinkle with ½ cup slightly crushed Kashi GOLEAN Crunch, if desired.

Nutritional information: Each serving has 160 calories, 3 g protein, 29 g carbohydrates, 4 g fat (3 g saturated), 0 mg cholesterol, 5 g fiber, 55 mg sodium, 17 g sugar.

Kashi
The Seven Whole Grain Company

Triple Berry Hand Pies
Kirkland Signature/Rader Farms

3½ cups frozen Nature's Three Berries, thawed

Juice of 1 lemon

1 tablespoon cornstarch

⅓ cup plus 2 teaspoons sugar

½ teaspoon ground cinnamon, divided

¼ teaspoon grated nutmeg, divided

18 9-by-14-inch sheets phyllo dough, thawed

Cooking spray

1 cup plain nonfat yogurt

3 tablespoons maple syrup or golden syrup

Mix berries, lemon juice, cornstarch, ⅓ cup sugar, ¼ teaspoon cinnamon and ⅛ teaspoon nutmeg. Strain, saving the juices.

Working in batches, place 1 phyllo sheet on work surface; lightly coat with cooking spray. Repeat process, stacking 3 high. Cut lengthwise into 3-inch strips. Continue until all 18 sheets are used. Use 3 stacked strips for each hand pie.

Mound 1 heaping tablespoon of filling near the end of each stack (1 inch from corner). Fold 1 corner diagonally across the filling to the opposite edge to form a triangle. Continue folding down the length of the strip. Repeat with remaining strips.

Preheat oven to 400°F.

Place pies seam side down on a lightly sprayed cookie sheet. Spray the tops. Mix 2 teaspoons sugar and remaining cinnamon and nutmeg; sprinkle over the pies.

Bake for 10-12 minutes, or until golden brown. Cool slightly on a rack.

Mix berry juices, yogurt and syrup. Serve the pies warm with topping. Makes 18 servings.

Note: Phyllo dough is fragile and may tear easily.

Mini Patriotic Pies
Andrew & Williamson/Curry & Company/Gourmet Trading Company

3 ounces blueberries

3 ounces strawberries

8 prepared mini tart shells (1.75 inch)

2½ cups prepared vanilla or lemon pudding

Rinse blueberries and strawberries.

Cut off the tops of the strawberries.

Fill the mini tart shells with pudding.

Top with blueberries and strawberries. Serve immediately. Makes 8 servings.

Double Nut Berry Yogurt Pie

Quick & Easy

J&J Snack Foods

10 Kirkland Signature double nut cookies, divided

1 cup blueberry yogurt

1 8-ounce container whipped dessert topping

¾ cup blueberries, divided

Coarsely chop 8 cookies. Press the cookie pieces into a 9-inch pie dish.

In a bowl, mix yogurt and whipped topping until well blended. Gently fold in ½ cup blueberries. Pour into the pie dish. Chill for 30 minutes.

To serve, decorate with the remaining cookies and blueberries. Makes 8 servings.

Apple Sharlotka

New York Apple/Pennsylvania Apple

7 Eastern apples – Red Delicious, Empire or Jonagold – peeled and cut into ½- to 1-inch cubes

3 large eggs

1 cup granulated sugar

1 teaspoon vanilla extract

1 cup all-purpose flour

1 teaspoon baking powder

½ teaspoon cinnamon

⅛ teaspoon grated nutmeg

Confectioners' sugar, for dusting

Ice cream or whipped cream, for serving

Preheat oven to 350°F. Line the bottom of a 9-inch springform pan with a circle of parchment paper. Butter the pan and paper.

Place diced apples in the prepared pan.

In a mixing bowl, combine eggs and sugar, beating well. Add vanilla, then stir in dry ingredients just until blended. Pour the batter over the prepared apples, smoothing it over and into the apples. Gently tap the pan on the counter to evenly distribute the batter.

Bake for 45-50 minutes, or until a cake tester comes out clean.

Let cool in the pan for 20 minutes. Flip the cake onto a plate, then again onto a serving platter.

When cool, dust with confectioners' sugar. Serve with ice cream or whipped cream. Makes 8 servings.

Eastern **Apples**

CRISPIER • JUICIER • TASTIER

Lemon Curd Tart with Pistachios
Paramount Citrus

3 large eggs

2 large egg yolks

¾ cup plus
  2 tablespoons sugar

⅔ cup freshly squeezed
  juice from about
  3 Paramount Citrus
  lemons, divided

½ cup unsalted butter,
  frozen in pieces

2 tablespoons finely
  chopped toasted pistachios

TART SHELL

1¼ cups flour

⅓ cup confectioners' sugar

Dash of salt

½ cup cold unsalted
  butter, cut in chunks

Prepare the tart shell: Preheat oven to 350°F. In a food processor, whirl flour, sugar and salt. Add butter and whirl until it starts to clump. Press into a 9-inch tart pan with removable sides. Prick the bottom and sides well with a fork. Bake until lightly browned, 18-20 minutes. Cool.

Combine eggs, yolks and sugar in a metal or glass bowl. Set the bowl over a saucepan of simmering water (bowl should not touch water). Whisk constantly until opaque and thick, about 25 minutes. Add ⅓ cup lemon juice and whisk until thickened. Whisk in remaining juice until thickened.

Remove from the heat and whisk in butter. Cool for 10 minutes. Pour into the tart shell.

Broil 6 inches from the heat until lightly caramelized, 1-2 minutes. Sprinkle with pistachios. Chill. Makes 8 servings.

Adapted from a recipe by Michael Sandoval, chef de cuisine, Bouchon Bistro, Napa.

Peanut Butter Banana Cream Pie
J.M. Smucker Co.

1 3.4-ounce package
  instant vanilla pudding

1 12-ounce can PET
  Evaporated Milk

¾ cup Jif Creamy
  Peanut Butter

⅛ teaspoon almond extract

2 bananas, cut into
  ⅛-inch slices

1 6-ounce prepared
  chocolate cookie crust

¼ cup Smucker's Hot
  Fudge Topping

1 cup frozen whipped
  dessert topping, thawed

¼ cup chopped
  cocktail peanuts

In a large bowl, combine pudding mix, evaporated milk, peanut butter and almond extract; beat on medium speed with an electric mixer until smooth.

Place a single layer of bananas on the bottom of the crust. Pour the pudding mixture over the bananas. Place another single layer of bananas over the pudding mixture.

Drizzle fudge topping over the bananas. Spread whipped topping over the fudge topping. Sprinkle with peanuts. Chill for 2 hours. Makes 8 servings.

Cranberry-White Chocolate Bread Pudding

La Brea Bakery

4 La Brea Bakery Torta Sandwich
  Rolls, cut into ½-inch cubes

½ cup sugar

6 large egg yolks

2 large eggs, whole

1 teaspoon vanilla extract

4 cups heavy cream

1 cup whole milk

12 ounces white chocolate, chopped

1 cup cranberry sauce or jelly

Preheat oven to 350°F. Place bread cubes on a baking sheet and bake for 10-15 minutes, until dry and lightly toasted.

In a mixing bowl, whisk sugar, yolks and eggs, and vanilla extract until smooth.

In a saucepan, bring cream and milk to a simmer. Reduce the heat to low and add chocolate, stirring to prevent it from sticking. Very slowly whisk 1 cup of the hot mixture into the eggs and sugar, whisking constantly. Add the remaining hot cream, whisking constantly until well combined.

In an 8-by-8- or 9-by-9-inch nonstick baking dish, put half of the diced bread, spreading evenly to cover the bottom. Add half of the cream mixture to cover the bread. Using a spoon or spatula, place small amounts of cranberry sauce or jelly evenly over the bread.

Add the remaining bread and cover with the remaining cream mixture. Press lightly on the bread to absorb the liquid. Cover with foil and bake for 30 minutes. Remove the foil and bake for 15 minutes, or until the top is lightly browned and the pudding is cooked throughout. Remove from the oven, cut into pieces, and serve. Makes 4-6 servings.

LA BREA BAKERY

Apple Rice Pudding
Oneonta Starr Ranch Growers

½ cup packed light brown sugar

2 large eggs, beaten

1 Starr Ranch Growers medium-size Gala apple, peeled, cored and grated

1 cup cooked rice

2 cups milk

½ cup raisins

½ teaspoon vanilla extract

¼ teaspoon salt

Sprinkle of freshly grated nutmeg

Cream or milk, for serving (optional)

Preheat oven to 325°F.

Make this old-fashioned recipe right in an 8-inch square baking dish. Combine sugar, eggs, grated apple and cooked rice; stir well to blend. Mix in milk, raisins, vanilla and salt. Sprinkle with nutmeg.

Place in a larger pan of hot water and bake for about 1 hour, or until set.

Serve warm or cold with a pitcher of cream or milk. Garnish with thin apple slices if desired. Makes 6-8 servings.

ONEONTA
STARR RANCH
growers

Banana Maple-Pecan Pudding
Nature's Path Organic Foods

Egg replacer equivalent to 2 large eggs

2 cups whole milk

½ cup maple syrup

1 teaspoon vanilla extract

¼ teaspoon ground cinnamon

1 cup pecan (or walnut halves), divided

4 firm, ripe bananas, peeled and sliced

1½ cups Nature's Path Pumpkin Flax Plus Granola

Position rack in the center of the oven. Preheat oven to 350°F.

In a 2-quart ovenproof baking dish, whisk together egg replacer, milk, maple syrup, vanilla and cinnamon.

Coarsely chop ½ cup pecans. Stir the chopped pecans, bananas and granola into the liquid.

Arrange the remaining pecan halves on top.

Bake, uncovered, until set, about 40 minutes.

Place on a cooling rack and let sit for 10 minutes or longer before spooning into dessert bowls or long-stemmed glasses. Serve warm. Makes 6 servings.

Vegan variation: Use organic unsweetened soy milk instead of dairy milk.

No-Bake Vegan Coconut Chocolate Pudding

Vita Coco

2 bananas

½ cup Vita Coco pure coconut water

¼ cup cocoa powder

2 teaspoons maple syrup

2 teaspoons toasted unsweetened coconut flakes, divided

In a blender, combine bananas, coconut water, cocoa powder and maple syrup. Blend until smooth.

Pour into 2 ramekins or small bowls. Top each pudding with 1 teaspoon toasted coconut. Makes 2 servings.

Tip: Refrigerate overnight if you want a thicker pudding.

Blueberry Lemon Trifles

Family Tree Farms

1½ cups fresh blueberries, rinsed, plus more for optional garnish

2 tablespoons granulated sugar

2 tablespoons water

1 8-ounce package cream cheese, softened

¼ cup confectioners' sugar

Juice of 1 lemon (2-3 tablespoons)

Grated zest of 1 lemon

1 3.4-ounce package instant lemon pudding

2 cups milk

1 prepared vanilla pound cake, cut into 1-inch cubes

Ginger or shortbread cookies, crumbled (optional)

In a saucepan, combine blueberries, sugar and water. Cook over medium heat, stirring occasionally, for 8-10 minutes. Remove from the heat and let cool.

In a mixing bowl, combine cream cheese, confectioners' sugar, lemon juice and lemon zest. Beat with an electric mixer until very smooth.

Prepare pudding mix according to package directions. Add to the cream cheese mixture. Mix at medium speed until creamy.

To prepare the trifles, place 1 layer of pound cake cubes in 4 glasses. Top with a layer of cream cheese mixture. Next add ¼ of the blueberry sauce to each glass. Repeat with another layer of pound cake and cream cheese mixture. Serve immediately or refrigerate for several hours.

Just before serving, top with crumbled cookies and fresh blueberries, if desired. Makes 4 servings.

Tuxedo Cake Trifle

France Délices/Ticklebelly Desserts

1 Kirkland Signature Tuxedo Chocolate Mousse Cake (see note)

5 cups 35% whipping cream

½ cup confectioners' sugar

2½ pounds fresh strawberries, sliced

Mint leaves, for garnish

Special equipment: 1-gallon glass bowl

Freeze the cake for 2 hours.

Whip cream and sugar until stiff peaks form.

Cut eight 1-inch-thick slices of cake. Cut each slice into 3 pieces. Spread ⅓ of the cake pieces in an even layer in the glass bowl.

Delicately spread 2 cups of whipped cream over the cake pieces.

Top with some sliced strawberries. Repeat whipped cream and strawberry layers. Add remaining cake slices. Top with remaining whipped cream.

Chill the trifle for 2 hours. Garnish with mint. Makes 12 servings.

Note: You will need ¾ of the cake for this recipe—the leftover piece will be for pure indulgence.

KIRKLAND *Signature*

Tropical Panna Cotta

Nature's Partner/Mulholland Citrus/Sequoia Orange

1½ tablespoons powdered gelatin, unflavored

3 tablespoons fresh-squeezed navel orange juice

2 cups heavy cream

2 cups canned coconut milk (full fat)

1 cup sugar

½ teaspoon freshly grated navel orange zest

1½ teaspoons vanilla extract

TOPPING

4 California-grown mandarins, peeled and segments separated

1 nectarine, pitted and sliced

½ cup red or green seedless grapes, halved

2 kiwifruit, peeled and sliced

½ cup blueberries

In a small bowl, sprinkle gelatin evenly over orange juice. Set aside while the gelatin dissolves.

In a saucepan, mix heavy cream, coconut milk, sugar, orange zest and vanilla. Bring to a gentle boil and stir to dissolve the sugar. Remove from the heat.

Add the gelatin to the cream mixture and gently stir to combine. Strain through a sieve and pour into 4 small ramekins. Refrigerate until set, about 4 hours.

Prior to serving, gently fold the topping ingredients together. Spoon the fruit mix on top of the panna cotta and serve. Makes 4 servings.

Grape Dessert Bowls
Four Star Fruit

1 pound *each* (about 3 cups total) Four Star Fruit red and green seedless grapes, stemmed, rinsed and drained

4 kiwi, peeled and cubed, *or* 1 14-ounce can mandarin oranges, drained

2 cups pineapple chunks, fresh or canned (drained)

8 ounces semisweet chocolate

6 4-inch waffle bowls

1 teaspoon freshly grated nutmeg

1-2 cups vanilla-honey Greek yogurt, or your flavor choice

½ cup toasted coconut flakes (optional)

In a large bowl, combine fruit. Set aside.

Melt chocolate in a double boiler. When the chocolate is melted and smooth, dip the top edge of each waffle bowl into the chocolate. Turn right side up and let stand until the chocolate hardens.

To serve, divide the fruit mixture among the bowls. Grate nutmeg over the fruit. Top with a generous dollop of yogurt and toasted coconut. Do not put the fruit in the bowls until right before serving or it might make the bowls soggy. Makes 6 servings.

Variations: Place yogurt in the bottom of the bowls and the fruit on top, then sprinkle with nutmeg and coconut. For a fun presentation, after the chocolate has cooled and set a bit, press coconut into the chocolate. Strawberries can be substituted for the pineapple.

Recipe developed by Christine W. Jackson, food stylist.

Citrus Dessert
Greene River Marketing

2 large red grapefruit
2 large oranges
1 cup fresh pineapple chunks
½ cup packed light brown sugar
2 tablespoons butter, softened

Preheat the oven broiler and set the rack about 6 inches from the top.

Cut grapefruit in half horizontally. Cut all around the inside edges and between the membranes to release the segments. Remove all the membrane from the grapefruit halves.

Peel oranges and separate into segments.

Place grapefruit sections, orange sections and pineapple chunks in an 8-by-8-inch baking dish.

In a small bowl, stir brown sugar and butter together. Spread the mixture evenly across the fruit.

Broil the fruit until the sugar is bubbly, about 5-6 minutes. Let cool for several minutes and place in the empty grapefruit halves. Makes 4 servings.

Creamy Fruitcake Toast
Dawn Food Products

1 Kirkland Signature fruitcake
Nonstick cooking spray
½ cup prepared cream cheese frosting
White chocolate shavings, for garnish (optional)

Remove fruitcake from the packaging. Remove the loose nuts and candied fruits from the top of the cake and set aside.

Using a serrated knife, slice the cake into ¾-inch slices.

Heat a sauté pan coated with cooking spray over medium heat. Working in batches, place the cake slices in the pan and heat for 1 minute to toast; turn and toast for another minute. Remove from the pan and let cool on a rack for 20 minutes.

Using a piping bag, pipe frosting onto the cake slices. Garnish with nuts and candied fruit. Top with white chocolate shavings if desired. Makes 32 servings.

Peach Crisp Cobbler
Wawona Packing Company

12 fresh Wawona peaches
1 cup sugar
4 tablespoons cornstarch
3 tablespoons lemon juice

TOPPING
1 teaspoon ground
  cinnamon
Pinch of nutmeg
3 tablespoons
  granulated sugar
½ cup biscuit mix
¾ cup lightly packed light
  brown sugar
2 cups rolled oats
4 ounces (1 stick) butter,
  softened

Preheat oven to 350°F.

Prepare the topping: In a small bowl, combine cinnamon, nutmeg and granulated sugar. In a medium bowl, mix biscuit mix, brown sugar and oats. Stir in the sugar mixture. Add softened butter and mix well. Set aside.

Peel and slice peaches. In a small bowl, mix sugar and cornstarch together.

In a large bowl, combine the peaches, the sugar mixture and lemon juice; stir to blend evenly. Place the peaches in a 13-by-9-inch pan. Spread the topping evenly over the peaches.

Bake for 60 minutes, or until golden brown. Makes 12 servings.

Cherry Cloud Cream Puffs
M&R Company

1 cup water
½ cup unsalted butter
1 cup flour
½ teaspoon salt
3 large eggs
  (room temperature)

FILLING
4 ounces Neufchâtel
  or cream cheese
1-2 tablespoons sugar
1 teaspoon vanilla extract
2 cups sweet cherries, pitted
  and chopped, divided
6 ounces whipped
  dessert topping

Prepare the filling: With a mixer, beat cream cheese, sugar and vanilla until smooth and fluffy. Blend in half the cherries. Fold in whipped topping and remaining cherries. Chill.

Bring water to a boil in a heavy saucepan over medium heat. Add butter and stir until melted. Blend flour and salt, then add all at once to the boiling water. Stir with a wooden spoon until a ball forms. Remove from the heat and beat in eggs one at a time; dough should still be stiff after last egg is beaten in. Let rest for 10 minutes. Preheat oven to 375°F.

Put dough in a ziplock bag and snip ½ inch off one corner. Pipe onto a parchment-lined cookie sheet in 2- to 3-inch-diameter mounds, 2 inches apart. Bake for 25-35 minutes, or until medium golden brown. Cool on a rack.

Slice puffs horizontally in half and fill with 1-2 tablespoons of filling. Makes 20-24 servings.

Recipe developed by Christine W. Jackson, food stylist.

Lemon Bars
Bee Sweet Citrus

1 cup butter, softened

2¼ cups all-purpose flour, divided

2 cups granulated sugar, divided

4 large eggs

Juice of 2 Bee Sweet lemons

Confectioners' sugar, as needed

Lemon wedge, for garnish

Preheat oven to 350°F.

In a medium bowl, blend together butter, 2 cups flour and ½ cup sugar. Press into the bottom of an ungreased 13-by-9-inch pan.

Bake for 15-20 minutes, or until firm and golden.

In another bowl, whisk together the remaining 1½ cups sugar and ¼ cup flour. Whisk in eggs and lemon juice. Pour over the baked crust.

Bake for an additional 20 minutes. The bars will firm up as they cool.

Once the pan has cooled, cut into 2-inch squares; dust with confectioners' sugar, if desired. Arrange in a checkerboard fashion on a dessert tray. Garnish with a lemon wedge. Makes 24 servings.

Bee Sweet
PREMIUM CALIFORNIA CITRUS

Medjool Date Cashew Bars
SunDate

1½ cups pitted and chopped SunDate Medjool dates

1 teaspoon vanilla extract

¼ cup lightly packed brown sugar (light or dark)

½ cup water

1 teaspoon grated orange zest

PASTRY

1½ cups all-purpose flour

1 cup rolled oats

1 cup lightly packed brown sugar (light or dark)

¼ teaspoon salt

⅓ cup chopped dried cranberries (optional)

½ cup chopped cashews

¾ cup butter

Preheat oven to 350°F. Grease and flour a 9-by-9-inch baking pan.

In a saucepan, combine dates, vanilla, sugar, water and orange zest. Bring to a boil, then simmer for 5 minutes, stirring frequently, until the mixture resembles a thick paste. Set aside to cool.

Prepare the pastry: In a mixing bowl, combine flour, oats, sugar, salt, dried cranberries and cashews. Cut in butter to form a semi-dry dough. Reserve about 2 cups of the mixture for the topping. Press the remaining mixture into the bottom of the pan. Spread the date filling over the pastry layer. Crumble the reserved pastry mixture over the surface.

Bake for 25-35 minutes, or until golden brown. Let cool, then cut into squares. Makes 9 servings.

Sun Date.

Snickerdoodles
Sun-Maid Growers

1 cup butter or margarine, softened

1½ cups sugar

2 large eggs

2¾ cups all-purpose flour

1½ teaspoons cream of tartar

1 teaspoon baking soda

¼ teaspoon salt

1½ cups Sun-Maid Natural Raisins

CINNAMON SUGAR

2 teaspoons cinnamon

2 tablespoons sugar

Preheat oven to 375°F. Grease cookie sheets.

In a mixing bowl, combine butter and sugar; beat until light and fluffy. Add eggs and blend well.

In another bowl, combine flour, cream of tartar, baking soda and salt. Add to the butter mixture and mix well. Stir in raisins.

Shape the dough into 1-inch balls.

Blend the cinnamon and sugar in a small bowl. Roll the balls of dough in the cinnamon sugar to coat. Place 2 inches apart on the greased cookie sheets.

Bake in the upper third of the oven for 10-12 minutes (do not overbake). Let cool for 1 minute, then transfer to wire racks to cool. Makes 3½ dozen cookies.

Delicious Whole-Wheat Dark Chocolate Pecan Cookies
Kirkland Signature/La Nogalera

½ cup butter, softened

½ cup dark brown sugar

½ teaspoon Kirkland Signature pure vanilla extract

1 large egg

1⅓ cups unbleached organic whole-wheat flour ♥Organic

½ teaspoon baking powder

⅔ cup chopped Kirkland Signature pecans

4 ounces dark chocolate chunks

Preheat oven to 350°F. Line a cookie sheet with parchment paper.

In a large bowl, mix butter, sugar and vanilla with an electric mixer until light and creamy. Add egg and beat until it is well incorporated.

Combine flour and baking powder; add gradually to the butter mixture.

Using a wooden spoon, mix in pecans and chocolate chunks.

Roll the dough into small balls about the size of an in-shell pecan and space them an inch apart on the baking sheet. Bake for 15 minutes. The cookies should be a light golden color and slightly crunchy.

Remove the cookies to a rack and let cool. Makes 32 cookies.

Cake Pops
Rich Products

Leftover Kirkland Signature half-sheet cake

Chocolate chips

Lollipop sticks

Almond bark (white or chocolate)

Toppings: confetti sprinkles, jimmies, edible glitter, chopped nuts and/or candies

Lollipop bags

Remove icing from cake and set aside. Place cake in a large bowl and beat on low speed with a hand mixer or in a stationary mixer with a paddle. Add frosting as needed to incorporate all of the cake crumbs.

With a melon baller or small ice cream scoop, mold the mixture into balls. Place the cake balls on a cookie sheet lined with waxed paper.

Melt some chocolate chips in the microwave. Dip a lollipop stick in the melted chocolate and insert into the center of each cake ball. Place in the freezer until set.

In the microwave, heat almond bark and chocolate chips on high for 20-second intervals, stirring, until melted.

Dip each cake pop into the melted chocolate, letting excess drip off. Sprinkle with desired toppings.

Stand upright to dry, then slip into lollipop bags and secure with twist ties.

Movie Night Snack Mix
Kirkland Signature/Jelly Belly

1 tablespoon sugar

1 teaspoon ground cinnamon

2 cups prepared air-popped popcorn

1 cup bite-size crispy wheat squares cereal

½ cup dried cranberries, cherries or raisins

Nonstick cooking spray, butter flavor

2½ cups Jelly Belly jelly beans, assorted flavors

2 cups fat-free mini pretzels

In a small bowl, combine sugar and cinnamon.

In a large bowl, combine popcorn, cereal and cranberries. Spray the mixture lightly for 4-5 seconds with cooking spray, then quickly toss with the sugar-cinnamon mixture.

Stir in jelly beans and pretzels. Store in a covered container. Stir well before serving. Makes 4 servings.

Tip: For a fun hostess gift, spoon into a clear container and finish with a pretty ribbon.

Index

Supplier Listing

AJ Trucco, Inc., 187
www.truccodirect.com
718-893-3060

Alaska Glacier Seafoods, Inc., 166
www.alaskaglacierseafoods.com
907-790-3590

Alpine Fresh, Inc., 136, 137
www.alpinefresh.com
305-594-9117

Alsum Farms & Produce, Inc., 38
www.alsum.com
800-236-5127

Altar Produce LLC, 14
www.altarproduce.com
760-357-6762

Amazon Produce Network, 57, 69
www.amazonprod.com
856-442-0410

AMC Direct, 223
www.amcgrupo.eu
856-241-7977

American Pride Seafoods, 187
www.americanprideseafoods.com
508-997-0031

Andrew & Williamson Fresh Produce, 227
www.andrew-williamson.com
619-661-6004

Anthony Vineyards, Inc., 65
www.anthonyvineyards.com

Apio, Inc., 196, 197
www.apioInc.com
800-454-1355

Aquagold Seafood Company, 171
954-888-9445

Arthur Schuman, Inc., 37
www.arthurschuman.com
973-227-0030

Atlantic Capes Fisheries, Inc., 118, 119
www.atlanticcapes.com
508-990-9040

Atlantic Veal & Lamb, LLC, 130, 131, 132
www.atlanticveal.com
800-222-VEAL

Babé Farms, Inc., 77
www.babefarms.com
800-648-6772

Bard Valley Medjool Dates, 187
www.bardmedjool.com
928-726-9191

Basin Gold Cooperative, 52
www.basingold.com
509-545-4161

BC Hot House Foods, Inc., 55
www.bchothouse.com
604-881-4545

Bee Sweet Citrus, 237
www.beesweetcitrus.com
559-834-5345

Better Than Bouillon, 58, 204
www.superiortouch.com
706-291-6528

Big Chuy Distributors & Sons, Inc., 211
www.bigchuy.com
520-281-4909

Blossom Hill-Lucich-Santos Farms, 72
www.blossomhillapricots.com
209-892-6500

Blumar Seafoods, 76
www.blumar.com
954-734-2721

Borton & Sons, Inc., 47, 219
www.bortonfruit.com
509-966-3905

Boskovich Farms, 61
www.boskovichfarms.com
805-487-2299

Butterball, 128, 129
www.Butterball.com
1-800-Butterball

C & M Mushrooms, 165
www.cmmushrooms.com
610-268-2099

Cabot Creamery Cooperative, 25
www.cabotcheese.coop
888-792-2268

Cal-Maine Foods, Inc., 211
www.calmainefoods.com
601-948-6813

Calavo Growers, Inc., 18, 80
www.calavo.com
805-525-1245

California Avocado Commission, 18, 80
www.CaliforniaAvocado.com
949-341-1955

California Pear Advisory Board, 156
www.calpear.com
916-441-0432

California Walnut Board, 78
www.walnuts.org
916-932-7070

Camanchaca, 167, 194
www.camanchaca.cl
800-335-7553

Cargill Meat Solutions, 16, 143, 147, 149
www.cargillmeatsolutions.com

Castle Rock Vineyards, 64
www.castlerockvineyards.com
661-721-8717

Cecelia Packing Corp., 62
www.ceceliapack.com
559-626-5000

Cedar Key Aquaculture Farms, 186
www.cedarkeyclams.com
813-546-1186

Chairmans Foods, LLC, 28
www.chairmansfoods.com
615-231-4315

Chelan Fresh Marketing, 146
www.chelanfresh.com
509-682-4252

Chestnut Hill Farms, 74
www.chfusa.com
305-592-6969

Chicken of the Sea Frozen Foods, 74
310-469-7030

Chicken of the Sea International, 77, 78, 207
858-597-4522

Chilean Avocado Importers Association, 83
www.chileanavocados.org
831-689-0962

Christopher Ranch, 59
www.christopherranch.com
800-321-9333

Citterio USA, 37
www.citteriousa.com
570-636-3171

Clear Springs Foods, Inc., 181
www.clearsprings.com
800-635-8211

Coleman Natural Foods, 108, 109
www.colemannatural.com
800-442-8666

Columbia Marketing International,
10, 11, 222, 223
www.cmiapples.com
509-663-1955

ConAgra Foods, 17
www.conagrafoods.com
813-241-1500

Consolidated Catfish Producers, 183
662-962-3101

Copper River Seafoods, 31, 34
www.copperriverseafoods.com
888-622-1197

Corona College Heights, 221
www.cchcitrus.com
951-351-7880

Mountain View Fruit Sales/IM Ripe, 68, 190, 191
www.summeripe.com
559-637-9933

MountainKing Potatoes, 59
www.mtnking.com
800-395-2004

Mucci Farms, 28
www.muccifarms.com
866-236-5558

Mulholland Citrus, 42, 233
www.mulhollandcitrus.com
559-528-2525

Multiexport Foods, 163, 169
www.multiexportfoods.com
888-624-9773

National Beef Packing Co., LLC, 142, 143
www.nationalbeef.com
800-449-2333

Nature's Partner, 42, 233
www.naturespartner.com
213-627-2900

Nature's Path Foods, Inc., 231
www.naturespath.com
888-808-9505

NatureSweet Tomatoes, 29, 60, 61
www.naturesweet.com
800-315-8209

Naturipe Farms, LLC, 42, 66, 180
www.naturipefarms.com
239-591-1664

New York Apple Sales, Inc., 228
www.newyorkapplesales.com
518-477-7200

New York Style Sausage, 198, 209
www.newyorkstylesausage.com
408-745-7675

Nichols Pistachio, 186
www.nicholsfarms.com
559-584-6811

Nissin Foods, 150
www.nissinfoods.com
310-527-5713

Norpac Fisheries Export, 182
www.norpacexport.com
808-842-3474

North Coast Seafoods, 32, 182, 184
www.northcoastseafoods.com

NuCal Foods, 211
www.nucalfoods.com
209-254-2200

Nunes Company, The, 213
www.foxy.com
800-695-5012

Oakdell Egg Farms, Inc., 211
www.oakdell.com
801-298-4556

Oneonta Starr Ranch Growers, 220, 231
www.starranch.com
800-688-2191

Oppenheimer Group, The, 72, 155
www.oppyproduce.com
604-461-6779

Orca Bay Seafoods, Inc., 166
www.orcabayseafoods.com
800-932-ORCA

Pacific American Fish Company, Inc., 185
www.pafco.net
323-319-1515

Pacific Seafood Group, 172, 188, 189
www.pacseafood.com
888-742-3474

Pandol, 70
www.pandol.com
661-725-3755

Paramount Citrus, 63, 229
www.paramountcitrus.com
661-720-2500

Penn Cove Shellfish LLC, 185
www.penncoveshellfish.com
360-678-4803

Pennsylvania Apple Marketing Program, 228
www.pennsylvaniaapples.org
717-783-5418

Pescanova USA, 76
www.pescanovausa.com
800-990-6292

Pilgrim's/Gold Kist, 94, 95
www.pilgrims.com
970-506-8100

POM Wonderful, 38
www.pomwonderful.com
888-801-4162

Premier Citrus Marketing, 221
www.premiercitrusmarketing.com
772-794-5388

Premio Foods, Inc., 116, 117
www.premiofoods.com
201-909-2370

Pride Packing Co., 221
www.pridepacking.com
800-828-4106

Puratos Corporation, 133, 134, 135
www.puratos.us
856-428-4300

Rain Forest Aquaculture, 176
www.tilapia.com
877-522-8420

Rainier Fruit Company, 138, 139
www.rainierfruit.com

Ralcorp Frozen Bakery, 205
www.ralcorpfrozen.com
630-455-5200

Ready Pac Foods, 39, 80
www.readypac.com
800-800-4088

Regal Springs Tilapia Group, 178, 179
www.regalsprings.com
941-747-9161

Regatta Tropicals, 174
805-473-1320

Reser's Fine Foods, 149
www.resers.com
800-333-6431

Rikki USA, Inc., 202
www.rikkirikki.com
425-881-6881

River Ranch Fresh Foods, LLC, 195
www.riverranchfreshfoods.com
866-767-3931

Rivermaid Trading Company, 69
www.rivermaid.com
209-210-6800

Royal Flavor, 148
www.royalflavor.com
619-710-2020

RPE, Inc., 38
www.rpeproduce.com
800-678-2789

Rupari Food Service, 54
954-480-6320

Sabra Dipping Company, 35
www.sabra.com
914-372-3900

Sandridge Food Corporation, 202
www.sandridge.com
800-280-7951

Seald Sweet International, 47
www.sealdsweet.com
800-237-7525

Seattle Shrimp & Seafood, 193
www.seattleshrimp.com
206-812-2822

Supplier Listing

Sequoia Orange, 42, 233
www.sequoiaorange.com
559-592-9455

Setton Pistachio, 19
www.settonfarms.com
800-227-4397

Skagit Valley's Best Produce, Inc., 53
www.svbest.com
360-848-0777

Slade Gorton & Co., 177
www.sladegorton.com
617-541-3095

SM Products (BC) Ltd., 174
www.halibut.ca
604-946-7665

Smithfield Foods, Inc., 15, 157
www.smithfieldfoods.com
888-366-6767

South Coast Baking Co.,
www.southcoastbaking.com
800-478-4252

Southern Specialties, Inc., 191
www.southernspecialties.com
954-784-6500

Splenda, 22
www.splenda.com
800-7-SPLENDA

Starbucks Coffee Company, 48, 216
www.starbucks.com

Stellar Distributing, 44
www.stellardistributing.com
559-664-8400

Stemilt Growers LLC, 49, 67
www.stemilt.com
509-662-9667

Stevco, 40
www.grapeman.com

Sun Belle, Inc., 12
www.sun-belle.com
708-343-4545

Sun World International, 72
www.sun-world.com
661-392-5000

Sun-Maid Growers of California, 238
www.sunmaid.com
800-768-6243

Sundate LLC, 237
www.sundateusa.com
760-398-6123

Sunkist Growers, Inc., 33, 75, 152
www.sunkist.com

Sunny Delight, 48
www.sunnyd.com
800-395-5849

Sunny Valley International, 51
www.sunnyint.com
856-881-0200

SUNSET, 126, 127
www.sunsetgrown.com
519-326-3218

Sunwest Fruit Co. Inc., 11
www.sunwestfruit.com
559-646-4400

Tanimura & Antle, Inc., 82
www.taproduce.com
877-827-7388

Tarantino Gourmet Sausage, 123, 124, 125
www.tarantinosausage.com
619-232-7585

Taylor Farms, 52
www.taylorfarms.com
866-675-6120

Ticklebelly Desserts, 225, 233
www.ticklebellydesserts.com
303-375-9925

Tillamook County Creamery Association, 44
www.Tillamook.com
855-562-3568

Timco Worldwide A C.H. Robinson Company, 211
www.timcoworldwide.com
530-757-1000

Top Brass Marketing, Inc., 53
www.topbrassmarketing.com
661-393-4096

Townsend Farms Inc., 217
www.townsendfarms.com
503-666-1780

Trident Seafoods, 170, 175
www.tridentseafoods.com
866-413-4749

Trinity Fruit Sales Co., 113, 114, 115
www.trinityfruit.com
800-669-1600

True Nature Seafood, 88, 89
www.truenatureseafood.com
305-591-8873

Tyson Foods, Inc., 151
www.tyson.com
800-233-6332

Unifrutti of America, 64
215-425-2777

Unilever, 225
www.unileverusa.com
800-782-8301

Valley Pride Sales, Inc., 53
www.valleypridesales.com
360-428-2717

Ventura Foods, 30
www.venturafoods.com
800-591-3899

Victoria Island Farms, 186
www.victoriaislandfarms.com
209-465-5600

Vie de France Yamazaki, Inc., 207, 218
www.viedefrance.com
800-446-4404

Village Farms, 83
www.villagefarms.com
877-777-7718

Vita Coco, 232
www.vitacoco.com
212-206-0763

Wallace Farms, 53
www.wallacespuds.com
360-757-0981

Wawona Packing Company, 66, 236
559-528-4000

West Lake Fresh, 216
www.westlakefresh.com
877-WLFresh

West Liberty Foods, LLC, 212, 213
www.wlfoods.com
888-511-4500

West Pak Avocado, 18, 80
www.westpakavocado.com
951-252-8000

Western Fresh Marketing, 72
www.westernfreshmarketing.com
559-662-0301

Western United Fish Co., 173
www.westernunitedfish.com
425-558-7809

Wilcox Farms, Inc., 211
www.wilcoxfarms.com
360-458-3997

Windset Farms, 96, 97
www.windsetfarms.com
604-940-7700

Yakima Fresh LLC, 21
www.yakimafresh.com
509-453-9081

Notes

Notes